ADVANCE PRAISE FOR **THE FOOD ACTIVIS**

D0376814

....

"I have seen, with my own eyes, Ali transform the food ecosystem in her community through direct action and activism. **With her feet planted firmly on the ground, but her vision soaring far ahead, Ali lays out the road to change with boldness, courage, and passion.** Bravo, my friend!"

— **Walter Robb,** co-CEO, Whole Foods Market

....

"Comprehensive and empowering."

Economy

....

e roused,
ably, and

telligence

....

ır
oth big
ve tool

mily Table

....

"It's not enough just to eat healthy ourselves. **We must all become food activists** if we are to have a sustainable future. Bravo to Ali for so beautifully showing us the path forward."

— **Laurie David,** producer of *Fed Up* and *An Inconvenient Truth*

The mission of Storey Publishing is to serve our customers by publishing practical information that encourages personal independence in harmony with the environment.

EDITED BY Deborah Burns, Pam Thompson, and Sarah Guare
COVER DESIGN BY Jennifer Heuer
BOOK DESIGN BY Michaela Jebb
INDEXED BY Christine R. Lindemer, Boston Road Communications

INTERIOR ILLUSTRATIONS BY © Becca Stadtlander/The Bright Group International, Ltd., except page 3, by Jennifer Heuer; page 50 and page 117, based on a map created by the Mississippi Basin Alliance

© 2015 by Alice Jane Berlow

Storey Publishing
210 MASS MoCA Way
North Adams, MA 01247
www.storey.com

Printed in United States by Sheridan Books, Inc.
10 9 8 7 6 5 4 3 2 1

Library of Congress Cataloging-in-Publication Data

Berlow, Ali.
    The food activist handbook : big and small things you can do to provide fresh, healthy food for your community / by Ali Berlow.
        pages cm
    ISBN 978-1-61212-180-2 (pbk.)
    ISBN 978-1-60342-929-0 (ebook) 1. Food relief—United States. 2. Slow food movement—United States. 3. Nutrition—United States. 4. Consumer movements—United States. 5. Community activists—United States. I. Title.
    HV696.F6B464 2015
    363.8'830973—dc23
                    2014046828

ALI BERLOW

THE FOOD ACTIVIST HANDBOOK

BIG & SMALL THINGS YOU CAN DO TO HELP PROVIDE FRESH, HEALTHY FOOD FOR YOUR COMMUNITY

Storey

CONTENTS

ALI BERLOW EATS in a territory located between feast and famine. She lives with her husband and three sons in a kind of elaborate tree house above plots for vegetables and pens for livestock on an island off the coast of Massachusetts.

Her kitchen is at the end of a rough country road. When I walked into her home for the first time, I recognized at once our common cause: a desire to use our pots and pans to connect our families to the land and to justice, to pleasure, and to health.

Ali has watched obesity threaten to rob her of her father and food illiteracy and immersion in processed foods threaten the long-term health of her adopted son, a gifted athlete. She fought back with her fork, her farm, and her cell phone.

Hers is a food activist's handbook for every eater, for every body.

Ali sticks to basics. She makes lists. She curates essential triumph and trial food stories. Names the need-to-know names. Provides a basic bibliography. In writing close to the bones of what it means to be a food activist in 21st century America, she has created an elastic handbook that can be used in a wide variety of communities and tailored to fit individual needs. She uses her particular and perhaps particularly charmed experience to create an efficient guide to moving beyond eating ethically in a single home to eating ethically in a community, even in the harshest hard-luck place.

Her handbook is an open-ended system. She presents starting points, road markers, stumbling-block breakers, and bridges to engagement. She does not prescribe or predict what the outcome of the engagement will be. Her handbook will be useful to a food activist focused on saving a family beef farm as well as to a vegan interested in urban foraging using what used to be called food stamps and is now called SNAP.

Self-improvement is an old theme in American literature, and the subgenre of idealistic, ecologically informed self-improvement handbooks is rich. *The Food Activist Handbook* will take its place on my shelves alongside *The Whole Earth Catalog* and *Our Bodies, Ourselves* as favorite modern classics that embolden folks to start changing their lives without being dogmatic about the exact form the change should take. These volumes reserve their zeal for the central tenets of the genre: change is possible, hope is wise, and doing is good.

The particular genius of this little volume is that it restores poetry to process. Ali recognizes there can be grace in administration, and within these pages she coaches her readers in the art of achieving administrative grace in progressive food spaces.

This is the perfect book for every experienced food activist who has ever wished to have a week or a month or a year to walk someone through the process of becoming effectively engaged in transforming America's foodscape but cannot spare the time. It's a pocket coach that can be there when they can't be.

On behalf of all of us who want food to be safe, sufficient, and delicious; to connect us to the land and to justice; to be about, at once, in the same bite, health and deliciousness, innovation and tradition, I applaud Ali for writing a book that celebrates our diverse ways and means and common purposes.

— **Alice Randall,** author of *Soul Food Love*

Introduction

"Find a way."

— 64-year-old *Diana Nyad's* mantra during her record-breaking swim from Cuba to Florida, without a shark cage, on September 2, 2013

MY MOM KEPT a sketch of my father's heart on a piece of scrap paper taped to the inside of a kitchen cabinet. His cardiologist drew it to explain what my father's heart disease looked like, how his six-foot-four body was reacting to it, and what his impending heart surgery was to achieve.

By that time in his life, his mid-60s, my father was overweight, with high blood pressure and blocked arteries due to too much food, too much stress, and not enough exercise. The sketch showed how my father's body had creatively built a circumnavigation system to deliver blood and oxygen around the blockages in his heart. The slow, inefficient system was an energy drain, but his body made it work for a while, with Western medicine's help.

Despite its damaged state, my father's body made detours and relied on them.

That is what's happening with our food system today. The heart of our system is sick, but we have created alternative systems to get people their food. And so we have an entirely separate distribution system that began as emergency food banks and is now a thin and thinning thread of food security for 40 million people. We have a federal food and farm bill and policies that make real food more expensive while subsidizing raw materials like corn, soy, and rapeseed that are turned into processed food by adding sugar, salt, fat, preservatives, and so on. Our farm bill calls whole fresh food "specialty crops." Those crops include tomatoes, broccoli, cabbage, apples, and greens. It has become legal and profitable to ship chickens raised and slaughtered in the United States to China, where the meat is processed and then sent back to America as food. We allow U.S. citizens, including children, to labor unprotected in fields, planting and harvesting food that they themselves cannot eat because they cannot afford it. The 2014 poverty line for a family of four, defined by the U.S. Department of Health and Human Services, is $23,850 — and the average farmworker family of four makes just $17,500 (see Who Grows Our Food?, page 157). At the same time, the local food movement, which strives to create more resilient, just, fair, and equitable systems of food production, distribution, and consumption within identified regions, remains stuck, perceived and tagged as "elitist."

In a fable attributed to the Cherokee, an elder describes to his grandson a terrible fight going on inside him, a fight between two wolves. One is evil: he is anger, envy, sorrow, regret, greed, arrogance, self-pity, guilt, resentment, inferiority, lies, false pride, superiority, and ego. The other is good: he is joy, peace, love, hope, serenity, humility, kindness, benevolence, empathy, generosity, truth, compassion, and faith. The same fight is going on inside you, and inside every other person, the elder tells his grandson.

The boy wants to know which wolf will win.

The one you feed, the old man says, simply.

Which system are we feeding? We have a choice. There is a daily balancing act in the struggle to meet human needs. People on a large scale must have food, but thinking only on that large scale has led to an emphasis on quantity over quality. In the contrails of the Green Revolution, we are feeding seven billion people on our planet. And we are balancing an outsized, industrialized, corporate consolidation of food production and processing that ultimately wreaks

CHICKEN DETOURS

U.S. chicken goes to China and back again. Crazy!

havoc on public health, the environment, and livelihoods with small-scale production and locally focused economically sustainable growth, processing, and distribution of whole, fresh foods. Creating access to healthy foods for everyone, so that we can escape the downward spiral of an inefficient and unjust food system, requires action and forward thinking. Like my father's heart, our food system has reached a crisis point, and we need to make it healthy again.

There is great hope for our food system because people like you are taking action, in real time, in culturally appropriate ways, where you live, in a variety of sectors — from public health to education, in government agencies and arts organizations, and so many other fields and places. We're peeking out of our individual silos to collaborate and share information. The richness in, say, a farm to school program, illustrates the many, varied, creative, and innovative ways communities are making transformative, positive change. We're thinking about our children, about what kind of education we can provide, so they may be wise, critical thinkers, as they inherit a complex, unbalanced national and international economy and food system.

This book is a glean. The materials in it are gathered from the vibrant community of activists of all stripes working to bring us better food.

Gleaning is a relationship in two acts. The first act is that of the farmer who consciously leaves food in his or her field. The second act is that of the harvesters who collect that food for themselves or those less fortunate or able so that they may be nurtured and fed. Each act does not exist without the other in any meaningful way. If for whatever reason a farmer leaves edible food in a field to rot, that may be considered wasteful, negligent, or maybe just bad luck. And if a person goes into a farmer's field to pick without permission, it's stealing. Gleaning is a two-act play of generosity, perhaps even a commandment, if you take the Bible or the Torah literally. Both parties are complicit: the farmer in leaving the food, the gleaner in culminating the first act by harvesting what's there.

In this book, the first act comes from grassroots programs, nonprofits, government initiatives, interfaith organizations, businesses, and individuals, all of which have purposefully created information about how to get healthy foods to more people. Time and money — investments from philanthropists, foundations, and our own tax dollars — have been spent researching agriculture, growing food, building structures, and educating people.

>>

The second act belongs to you and me. There is a wealth of information out there for gleaners like us to harvest. Some of it is hiding in plain sight; some of it is buried. This knowledge is vast, the experience deep, and the mandate is to share it. When we work in our own food communities, we can use the existing collective knowledge and apply it in practical, individual ways in our neighborhoods, hospitals, and schools. We can use it to affect zoning laws, regulatory agencies, and national policies. We can use it for our own children as well as for various groups: veterans, farmers, ranchers, fishermen.

You will not find in this book equations to determine the perfect size for a school garden or the exact number of shovels, hoes, and rakes it takes to build one. There's no single blueprint that a town or city can download when it builds its urban gardens, aquaponic greenhouses, or vertical farms. But among these pages you will find resources that will allow you to dig deeper.

I want to offer something practical on every page of this book. Something inspiring. Each chapter includes a variety of actions, labeled "You Can Do This," that you can take to improve your community's food. Interspersed with these are gleanings from the big world of community action. You'll find tool kits, snippets of advice, and essays that can get you started or inspire you to dig deeper, whoever you are, whatever your skill set. Maybe school food or food education is your passion. Or perhaps you'll be inspired to talk at a place of worship, a Boys & Girls Club, or a community center about your garden, your farm, or your community supported agriculture (CSA) group — sharing with others what fresh, healthy food means to you. Maybe you will serve on a committee or a board and rewrite policies that impact the health of your community. You might screen a film, tell a story, or figure out how to get the day-olds from a restaurant to people who need them. Or perhaps you'll build a humane slaughterhouse. You may even just cook dinner tonight instead of going out to eat. Whatever you do, it will be something to behold.

"It's time for us to elevate the conversation about the food system to solutions." — Oran Hesterman (see page 289)

THE LIST

START small. Do something big.

INVITE farmers or fishermen to dinner. Ask questions about what they need. Listen, take notes, then figure out how to support them.

GET fresh, local food in your school's cafeteria, even if it's just one thing. Even if that one thing is simply parsley as a garnish, it's a start.

SCREEN a film about food, whether the genre is politics, pleasure, documentary, or art. Show it to your friends, at your YMCA, or in your community center. See what fires it ignites, and use it to start the dialogue and inform your next moves.

DIG a community compost. You'll turn waste into nutrient-rich fertilizer.

BUILD a community garden, be it on a roof, in a park, at a school, or in an abandoned lot. Help people grow their own food.

CELEBRATE a "day." There's Food Day, Earth Day, World Food Day, and more (though April 17, National Cheese Ball Day, may not be the message you're going for).

FIND OUT what your community needs to promote, develop, and support local food entrepreneurs. Community kitchens come in many forms.

MAKE a home-cooked meal with fresh, seasonal local food. Feed your taste buds. Eat with family members or friends.

START a home kitchen garden. Start small with something you love, like basil, tomatoes, or green beans. Or try something different, like grains, shoots, or roots.

GROW food that comes from your ancestral roots. What did your grandmother eat? Taioba, jiló, kohlrabi, calabaza, water spinach, Florida butter beans, Turkey hard red winter wheat?

TEACH a whole foods cooking class. Offer it at your food pantry, hospital, church, synagogue, mosque, school library, or local cooking supply store.

IMPROVE your booster club's food, be it at baseball, football, hockey, field hockey, soccer, or basketball games. Your family, friends, and fans will eat a better burger and hot dog if you offer it to them.

>>

SNUB the sodas and sports drinks. Water is the new in. Tweak the beverage lineup and take a pass on plastic bottles.

DESIGN a "local food miles" sticker campaign at your local grocer. It's good marketing and geography all rolled into cool signage.

HOST an open house on your farm. Invite your neighbors, customers, and health agents to see how you grow, what you grow, and why you grow.

LAUNCH a Harvest of the Month program at your local school. Foster local, seasonal, and healthy eating.

START an apprentice program for farmers. There's no better way to pass on firsthand knowledge and to get boots-on-the-ground experience.

DRIVE-IN fresh. Organize a farmers' market at a rest stop on the highway.

BUILD something mobile. Farmers' markets and slaughterhouses are on the move.

INTRODUCE yourself to your state's department of agriculture. Invite its members to tour your farms and cafeterias.

SAY no to marketing junk food to kids at school. Dump the cereal box

and soda bottle cap "incentives," "rewards," and "giveaways" in the name of education.

GET chocolate and strawberry milks out of the kids' reach at school, and quick! They do not come from cows. They come from lots of sugar, artificial flavoring, and coloring.

BUILD a garden with and for elders.

START a sustainable book club or a community read. Read, discuss, share ideas, and eat well while you do it.

HAVE some land? Lease it to a farmer.

START a food recovery program.

BECOME a language interpreter for the local food bank, mobile farmers' market, or a farm to school program; Spanish, Chinese, French, Vietnamese, and Tagalog speakers sought.

BUILD a school garden. It'll survive the summer. And yes, you can let kids eat the food you grow, no matter what they tell you.

REVIVE indigenous food cultures with indigenous languages.

DONATE time, money, stuff, spirit.

LEARN what your town or city ordinances are so that if they get in the way of developing strong local food systems, you can change them if necessary.

SHOW OFF your cows. Walk them down Main Street. People will come from miles around to see your crazy, beautiful parade.

GIVE voice. Tell your story or tell others' stories.

WRITE letters about why local food is important to you. Send them to your representatives and newspaper editors. Tag them to a news or cultural event, an election cycle, or a book review.

GROW your legacy at your college. Build a food garden on campus for classes to come.

TRANSFORM your school's cafeteria into a place you'd want to eat in. Relax the lunch period. Get rid of the paper and the plastic. Paint a mural.

TAKE a food safety course. Once you have your food safety certification, you have options about where and how you work with food.

HOST a meet and greet between farmers and fishermen, chefs and restaurants.

SEEK more, learn more.

CONNECT your food and arts communities. Find the poets, potters, photographers, and painters. Host a workshop, a slam, a fund-raiser. Make art about food.

START a garden for veterans. Welcome them home. Grow peace.

TAKE a field trip to a community kitchen, a cannery, an ice cream factory, a living history museum, a slaughterhouse. See where food comes from and how it is made.

START a "grow-out," a program that encourages farmers and chefs to work together with heirloom vegetables and heritage breed animals specific and significant to a given region.

HELP migrant farmworker children who have virtually no access to healthy foods, including the very fruits and vegetables they plant, tend, and harvest, to break out of this disgraceful cycle.

ADVOCATE for genetically modified organism (GMO) labeling. It's your right to know what's in the food you're eating and feeding to your loved ones. Initiate a campaign.

COOK with one fresh, local ingredient today.

>>

CHANGE what you can see. We all see food through our own particular lens. Whether your perspective is from the kitchen, the land, the sea, or the fork, affect what you know.

HOST a public speaker. Call in the experts to inspire.

INVOLVE a youth group such as the Boys & Girls Club or the Scouts. Start by convincing the group's leaders to change the vending machine offerings in their facilities from junk food to healthy snacks.

START a food forest on public lands, or plant just one fruit tree outside a public building. Food for all.

BUILD an online food co-op.

RUN for public office: a planning board, board of selectmen, school board, or board of health. Be politically active.

REGISTER to vote, and vote.

FOLLOW the money. State and federal agencies, nonprofits, and foundations can provide funds for underserved and high-risk communities to build healthy food systems.

RESIST being fooled (or bought) by the greenwashing of corporate industrial agriculture and processed food lobbying groups while you're following the money.

RAISE money for a good food non-profit that reflects your passion and beliefs.

REINVENT food distribution for local markets and local economies. There are new routes to make, new routes to take.

THINK size-appropriate. Think scalable. If outsized regulations are barriers to small-scale food and agriculture enterprises, change them.

HOST a zero-waste potluck featuring fresh seasonal food.

SAVE seeds.

START a public seed library.

BRAINSTORM and identify all barriers great and small to your project. Figure out your strengths and the weaknesses in those barriers. Be smart and strategic.

GROW heirloom. Raise heritage.

ASK for heirloom vegetables. Ask for heritage meats.

ORGANIZE a local food festival.

REVIVE home economics classes.

BE an active, participating, positive board member. Build ethical and civil nonprofits.

BECOME a beekeeper. Healthy pollinators are essential to growing food everywhere.

START a cooking club.

RAISE healthy fish and grow fresh food in an aquaponic greenhouse. Aquaponics is by definition organic and, compared with other ways of raising food, requires less land, water, and energy when you do it right.

BE outspoken. Take action. No one else can do it for you.

START a gleaning program. Connect gleaned food to schools, food pantries, jails, and hospitals.

TEACH medical students how to cook.

BUILD a just, equitable, and fair food system for everyone. Start with the basic founding principles.

MAKE a farm map. Direct people to where and when fresh seasonal food can be bought direct from the farmer.

DRAW constellations. Every farm, ranch, fishery, school, hospital, farmers' market, grocer, and restaurant is a star. Learn all the stars in your sky, and connect them in new ways to build a more resilient good food system.

WAGE peace, grow food. Turn guns into farm tools.

SPIN the roulette wheel of school food reform all you want, but the house always wins. The game is rigged. Put your money where it's going to land: with the cafeteria staff. Support them with training and finances, and you will have reform.

ASK about that wellness policy at your school. Did you know you had one? How is it really going?

FIND OUT who is in charge of the food in the cafeterias, whether it's at school, at a hospital, or at a workplace. Once you know who controls what, then you can do something about it.

CAMPAIGN to raise the minimum wage and support good food education.

CAMPAIGN to tax the food and sugary drinks that make people sick, in order to subsidize whole, good food and good food education.

START 'em young. Initiate a farm to school program at a preschool.

>×<

CHAPTER 1

Start

I N BUILDING A strong food community, there's no right or wrong way to start. But not starting — now, that's a mistake. Be courageous wherever and whoever you are. Use everything you've got, from networks to technology to know-how. Do not be ashamed if what you start is not perfect. Fear of failure squashes creativity every time.

Look around you. What is the history of your place, the people, the culture? Food activism is not a recent phenomenon. We all stand on the shoulders of those who came before us. Who are the elders, activators, and instigators who came before you? What did they try to do, and what were their successes and failures? Ask them, while they're still around.

This is not about re-creating the past, but instead about incorporating lessons learned in order to build resilient food systems today, using all the resources and innovations we can to create better access to fresh whole foods for everyone. Ask, then: What food grows around you today, and what food used to be grown? Ask why it disappeared. Was it due to the weather, consumer mistrust, job loss, low wages, trends, unsustainable business or nonprofit practices, distribution, corporate consolidation, or some other reason?

Know your place, and get to know it all over again, through the lens of building a healthy and strong food community for everyone (page 20).

Start small, because even the seemingly small things take time, commitment, and follow-through. Hold a potluck with a purpose to learn more about your food system (page 23). Cook and serve food that's grown locally or regionally and that's culturally grounded to your place, by the seasons. Buying locally grown food supports growers and your area's economy, as well as health. And food from nearby just tastes better.

Learn more about what you can do to make a big difference; there are so many issues that you will have to narrow your scope and find one that interests you most (page 26).

Host a dinner at which you can meet with the farmers in your community and ask how you can support them (page 27).

As the poet Martha Postlewaite writes in her poem "Clearing,"

Do not try to save
the whole world
or do anything grandiose.

Just start. And keep your phone charged.

KNOW YOUR LOCAL FOOD COMMUNITY

Start with a sketch. As I noted in the introduction to this book, the doctor drew a picture of my father's heart because it is important to try to visualize what it is you want fixed. As you think about creating a more just and healthy food system, you will need to know how the one you have already functions. Who is in your food community? Who are your potential allies and your collaborators? Also, an important question is this: Who is left out?

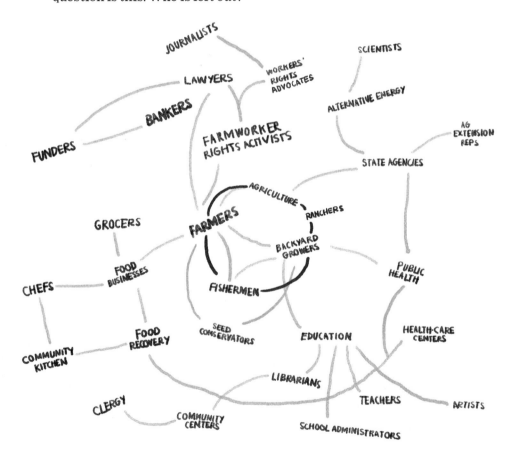

>><<

EVERYTHING YOU NEED

When my friend Julia Kidd moved to the small rural town of West Tisbury, Massachusetts, from New York City, she wrote on an index card, "This island has everything I need," and stashed it in her underwear drawer. I love this daily assurance. It tells you what you need to know: help surrounds you now. Today you have what you need. And if it's not right there in the immediate, it's probably only one or two degrees of separation away. Substitute the name of your town or village or neighborhood for the words "This island" in Julia's affirmation to help you work within your existing food system to change it into one that feeds and sustains rather than withholds; into one that that is resilient rather than rigid and destructive; and into one that is varied, vibrant, and meaningful.

As you think about ways that you can work to strengthen your local food system, keep collaboration and economic sustainability in focus. "Collaboration is the new competition," said John Hickenlooper, Colorado's governor. The advantages of collective local wisdom are enormous when facing the multidimensional issues related to good food against a backdrop of climate change and of the gazillions of lobbying and marketing dollars the processed food industry possesses. As federal grant monies dry up, we need creative collaborations now more than ever.

LOCAVORES ARE JUST EATERS

locavore (noun): One whose diet consists only or principally of locally grown or produced food. Origin: early 21st century: on the pattern of *carnivore*, *herbivore*, etc.

I hope the word "locavore" is forever included in future dictionaries as reflecting a kind of cultural apex when it was nominated the Oxford Word of the Year in 2007. Let's also hope that the concept will not be relegated to the dustbin of history, along with the avocado-green and autumn-orange kitchen appliances of the 1970s.

Unfortunately, however, this word has been pinned with a connotation of pretentiousness, preciousness, or snobbery. Some people who aspire to be locavores seem to suggest by their use of the word that good food is only for those who are somehow more aesthetically, cognitively, and emotionally aware than most others. They use it to turn their conversation into a kind of competitive tango of culinary elevation.

So even though "locavore" is kind of a cool word, because it does mark a shift and sparks debates and diets, it's not entirely inclusive. As we talk about food, I prefer the simple word "eater." This word includes all of us.

START COOKING

Perhaps you never considered yourself to have enough of whatever it is that's necessary to be a food activist. Perhaps you have let your fears and insecurities stop you from even imagining what you can accomplish. Perhaps you think you need a specialized degree to work in food systems (the phrase itself is kind of off-putting and clinical) and you don't have any credentials. Or maybe you think someone else, someone more qualified, is going to do it for you. You may also see time and money as barriers.

All these resistances live in each of us every day. But you know what? Light up those resistances with a blue flame! Start cooking, and invite others to your table. Find and connect with the collective wisdom held by people who live alongside you today. It's how my own story of becoming a food activist started — at the stove, in my kitchen, with one of the best potlucks I ever had.

In May 2005, I threw a handful of figurative darts at my community food web, finding some writers, fishermen, farmers, grocers, clergy members, beekeepers, gardeners — eaters, 35 in all — to come together for a working potluck dinner.

I was excited and nervous as I stood in my family's dining room in Vineyard Haven, Massachusetts, surrounded by friends, some of whom I knew, some I didn't yet know. The energy in the room was electric in the best possible of ways.

I remember the slow-cooked beef ribs the most (see page 25), how just a few bites of them steadied me. And there was a salad made by Jan, lamb from Clarissa and Mitch's Allen Farm, and farmed oysters provided by Rick of the MV Shellfish Group.

After we ate, we held a facilitated discussion about the "s" word: sustainability. We discussed what that word meant to us in that time and place — and, more important, what we were going to do about it. That evening, we were determined to end the discussion with actions, and we did.

Out of this gathering, a group of people eventually established the small nonprofit named Island Grown Initiative, of which I was the founder and first executive director. Another group came together to organize a Slow Food group (a convivium, in Slow Food parlance). As of this printing, both the Island Grown Initiative and Martha's Vineyard Slow Food still hold a presence in our community's local food system. Both groups contribute to food awareness and education. Both organizations work toward a more sustainable way of life that respects the water, energy, land, animals, food, and people.

YOU CAN DO THIS

HOLD A POTLUCK WITH A PURPOSE

The potluck I held in May 2005 changed forever how I view my community, neighbors, the local economy, the schools, the landscape, and the food I buy, cook, and eat. It's incredible what one night and a simple thing like sharing food — and a focused discussion with different perspectives coming together — can do.

Use the Know Your Local Food Community list on page 20 to help you identify allies in your local food web and invite them, whether you know them or not. Don't be shy.

Decide on a location that can comfortably fit anywhere from 10 to 35 people. This is a working potluck, and if you get much bigger than 35 people, the gathering may be difficult to facilitate. Choose a private home or perhaps a community center, Grange hall, YMCA, or library conference room. Check first to make sure that your chosen venue will allow you to serve food.

Designate a facilitator or cofacilitators. I'm a strong believer in having someone from the outside help facilitate your potluck. I've attended other "get started" potlucks and seen this guest facilitator phenomenon work wonders. We neighbors tend to behave better in front of guests. John Ash, a California-based cookbook author and teacher, was my cofacilitator, coconspirator, coagitator, and always a friend.

TIPS

PASS AROUND a sign-in sheet, and ask for best contact info.

SUPPLY name tags.

START and finish on time.

EAT TOGETHER FIRST, then get to the working part of the meeting.

LEAVE SCRAP PAPER and pens/pencils on the tables so that guests may take notes during the meeting.

DISPLAY THE AGENDA for all to see; use a whiteboard or large pad of paper to record your brainstorming and subsequent action items.

>>

A SAMPLE POTLUCK AGENDA

INTRODUCE the participants.
(5 to 15 minutes)

ASK some questions: What does a
healthy community food system mean
to us? What do we want to do about it?
(5 minutes)

CHOOSE your goals. For inspiration,
see The List on pages 13–17.
(5 minutes)

IDENTIFY what you already have
accomplished. (5 minutes)

FIND any gaps that need to be filled.
(5 minutes)

SUGGEST allies in funding, education,
and outreach. (10 minutes)

DETERMINE what actions you will
take, assign tasks, list the next steps,
and decide how you will follow up.
(10 minutes)

SUMMARIZE the meeting, and set the
time for the next meeting. Say good
night and thank you! (5 minutes)

*Note: If your community is already engaged and active yet you're looking to take on
another project or go to the next level, ask a more specific question around the topic you
want to develop. Maybe your goal is to build a community garden (page 131), or start a
seed conservation movement (page 129) or a farm to school initiative (page 34).*

"When people are ready to, they change. They never do it
before then, and sometimes they die before they get around to
it. You can't make them change if they don't want to, just like
when they do want to, you can't stop them." — Andy Warhol

ASIAN FLAVORED SHORT RIBS by John Ash

SERVES **4**

It's hard to screw up short ribs. You just need to cook them slowly and gently for the meat to become softened and luscious. Once cooked, they can be served as is or pulled from the bone and turned into a great topper for rice, noodles, or a fantastic hash. Since short ribs contain a fair amount of fat, I like to braise them ahead of time and then refrigerate them so that I can easily remove the congealed fat.

5   **tablespoons olive oil**

4   **pounds short ribs with bone, cut in 2-inch pieces**

Salt and freshly ground pepper

1½ **cups chopped green onions with green tops**

2   **tablespoons finely chopped fresh ginger**

1   **cup chopped carrot**

1½ **cups red wine**

4   **cups beef or chicken stock**

¼   **cup rice vinegar**

⅔   **cup low-sodium soy sauce**

¼   **cup brown or palm sugar**

2   **tablespoons chile garlic sauce**

3   **pieces dried tangerine peel or 3 tablespoons finely grated orange zest**

1   **tablespoon 5-spice powder**

2   **teaspoons cornstarch mixed with 2 tablespoons cold water (optional)**

1. In a heavy-bottomed Dutch oven or casserole with a lid, add 3 tablespoons of the olive oil and quickly brown the ribs, seasoning lightly with salt and pepper. Remove, set ribs aside, and pour off any fat.

2. Add remaining 2 tablespoons olive oil, onions, ginger, and carrot to pan and brown lightly. Add wine, stock, vinegar, soy sauce, sugar, chile garlic sauce, tangerine peel, and 5-spice powder and bring to a simmer. Add ribs, cover tightly, and place in a preheated 350°F oven for 2½ to 3 hours or until meat is very tender and almost falling off the bone.

3. Remove ribs, keeping a bone with each piece if desired, and cover with foil to keep warm.

4. Strain the cooking liquid and degrease. Return liquid to a clean pan, and boil down uncovered until reduced by a third or so, about 5 minutes. Add cornstarch mixture if desired to slightly thicken, and simmer for another 3 to 4 minutes. Season with salt and pepper if needed, and pour over ribs. (If making a day ahead, refrigerate strained broth to solidify fat for easy removal, and reheat ribs in the finished sauce.)

— John Ash © 2001

FIND YOUR ISSUE(S)

Get to the heart of the matter. Identify the issues that inspire and empower you. Meat is what got me hooked; within that broad topic, the two specific areas that concerned me were animal welfare and cooking healthy food for my kids. There are lots of angles, issues, and nuances around meat, and this is true about any food. Value this diversity, and use it to leverage change to support healthier food communities. Here are a few (!) of the issues that meat brings up:

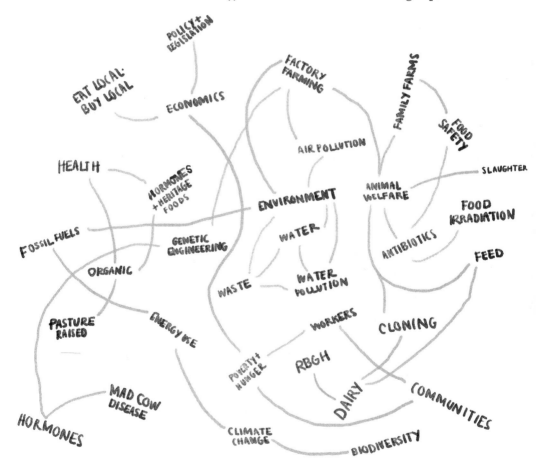

— Array of issues courtesy of The Meatrix (themeatrix.com)

WHEN YOU NEED INSPIRATION

Seek out these authors and speakers to learn, be inspired, stay informed on issues of food, health, economics, climate change, and agriculture: Wendell Berry, Mark Bittman, Malcolm Gladwell, Jean Glasgow, Jessica B. Harris, Frederick L. Kirschenmann, Bill McKibben, Wangari Maathai, Gary Nabhan, Marion Nestle, Raj Patel, Michael Pollan, Vandana Shiva, and Muhammad Yunus. Read a lot. Learn, take in the information, and transform it into doable actions.

YOU CAN DO THIS

HOST A FARMERS' DINNER

Feeding farmers is very satisfying. They are appreciative, and good eaters to boot. Since Island Grown Initiative was a small group committed to supporting local farmers, we needed to hear directly from *them* — rather than from industry insiders, state representatives, or consultants (a.k.a. lobbyists) — about how we could best give them that support.

We wanted to create a safe environment in which both we and the farmers could speak freely and respectfully. Our first farmers' dinner conversation took a bit of cajoling. We were all in uncharted territory and somewhat tentative. When we asked the farmers what they needed in order to keep growing the food we eaters wanted, their initial answers were things like "I need more fencing and a new tractor." We were casting about. Three themes finally arose: our local farmers needed skilled labor, more land, and access to a humane slaughter facility. With that information, we went back to our drawing board. In our community, land and labor were already being addressed to varying degrees by other nonprofits focused on conservation and affordable housing. A slaughterhouse, however, was not being pursued beyond lively talks over coffee at the general store that always started with, "We should . . ." and ended despondently with, "but it's never going to happen." As it turned out, we were able to make this happen (see page 104). The moral of this story is that you don't know where your farmers' dinner conversation will lead you. Start cooking to find out.

>>

DEFINE YOUR TERRITORY. County and town lines may be confusing when it comes to defining a community food system. Public school systems may help you focus your search radius. School systems are already delineated communities, so they can act as the hub of your food system, and they consist of a fairly predictable population of eaters.

HOLD YOUR FARMERS' DINNER IN A NEUTRAL LOCATION, not in someone's home. We had our first in the Agricultural Hall in West Tisbury.

SEND OUT POSTCARDS with date, time, location, agenda, and RSVP info. The winter is a good time to host a farmers' dinner. If it must be in the spring, summer, or fall, have a "twilight dinner" that begins after the workday is finished.

SEND OUT E-MAIL REMINDERS, or follow up by phone. Reach out and encourage people to come. Set the tone of conviviality, community, and mutual support.

DETERMINE YOUR AGENDA with time allotments. Post it on a whiteboard or a large piece of paper on the wall for all to see. See page 24 for a sample agenda. In the case of a first farmers' dinner, though, after the preliminaries, ask: How can we eaters support you? And plan to listen for at least a half hour. (Maybe throw out some ideas to get going; for example, help connect farmers to landholdings, develop a seed cooperative, start a gleaning program, build a slaughterhouse.)

IF YOU NEED A MICROPHONE, arrange for one beforehand and test it.

HAVE NAME TAGS and a sign-in sheet that asks for best contact information.

PROVIDE A HEALTHY, SEASONAL HOME-COOKED MEAL with a vegetarian option. Serve water, coffee, and milk but no alcohol.

ASSIGN TASKS to your working group for the day of your meeting: setting up the space, welcoming guests, preparing food, providing recycling and/or compost/pig buckets, doing cleanup, and removing trash.

ASSIGN A SCRIBE to take notes for your working group during the meeting.

HAVE A WHITEBOARD or flip pad of paper to record the group's ideas and thoughts.

PROVIDE PAPER and pencils for the table, for farmer-guests to use. Offer nuts and water on the table to let people keep their energy up.

ASSIGN ACTION ITEMS at the meeting. Plan to check in with the actions/people after the meeting.

STICK TO YOUR AGENDA. Start and end on time. End when you say you are going to end.

THANK YOUR COOKS, your hosts. Thank the farmers and the working group for coming out, and let them know you will send out follow-up notes to all in attendance. Let them know how to reach you or the contact person for the group. Be a good communicator.

>✕<

"Pay attention. Be astonished. Tell others." — Mary Oliver

ADAPTING THE FARMERS' DINNER MODEL

The Potluck with a Purpose casts a wide net into your community food system, whereas the farmers' dinner is more specific to a group of people you want to engage. But if it's not specifically farmers you're trying to reach, or if the project you want to jump-start hinges on working with a different target group, then go ahead and adapt the Farmers' Dinner model to fit your needs. For instance, if you want to support a food recovery program, then invite chefs, caterers, and food bank and community supper people. If you want to focus on seed conservation or pollination, invite garden club members from your region. If you want to plant fruit trees on public lands, invite orchardists and representatives from the parks department. For any group you decide to invite, have an agenda but also be open to going wherever the meeting takes you.

CHAPTER 2

Educate

THIS CHAPTER USES the word "education" in the broadest possible sense. Many of the suggested actions take place in schools, but education definitely doesn't stop in the classroom. We can always hone our critical thinking skills as we find, develop, and implement effective ways and means of changing whatever it is we set out to change.

One thing I have realized is that everyone I meet knows more about something than I do. Educators include everyone from the panelists at conferences (see page 44), to the Lunch Teachers (see page 48), to the FoodCorps members (page 54). As an aspiring lifelong learner (I learned that phrase from my kids' elementary school), I think asking questions, listening, and continuing an education while supporting the education for others (especially the youth) are all essential steps.

Farm to school is the foundation of good food activism. It is a stunning wave of one of the most important and long-view progressive movements happening today.

Farm to school programs connect local growers, fishermen, and other producers to schools with a steady, predictable market for produce, meat, fish, dairy, and value-added products. Such programs reach across socioeconomic and cultural divides because of the inclusiveness of the public school system. The movement is boundless and flourishing in all areas of the country — rural, urban, and suburban.

Teaching youngsters the value of eating good food and introducing them to the tastes of fresh seasonal fruits and vegetables will, in a very few years, pay off in terms of health care and diminishing food-related illnesses. School gardens create community within the school and can do so outside of it by connecting schoolchildren with elders, the underserved, and veterans.

Students who've been exposed to farm to school will more than likely become conscious consumers who use their pocketbooks to buy fresh, local, seasonal foods. If you're a farmer, you can't do better than a "buy local" marketing campaign, no matter how well designed another logo may be. You can tell that farm to school is the real deal simply because of how hard big agriculture and food conglomerates are lobbying *against* improved school food nutrition requirements.

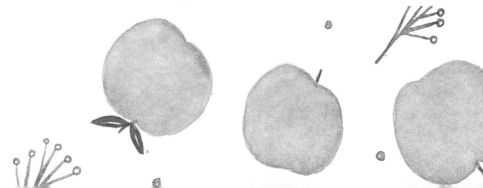

FIVE MYTHS ABOUT FARM TO SCHOOL

Here are some invaluable clarifications from Chelsey Simpson, communications manager for the wonderful National Farm to School Network.

Myth 1: Farm to school is only about local food in the cafeteria.

Fact: Farm to school programs are as diverse as the communities that build them, and school gardening, nutrition education in the classroom, and even cooking lessons are equally important aspects of farm to school. While integrating local food into the school cafeteria is the goal of many farm to school programs, studies have shown that without complementary education, kids might not even try the new foods being offered. It's also important to remember that most farm to school programs start small: container gardens, local apple taste tests, and field trips to farms are *all* examples of common and successful farm to school activities.

Myth 2: My school is too small/big/urban/rural/underfunded to have a farm to school program.

Fact: Farm to school programs are taking shape in all kinds of communities, from schools with fewer than 100 students in rural Montana to large schools in big urban districts in cities such as Chicago and New York. The key, again, is to remember farm to school's diversity and to do what you can, where you are, with what you have. Not enough money for a farm field trip? Start a farmer pen-pal program; farmers *love* to get letters from kids! Are supply problems thwarting your all-local salad bar? Buy a smaller quantity of cherry tomatoes in several varieties, and let kids sample them to determine a favorite. Every program has to start somewhere!

Myth 3: It's illegal for schools to buy local food.

Fact: Farm to school is taking place at more than 12,000 schools in all 50 states, and the USDA has made it clear that schools are allowed to give preference to locally sourced food during the bid process. You can read more about the geographic preference rule on our website. Every state and school district does have its own set of additional guidelines, however, so it's always best to check with someone locally to understand the lay of the land. The National Farm to School Network has state leads (a.k.a. local experts) who can help you navigate your community's regulations.

Myth 4: Purchasing local food is too expensive, and my school can't afford it.

Fact: Not necessarily. In some cases, studies have shown that the local option is *not* more expensive. For example, Michigan apples are very affordable during apple harvest season, and in Alaska fish is often less expensive than beef. There's also the possibility that your school is already receiving some local products from its regular distributor, but the staff either doesn't know it or isn't advertising it. Asking is the first step. Finally, we can't talk about cost without also talking about the link between food and health. Research shows that kids participating in farm to school programs eat as much as 1.3 additional servings of fruits and vegetables in their school meals and make healthier food choices at home, too. Spending a few extra cents on lunch today might save thousands of health-care dollars down the road.

Myth 5: Someone else is going to start a program for you.

Fact: The two most common questions we receive at the National Farm to School Network are, "Where can I apply to get a farm to school program?" and "How does my school qualify to receive local food?" Both hint at the misconception that farm to school is something that comes from outside a community (like being selected for *Extreme Home Makeover*) versus inside the community (like a barn raising). So I'm here to tell you this is a movement of grassroots movers and shakers, barn raisers, and seed sowers! Virtually every farm-to-table program in the country was started by someone just like you. And don't forget that we are here to help: in addition to contacting one of the National Farm to School Network's local experts, check out our Getting Started guide online, and join our network so that you can stay in touch. When your spuds have sprouted and your local hamburger is a hit, we want to hear about it!

— Excerpted with permission from the National Farm to School Network (farmtoschool.org)

YOU CAN DO THIS

START A FARM TO SCHOOL PROGRAM

Here are a few simple first projects from the National Farm to School Network. These are attainable goals that can help you prepare the ground for establishing a farm to school program in your community.

IDENTIFY menu items that you would like to transition to local products.

FIND a farmer or distributor to connect you to local items.

PLAN a local meal event.

DETERMINE training needs to assist food service staff with incorporating farm-fresh items in meals.

BRING a school garden planning team together.

IDENTIFY curricular opportunities to connect to a school garden.

BRING a chef into the classroom.

PLAN a farm field trip or host a tasting event featuring local produce.

CONTACT your state's School Nutrition Association to learn how others in your state are approaching farm to school in their school/district.

CONNECT with the Child Nutrition Program at your state agency (typically your Department of Education or Department of Agriculture).

— Excerpted with permission from the National Farm to School Network (farmtoschool.org)

>×<

The number of schools known to be participating in farm to school programs jumped from 400 in 2004 to more than 2,300 in 2011.

TIP When you introduce your farm to school aspirations to your community, share an inspiring program from your region to make the connections stronger and to preempt skepticism.

NOLI TAYLOR

The Summer Months: A School Garden's Achilles' Heel?

Noli Taylor, founder and program leader at Island Grown Schools (IGS), has some very good advice on what to do when school lets out, a common barrier that keeps many schools from even getting started with a garden.

We have found that irrigation systems are a huge help in sustaining gardens over the summer months. If there is a way to have a regular irrigation system installed, on a timer so it happens regularly each week, that is an ideal system. We asked a local irrigation installation company to donate time and materials to one of our school gardens, and they happily complied.

Even with careful planning in the garden to make sure that harvesting happens mostly before school is out and once it resumes, and even with irrigation systems, gardens still need care over the summer, and there is always some harvesting to be done during these important growing months. Our schools on the island approach this a few ways.

Adopt-a-Garden

Some schools asked families to "adopt" the garden for a week or more during the summer months. In exchange for one to three hours of service, the families can harvest whatever is ready during their week to bring home and eat. This is a great way to keep kids engaged with their gardens even while school is out of session, and to expand garden experiences and skills in food production to parents and caregivers.

The adopt-a-garden schools set out a sign-up sheet at least a month before school lets out for families to commit to taking care of the garden. The sign-up sheets always make clear that no previous garden experience is necessary. Before summer break begins, the IGS staff leads a short after-school session on garden care (with snacks provided), to help families that have signed up prepare for their summer responsibilities and to thank them for taking this on.

The week before a family's designated garden care week, a staff member will call to remind them and, ideally, set a date to meet with them in the garden during their week to go over that week's needs (e.g., weed the beans, water, harvest *x*, *y*, and *z*) and give a little training if needed on how to fill those needs (e.g., "Here's how to harvest kale so it will keep coming back"). If the family can't meet with our staff in the garden, a staff member will explain

>>

the needs over the phone and/or on a message board at the garden site. We always try to find a way to recognize these families' service, whether it's through a note in the school newsletter once school is back in session or a letter to the editor of the local paper.

Some schools have summer programs happening on their campuses while school is out of session. Some summer program leaders commit to maintaining the gardens with their students over the summer.

IGS runs a youth agricultural service learning program during the summer months, and these teenagers commit some time each week to supporting school garden maintenance needs. Many high school students who are looking for community service opportunities, either to fulfill school requirements or for college application credentials, find a way to connect and keep the school garden growing strong. Connecting with them can inspire their involvement in food system change while keeping the garden vibrant during the summer months.

Some farm to school organizations work with companies and private businesses in their local communities to organize days of service. Staff service activities/days are a great way to connect with more folks in the community, get them engaged in your mission, and get maintenance needs done in the gardens, while helping the businesses fulfill their team-building and community service goals.

Sometimes you'll find that no matter what you do, school gardens will still need staff to keep them vibrant over the summer. While we are constantly working to develop creative systems and solutions that engage students and families in maintaining their school's garden at all of our schools, at some schools, this can be a difficult thing to put in place and sometimes our staff ends up needing to be on-site during the summer to keep the gardens growing. We are always experimenting with different approaches to see what can work in our school communities, and the investment in time and creative resources in reaching out to engage caregivers and students in summer garden maintenance feels worthwhile and important. You never know who will "grow" into your next new student and/or adult leader!

— Excerpted with permission from Noli Taylor, Island Grown Schools (islandgrownschools.org)

TIP Join the National Farm to School Network (farmtoschool.org). Listen to one of their Lunch Bites, brief free webinars on such topics as "School Composting Made Easy."

VERMONT FEED AND THE 3 C'S

Shelburne, Vermont

The farm to school program Vermont Food Education Every Day (FEED) is a partnership between two nonprofits: the Northeast Organic Farming Association of Vermont (NOFA-VT) and Shelburne Farms. As noted on its website (vtfeed.org), the organization's mission is to work "with schools and communities to raise awareness about healthy food, good nutrition, and the role of Vermont farms and farmers."

Vermont FEED is a great model founded on what it calls the 3 C's:

COMMUNITY · CLASSROOM · CAFETERIA

All of its guidebooks are downloadable for free at its website, and its DVD "Grow Up Fresh" is a terrific short introduction to the potency of a farm to school program. Show it at your first community meeting!

Finding Vermont FEED was a real boon to our baby farm to school program on Martha's Vineyard. Because we're based in New England, looking, say, all the way to California to chef Alice Waters's Edible Schoolyard Project (edibleschoolyard.org), as aspirational as it is, would not have played well in our local culture. But Vermont was right in our neighborhood, so we took a page from Vermont FEED's playbook. Who are the muses in your region?

WHEN FACED WITH ROADBLOCKS

It was surprising to me when a school cafeteria worker and local board of health roadblocked students' access to the food grown in their school's own garden. The reasoning, apparently, was that the tomatoes, basil, and carrots hadn't come from "approved sources." Yet what constituted an approved source remained ambiguous and open to interpretation. It seems that "approved source" is one of those open-ended insider phrases that keeps people, including activists and organizers, at bay. It implies that there is some greater authority (also undisclosed and hidden away) who decides what's acceptable and warranted and good. In the most cynical of perspectives, underlying this obfuscation are the food service contracts locking in what schools can buy and from whom. A less sinister contributing factor is that local boards of health and local school cafeteria personnel may not know yet how to go about including food grown at the school, so it's easier to say no, with a little intimidating language thrown in.

>>

But instead of getting roadblocked, a group of good food activists from around the country (including Noli Taylor of Island Grown Schools) wrote some boilerplate text for you activists to hand over to your local boards of health when you start your own school garden. This language is available to schools and school districts around the country and can be adapted as needed. All together now: school garden best practices!

>><<

INSTITUTE BEST PRACTICES
AT YOUR SCHOOL GARDEN

The following best practices were created as a collaborative effort among school garden practitioners from across the country. Thanks to Kelly Erwin, Deb Habib, Tegan Hagy, Dana Hudson, Emily Jackson, Marion Kalb, Catherine Sands, Noli Taylor, and Amy Winston. These recommendations were created with the support of the National Farm to School Network (farmtoschool.org).

School gardens serve as exciting living laboratories and are an important component of farm to school efforts. The bounty from school gardens can contribute to the school cafeteria, to students' families, or to classroom and after-school taste-testing activities.

The following practices are intended to provide basic food safety guidelines for those involved with school gardens. They include principles from good agricultural practices and safe-handling procedures and are intended to serve as a framework that may easily be adapted to meet individual school settings and regional requirements. The safety benefits of fresh food grown on-site include the avoidance of potential contamination that accompanies long-distance travel (where products frequently change hands) and control over the supply chain direct from garden to table.

Safe-handling information should be provided to students, teachers, and others involved in growing, harvesting, and preparing food. In addition to the many benefits of fresh food, healthy activity, and learning, your school garden can be an educational tool that helps teach students about food safety procedures.

Recommendations

Those planning and planting the school garden should review your school's rules and regulations. Some plants that can cause serious allergic reactions may be prohibited.

If the garden is near parking areas or other high-traffic zones, consider testing for contaminants before growing fruits and vegetables. Many states have agriculture Extension services that can help with this. If building a raised-bed garden, consider purchasing soil meant for food production from an established retail entity to ensure soil safety and traceability.

If your school has a composting program for cafeteria waste, use the resulting compost for flowers, ornamental plants, and trees rather than for garden beds where food is grown. Compost that comes from garden waste can be applied to food-growing beds if deemed appropriate by the school garden supervisor and/or compost coordinator.

Be sure to coordinate with school groundskeeping or custodial staff about your garden's goals, protocols, and maintenance plan. If you are concerned about the presence of pesticides on or near your garden, be sure to communicate that, too. Consider using your school garden as an educational tool that can teach students about food safety procedures, and incorporate curricula that teach to these issues in your garden educational plan.

Be sure that your school garden program is aligned with any relevant school district policies, including but not limited to wellness policies, school procedures for receiving gifts and donations, working with parent and community volunteers, and liability policies.

>>

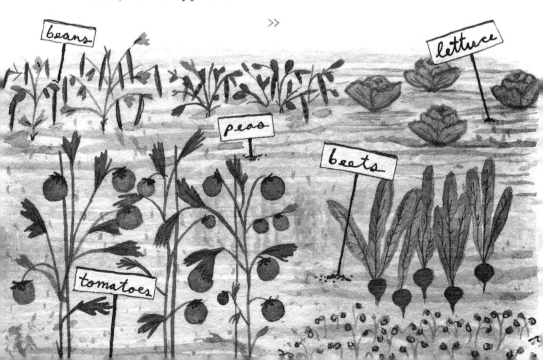

Growing Practices

All organic matter should be fully composted in aerobic conditions and at high temperatures prior to application. Avoid raw manure, and limit composted manure to what can be purchased from a commercial outlet to ensure traceability.

When using water for irrigation, make sure it is potable and from a tested source. Check with your state Cooperative Extension for simple testing kits.

If soil used for growing is coming from school property, test for contaminants before planting. Testing kits are usually available through your state, same as water testing, above.

There are many places to purchase seeds for your school garden, so be conscious of where your seeds come from and consider source and quality. Look for those that are non–genetically modified and come from companies that have taken a "safe seed pledge."

No synthetic pesticides or herbicides should be used, preventing toxic residue on food and avoiding human and environmental exposure to pesticides.

Materials used for garden beds should be constructed of nontoxic, nonleaching material (no pressure-treated wood or used tires).

Harvesting and Handling

Everyone involved in harvesting should wash hands thoroughly in warm soapy water for at least 20 seconds prior to harvesting. Anyone with open cuts or wounds should not participate in harvest until those wounds have healed.

All harvesting tools — scissors, bowls, tubs — should be food-grade and/or food service approved and designated solely for harvest and food handling. The tools should be cleaned regularly with hot water and soap, then dried.

School garden produce delivered for use in a school cafeteria should be received and inspected by food service personnel upon delivery with the same system used to receive and inspect all other incoming products.

If storage is necessary, produce should be cooled and refrigerated promptly after harvest. Temperatures vary on type of produce being harvested; specific postharvest storage and transportation temperatures can be found at the University of California–Davis's Postharvest Technology website (postharvest .ucdavis.edu/producefacts).

School garden produce should be handled according to the same standards that the cafeteria has in place for conventionally received produce. A person with ServSafe (page 42) or comparable food safety certification should supervise students, parents, or staff who participate in any food preparation events (e.g., taste tests or special cafeteria events).

ISLAND GROWN PRESCHOOLS

In 2011, the National Farm to School Network created the Farm to Preschool Subcommittee (farmtopreschool.org). This essay underscores the value of collaboration.

On a recent spring day in a school garden, the children were watering their peas. One of the students looked at the pea shoots poking out of the ground and exclaimed, "Oh, so that actually works?!"

Preschool is an important age to create and inform future eating habits, and it is an ideal time to connect with families about nutrition and offer practical cooking skills. We aim to engage the whole family to empower them to make healthy eating choices, learn to grow food, and connect with local farms and farmers. To that end, Island Grown Preschools partnered with Vineyard Nutrition (a local nutrition consulting business). Vineyard Nutrition in turn collaborated with the state's Health and Human Services Department to create a healthy family cookbook, which they offered as a free download. The cookbook offers suggestions for budget-friendly, kid-approved, healthy dishes for breakfast, snack, lunch, and dinner. Through Island Grown Preschool's partnership with Vineyard Nutrition and Martha's Vineyard Community Services, we were able to offer parent/child cooking classes to help families foster traditions of cooking healthy foods together.

Throughout the school year, students participate in indoor and outdoor activities. Garden activities naturally relate to other lessons that preschoolers are learning such as counting, writing, reading, motor skills, and working together. Everything can be taught through the lens of food.

The success of the program at the preschool level is due in large part to commitment by the schools to educating kids and families about food, nutrition, and gardening. Some preschools have overhauled their snack programs to include whole foods with an emphasis on fruits and vegetables. I work with the kids to make a healthy dinner for their parents so that when the parents pick the kids up, everyone enjoys salad and soup and homemade bread together before going home. This holistic approach, together with school buy-in, has made this collaborative program such a success.

— Excerpted with permission from Emily Armstrong and Island Grown Preschools

YOU CAN DO THIS

GET CERTIFIED

....

Overcome one of the barriers to working or volunteering in a school cafeteria (or a food recovery program, page 250) by getting a food handler certification. The National Restaurant Association has established the ServSafe Food Safety Training Program (servsafe .com) to certify food service professionals. You can use the ServSafe website to find a nearby class, or you can complete the training and exams online. Trainings are available in Spanish, Korean, and Chinese, as well as English. The classes and exams do cost money, however. If you are part of a nonprofit organization, you could ask your donors to cover the costs or submit a grant proposal to an appropriate foundation. Becoming a certified food handler will pay off in confidence and competency, and in many instances it may be required.

>×<

HAVE A FUN-RAISER

If you're lucky, your school has everything from sports teams to debate teams, and each of those teams has its own fans. Now here's a chance to rile up your fans for your school's good food program and raise awareness about it in your community. By throwing a party that's one part fund-raiser and one part fun-raiser, you invite people in.

The goal is to raise community awareness and to celebrate your school's commitment to its garden, to its cafeteria, to good food, and, most important, to its students. You want to shoot for breaking even or perhaps for making a little money to go into your program's coffers. To that end, make it affordable and open to the public.

Find a location that suits your needs. Does it have parking? Do you need a kitchen? If so, does that kitchen work in terms of storing, prepping, and cooking food; serving guests; and cleaning up?

Give yourself time to plan. Schedule the event when you think your audience can attend. Avoid school vacation weeks, major holidays, exams, proms, big games, and school plays.

Ask community businesses to sponsor or support you with gifts of goods and services. Maybe one company can print the posters, maybe a grocer or caterer will donate food, or maybe some employee groups will volunteer their time.

Get volunteer commitments by asking people for the specific kinds of help you need, such as publicizing, planning, cooking, welcoming, serving, and cleaning up. Make sure to thank your volunteers.

Serve seasonal and simple good food, like sloppy joes, pulled pork, or tacos made with quality meat, chicken, or fish. Use the best ingredients you can, whether those include local meat, cheese, bread, veggies, or fruit.

Do not serve processed foods or sugar-sweetened beverages, such as soft drinks, sports drinks, or flavored milk. Model by serving the food and drink you want to support in your program.

Serve the dinner on cafeteria trays. You can find them at a restaurant supply store or online. They're durable and reusable, and they will fit the theme of your event.

>>

Identify one or two people to speak at the event. Welcome your guests. Tell them a little about why the program is important, whom it reaches, how it does what it does, where their money is going. Share your story about why you think this work is important. Thank your host, whether that's the director of the school cafeteria or another venue such as a Grange hall or a community center. Publicly thank your volunteers, teachers, cafeteria staff, and anyone else who has supported you in your fun-raiser.

>><<

YOU CAN DO THIS

GO TO A CONFERENCE

Whether you're interested in public health, public policy, clean water, workers' rights, indigenous cultures, sustainable agriculture, urban gardens, food recovery, or farm to school, there is a conference for you. By volunteering, you may qualify for free entry into workshops and panels. Often, national organizations such as the Farm to School Program hold regional conferences. One way to stay on top of the conference calendar is to create a Google Alert for your area of interest and/or your preferred organization.

Here's a sampling of some organizations I watch that host either national or regional conferences and/or workshops:

» **Slow Food USA** (slowfoodusa.org)

» **First Nations Development Institute** (firstnations.org)

» **Southern Foodways Alliance** (southernfoodways.org)

» **Women Food & Ag Network** (wfan.org)

» **National Farm to School Network** (farmtoschool.org)

» **Native Seed/SEARCH** (nativeseeds.org)

>><<

CONNECT ATHLETICS TO HEALTHY EATING

Work with the school booster club to sell better-quality food at your school's sports games. Look to upgrade to organic hot dogs and beef burgers for the grill. Bring in ketchup that's free of high-fructose corn syrup. Ax the sodas and sports drinks, and promote drinking more water instead. (For more on how to limit food and beverage advertising in schools, see page 46.)

Leverage student athletes' desire to improve their athletic ability by making the connections between healthy eating, good workouts, and improved performance. Look for strategic entry points to your athletic programs. Is going straight to the top and talking to the athletic director the best approach, or will you have a better chance bending the ear of a coach? Write up what you are doing so that you have an articulated purpose and plan. If the teams travel, maybe a good place to start is a backpack program for student athletes that includes fresh fruit, nuts, whole food bars, and reusable water bottles.

Another approach to consider is implementing the "study table" model that some college athletic programs provide for their teams. A study table is a designated place where student athletes are encouraged (and in some cases required) to be at a designated time. At study table the athletes can meet with tutors, do their schoolwork, and, most important, get a good, hot, healthy meal. Eating together not only promotes team building and develops social skills but also has the potential to shift what kinds of foods athletes are getting and innately teach healthier food choices. But of course you've got to serve good, healthy whole foods to make study table work as it should.

RESTRICT FOOD AND BEVERAGE ADVERTISING IN SCHOOLS

From display ads for soft drinks on vending machines to fast-food logos on book covers and sports scoreboards, students are often surrounded at school by promotions for unhealthy foods. While these ads can bring much-needed revenue to cash-strapped schools, they also promote unhealthy food choices and compromise the educational environment. The good news for parents, nutrition advocates, and school administrators is that schools have broad authority to control commercial messages on their campuses. ChangeLab and the National Policy & Legal Analysis Network to Prevent Childhood Obesity (NPLAN, a project of ChangeLab Solutions) have outlined some steps a community can take to create a school district policy restricting food and beverage advertising.

1. Review state law to determine whether it may affect the district's ability to adopt a policy.

Some states directly control the process through which schools can enter into a contract that grants advertising rights. Other state legislatures are currently introducing new laws on the issue. Familiarize yourself with the law in your state (you can contact your state school board association for guidance) before suggesting that your school district develop a policy restricting advertising.

2. Determine the scope of the policy you wish to adopt.

If state law permits, the school district can approve a districtwide policy that restricts the advertising of foods and beverages on school property. Three main options are to:

» Ban all advertising on campus

» Ban the advertising of all foods or beverages on campus

» Ban the advertising of those foods and beverages that the district does not allow to be sold on campus

3. Select one of NPLAN's two model policies and adapt it for your district. NPLAN's website, nplan.org, contains model policies for the second and third options (outlined in the previous list), which school districts can adapt for their use.

Because the First Amendment to the U.S. Constitution limits the government from imposing certain restrictions on speech, concerns can emerge when a public school district (a government entity) limits food and beverage company advertising. But fortunately, the First Amendment should not stand in the way of carefully crafted advertising restrictions on public school property because, in legal terms, a public school is a *nonpublic forum*. A public forum is a place that, like a public park or city square, has for many years been made available to a wide variety of speakers. The First Amendment makes it very difficult for the government to restrict speech in public forums. Because public schools have a basic and far-reaching mission to educate students, courts have ruled repeatedly that K–12 schools are *nonpublic forums*.

As a nonpublic forum, a school district may limit advertising as long as any restriction is both reasonable and viewpoint neutral. A policy is reasonable if it is consistent with the district's legitimate interest in preserving the property for its dedicated use: learning, rather than commercial activity.

— Excerpted with permission from ChangeLab Solutions (changelabsolutions.org)

"The percentage of school districts that allowed soft drink companies to advertise soft drinks on school grounds decreased from 46.6 percent in 2006 to 33.5 percent in 2012!"

— U.S. Centers for Disease Control and Prevention, 2013

GREG REYNOLDS
Delano, Minnesota

In a YouTube video sponsored by the University of Minnesota Extension Family Development called "Partnering with Schools — Advice for Farmers," farmer Greg Reynolds has this straightforward advice for farmers who'd like to sell their produce to schools: treat the schools "like a new account, a wholesale account." If you're a farmer looking to connect with schools, watching this video is one of the best ways you'll ever spend 3 minutes and 13 seconds. Some tips:

GO to the back door as you would at a restaurant or a grocery store, with a sample of your ripe, raw, and ready produce for the cafeteria managers to try. Include a few copies of your card.

COMMUNICATE well throughout your dealings. Let the school officials know what you have coming, when it'll be ripe, and what you plan to be picking, and follow through with delivery and invoicing.

COOK FOR AMERICA®
"Where School Food Is the Solution, Not the Problem"

Every school meal served is a chance to teach and an opportunity for learning. That's why chef Kate Adamick of Cook for America, a company that trains school cooks to provide healthy made-from-scratch lunches, doesn't like the disparaging nickname "lunch ladies" or the sterile-sounding "cafeteria personnel" and instead trademarked the moniker "Lunch Teachers" to emphasize the positive impact and the potential of these frontliners. Kate and her team conduct "Lunch Teachers® Culinary Boot Camps," transforming lunch ladies into Lunch Teachers across the country and empowering them to instill self-respect as they impart knowledge about budgeting, culinary arts, and food safety. Kate is also the author of the book *Lunch Money: Serving Healthy School Food in a Sick Economy.* This book, a must-have for understanding the complexities of institutional food systems, contains invaluable worksheets for the activist who delves into the crux of the issue: money.

BY THE NUMBERS: **HEALTH IMPLICATIONS OF SUGARY DRINKS**

43% INCREASE

in daily calorie consumption from 1977 to 2001 in the United States that was due to sugary drinks

55% increase

in the likelihood of a child being overweight or obese if they drink at least one serving of sugary drinks a day, compared to children who rarely drink sugary drinks

10%

of teenagers' daily calories come from sugary drinks

20% INCREASE

in levels of bad cholesterol and triglycerides in the blood of young men and women after drinking three cans of soda a day for two weeks

26% increase

in the risk of developing type 2 diabetes when consuming one to two servings of sugary drinks a day

27% INCREASE

in likelihood of an adult being overweight or obese if they drink one or more sugary drinks a day, compared to those who do not drink sodas, regardless of income or ethnicity

— publichealthadvocacy.org
(October 2013)

START A HARVEST OF THE MONTH PROGRAM

Harvest of the Month, a program that has its origins in California, with Champions for Change Network for a Healthier California, has been adapted in Oregon, Vermont, and Massachusetts. Our own Island Grown Schools compiled the art from Harvest of the Month posters as a calendar, sold to the public to benefit the program.

Fact sheets, calendar templates, program materials, and impact evaluations can be downloaded for free at the Harvest of the Month website (harvestofthe month.cdph.ca.gov) and are not California specific. Expand and integrate your Harvest of the Month programming beyond the cafeteria. Encourage the library to showcase books about that month's harvest, host book readings, and engage art classes to make art for the cafeteria around and about the featured crop or ingredient.

>><<

Harvest of the Month Tally Sheet
Contributed by Island Grown Schools

To be filled out by teacher: **Mr. Aaron**

This Month's Harvest of the Month: **Kohlrabi**

Grade Levels Participating: **5TH**

Served (check all that apply):

☑ In lunch line

☑ As separate taste tests

To be filled out by students:
Place a tally mark below if you **tried**

Kohlrabi
卌 卌 卌 ||

Place a tally mark below if you **liked**

Kohlrabi
卌 卌 |||

COLLECT DATA

Keep track of every ounce and pound of food that is being grown in your school garden, eaten in the school, or taken off the premises for another's kitchen. School-garden-grown carrot, pea, basil, parsley, and sweet potato facts and figures add up, proving their worth in both sustenance and education.

Assessments are important tools to have in place as early as you can. There are a lot of moving parts even when you start small, but being able to collect the information about how your program is making an impact is important not only for you but also for potential donors and any grant proposals you may write. It's also good to know the facts and figures when you are speaking to someone in the media, whether that person is a local television show producer or a blogger. Assessment information is also helpful if you are trying to include your program as part of the school budget. The stronger the case is for the positive impacts of a farm to school program — in the myriad of ways it affects learning, health, and well-being — the better shot you have of sharing or even passing on the fiscal responsibilities to the school or school district.

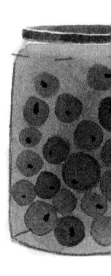

STEWARDSHIP

Here Noli Taylor, the Island Grown Schools founder and program leader, shares what's she's learned over the years. Note that she starts out by talking about "perceived" barriers rather than real ones. That's something to remember, over and over.

As we've worked toward school food change, we've faced a lot of challenges that have turned out to be perceived barriers rather than real ones. Reading the small print and calling state regulators to get the straight story on what rules really govern the work we are trying to move forward have been important time and time again in clearing up misconceptions about why farm to school was thought to be impossible.

When we started trying to move cafeteria staff to use local food in school meals, some thought that any farms they purchased from had to have special permits or certifications. At the scale we were looking at in our small rural community, this turned out not to be an issue. Nothing along these lines was written into the corporate food service contracts that governed some of our schools.

At another point, a board of health agent was concerned about the safety of food coming out of the school garden. We worked with a team organized by the national Farm to School Network to create safe food-handling protocols that set our local board of health agents at ease about the care that was being taken with the food in the gardens (page 38).

One of our schools' kitchens wasn't equipped to do scratch cooking. When we started looking into what it would cost to expand the kitchen so it could do full meal prep using fresh, locally sourced ingredients on-site, administrators estimated the project would cost $750,000, a figure so high that no one thought this would ever be possible. Tradespeople with children in the school — builders, plumbers, electricians, and others — offered to volunteer their time to bring down the cost of the project. When school committee members told us this would violate regulations, we spoke with the people at the state labor board who clarified that under certain circumstances, including this project, volunteer labor could be permissible. With the dedication of these parents and community members, the project was completed over the summer for less than $100,000.

Finding Balance

Beyond persevering, reading the fine print, and going to the source of regulations to understand what real challenges and opportunities there are to move farm to school ahead, there are personal challenges to running farm to school programs. Most of the people I've met involved in this movement are parents, usually moms, with children. Finding a balance between this important work, which can always use more time and energy, and the responsibilities of family life is a challenge. Creating an environment where people with these competing demands on their time can feel supported is an important part of the success of our program. We hire a teenage daughter of one of our staff members to provide child care during staff meetings for other employees' young children. We allow our staff to work flexible hours that fit with their families' schedules. Honoring the competing needs of the dedicated, bright, and motivated people who want to do this work is a critical part of building a farm to school movement that follows the values we are hoping to create in our world and that can be sustained over time.

— Noli Taylor, Island Grown Schools (islandgrownschools.org)

FOODCORPS
New York, New York

FoodCorps, a fairly recent addition to the AmeriCorps team, was started in 2009 with the goal of giving "all children an enduring relationship with healthy food." Their three main goals are educating students about food and nutrition; helping students to create and tend school gardens; and encouraging the use of healthy, local food in the school cafeteria. As of now, they have 125 service members working at 108 sites in 15 states. FoodCorps is funded by a number of different private companies and foundations, as well as some federal USDA and AmeriCorps money.

YOU CAN DO THIS

MAKE OVER McDONALD'S

This idea for action is by Genna Cherichello, a FoodCorps service member with the University of Maine Cooperative Extension.

If you'd like to bring your hamburger out of the fast-food lane and into your kitchen classroom, follow the recipe on the facing page. Broadened minds and strengthened community will remain long after the aroma of bacon dissipates.

"Who digs these burgers?" We all raise our hands. Beef, bacon, onion, and cheddar blend together on the bun. Consensus settles that these are among the best burgers anyone in the class has ever had.

INGREDIENTS

» 1 innovative teacher

» 1 class of skeptical students

» 1 supportive neighboring food co-op

MATERIALS

» *The Omnivore's Dilemma, Young Reader's Edition* by Michael Pollan

» 1 kitchen

» 1 nonprofit youth organization

» 1 FoodCorps service member

SERVES: Students and local farms

1. Together as a class, read Section One, "The Industrial Meal," of *The Omnivore's Dilemma, Young Reader's Edition.* Any class will do, but my students are at Oceanside East High School in Rockland, Maine, where they are enrolled in an alternative education program that focuses on sustainable living.

2. Have the students figure out the ingredients of their favorite McDonald's meal. Identify the corn-derived ingredients. In addition to obvious choices like corn meal and high-fructose corn syrup, be sure to include meat and dairy products from corn-fed cows as well as substances like maltodextrin.

3. Calculate the percentage of corn-derived ingredients in your favorite meal, and determine class average. It will likely hover around 40 percent.

4. Vote on a McDonald's meal to make over. We settled on the Angus Cheddar, Bacon, Onion Burger.

5. Pick up burger ingredients. Our class has a great relationship with Good Tern Natural Foods Co-op & Café in Rockland, Maine. We receive store credit in exchange for writing weekly lesson plans to educate K–8 students about the snacks they receive from the co-op through the Fresh Fruit & Vegetable Program (FFVP), a federal program administered by the U.S. Department of Agriculture's Food and Nutrition Service. Generally, states then administrate FFVP via their departments of education.

6. Find a kitchen. The kitchen we use, flush with utensils and gadgets, belongs to YouthLinks (youthlinksonline.org), a nonprofit youth development program stationed in a house on the school grounds. The short walk there also allows us a glimpse at our garden space!

7. Start cooking. Address any number of topics: appropriate portions, how to cut an onion, food safety, whole-grain versus white-flour buns, or food miles.

8. Acknowledge and appreciate the farms and systems that provided your meal. Compared with the experience outlined in Section One of *The Omnivore's Dilemma* and most meals at McDonald's, the ingredients in our burgers are traceable.

— Excerpted with permission from Genna Cherichello and FoodCorps, who give special thanks to Caldwell Farms in Turner, Maine, for raising the cattle for the ground beef; Sonnental Dairy in Smyrna, Maine, for making the cheddar cheese; A Wee Bit Farm in Orland, Maine, for producing the bacon; and Hope's Edge Farm in Hope, Maine, for growing the onions.

>><<

SWEET POTATOES FOR THANKSGIVING

This essay is by FoodCorps service member Sebastian Naskaris. Like Genna's piece (page 54), Sebastian's story might suggest action you'd like to take, too.

Getting local food into local schools is not impossible. In fact, this November, for the first time since anyone can remember, my county school system will be serving local sweet potatoes.

I am a young farmer and cook who is taking a year to serve with FoodCorps, a great new national nonprofit made up of 50 leaders who are trying to foster some much-needed change in our nation's school food system.

One of the ways we do this is through getting local produce into our school cafeterias. Our goal is to make a big impact on the health of our nation's kids, while making a smaller impact on the health of our nation's environment. Side effects include stronger local economies, sustainable development, farmer support, a decreasing carbon footprint, and expanding entrepreneurship opportunities.

I serve in Moore County, North Carolina, with the Communities in Schools (CIS) program's FirstSchool Gardens. The 12,500 students in my school district eat at school three times a day, but my district hasn't used the farm to school program for four years, so I set out to figure out why that was, and how I might change it. Here's what happened.

First, I met with the childhood nutrition director (CND). She helped me identify the hurdles facing the national farm to school program in our county. CNDs must procure food through bids, and my CND had already contracted with her bidders for the year. Right away, we realized that we were too late to sign up for the program. But then she suggested trying to move local produce through the distributor she already used. Brilliant!

Then, out of the blue, the CND called me and said that, in just four weeks, she wanted to put sweet potatoes on the lunch menu — the very crop we had already certified!

I had to move quickly. First, I got the contact info for our CND's distributor and started calling. I called for two weeks until finally he agreed to meet with me. Then, I got a price quote from the Extension agent working as representative for our certified farmer.

Next, I jumped in my truck and drove up to Raleigh to meet with the distributor. I needed to figure out how to get our sweet potatoes into our schools — and see if I could do it while also getting our farmer's demands met. But what if this head of distribution lived up to the stereotypical image I had in my head, sitting fat in a chair and leeching off the hard work of our producers? I pictured cigar smoke and the smell of french fries. I began reciting a sort of mantra about the need for healthy children and strong local economies. I was channeling Jimmy Stewart in *Mr. Smith Goes to Washington.*

I arrived at the distributor's office, told him our situation and our deadline, and started my Jimmy Stewart tirade. To my surprise, he sweetly listened, even agreed. And his office didn't smell like cigars or french fries. I stated our farmer's demands — his required price point and the ability to deliver the sweet potatoes himself. The distributor didn't bat an eye. Though he told me he preferred to use his own trucks for delivery, allowing the farmer to deliver his own product was not a deal breaker. The meeting ended; we shook hands in one of those business deal–type handshakes. Brilliant!

That is, until my farmer called. The spuds wouldn't be ready until a month after the due date. And so begins the portion of the story that is akin to running suicides in gym class (read: lots and lots of back-and-forth). Negotiating, calling, harvesting, explaining, changing menu dates, calling chief financial officers, holding the farmer's hand as he called the distributor, and running to hold the distributor's hand to pick up his phone. All of this while we sent scores of e-mails and made tons of calls to build support for these local spuds. The anxiety made me wanna barf.

Finally, the big day came. I was busy trying to replicate the process with a local carrot farmer when I learned that the delivery had been made. We'd done it!

Did you ever play on the monkey bars when you were little? That's what getting local produce into a local school is like. You don't know you've reached the bar you want until you are onto the next bar.

The steps you need to take to bring local food into your cafeteria may look quite different from the ones I've just described, but it's important to find comfort in the process. You may be called upon to do things you'd never have guessed you'd do. You may feel like you're running suicides, but the end line is supporting healthy lives; it's well worth the struggle. Of course, once you establish the supply line from farm to school, the problem becomes getting kids to eat the foods you've provided. After all, it's only healthy if it goes down. I call it monkey bar-ism.

— Excerpted with permission from Sebastian Naskaris and FoodCorps

VISIT YOUR SCHOOL CAFETERIA

The best way to learn about school food is by experiencing it first-hand, and by getting to know the staff who work hard to prepare the food. As you come to understand their challenges and their points of pride, then you can begin to make transformative positive changes.

Cafeteria personnel begin readying their kitchens a week or two before students arrive to start the school year. Schedule an informational visit and tour of their facilities when it's best for them. A phone call seems to work better than e-mail, and in person is the best. In our community, the window of opportunity between breakfast and lunch, around 9:00 a.m., seems to work well for the staff.

Ask your Lunch Teachers (page 48) what they love about their cafeteria, what they would like to do more of, and what they need to do so (see Ask What *Is* Working, page 68). Then throughout the school year, eat breakfast or lunch in the cafeteria with the students. Observe how it works, how much time the kids have, what it sounds like in there, what the kids eat, what gets thrown away. Eat with the kids (if they'll let you!). Ask the students what they like about the school food and what they'd like to do to make it better.

HEALTHY TOOLS FOR ALL SCHOOLS

The author, chef, and educator Ann Cooper, popularly known as the "Renegade Lunch Lady," has created online tools for schools and cafeterias on her website The LunchBox (thelunchbox.org) to assist in the scaling of recipes, menu planning, and preparing cycling and production reports. School cafeteria staff members can create an account, sign in, and get the support they need. Watch the tutorial videos to get started.

SUSPEND JUDGMENT

After visiting one of the cafeterias in my town during lunchtime, I was talking to my neighbor about what I saw: lots of Go-Gurts, Lunchables, chips, sugary flavored milk, Gatorade, and all the trash those products generate. And this was on a day when the salad bar was full and the cafeteria director was serving soup out of a Crock-Pot along with chicken and biscuits. My neighbor was quiet. She listened to my rant. Her two kids had graduated from that school. She knew it well. When I was done, she told me a story that I recall here, because as with many good stories, there's a moral to share. Here's the gist of what she said.

"When my son reached middle school age, I couldn't get him to take lunch to school or eat anything they served. He wouldn't do it. He never really explained why — he'd just come home after school voracious. We've always had family dinner together, so I knew he'd be eating well. And he left for school in the morning on a full stomach. But there was only one thing he would let me pack for him: fluffernutter sandwiches. And I would. White bread, peanut butter (Jif was what he liked), and Marshmallow Fluff. He had to eat something, and as a mother, I couldn't not give him something to eat, even if it was a fluffernutter. He eventually grew out of it. So what I'm saying to you is, if you'd dropped in on that cafeteria on that day and seen my son eating a fluffernutter, what conclusions would you draw? What would you think about him, or me as a mother, or even the cafeteria?"

TIP   Beautify the school cafeteria. Make it a comfortable, welcoming, and congenial place to eat together.

START A COLLEGE FARM

If you want to start a student farm, these 12 suggestions from Laura Sayre and Sean Clark's *Fields of Learning* can be summed up in three words: go for it. But you'd best read what they have to say first.

1. FORM YOUR CORE GROUP. Identify a few people who are not just interested but willing to work to make this thing happen. Many community supported agriculture (CSA) programs work on the core group principle. You need to be able to brainstorm ideas, tag-team on specific tasks while you're all juggling various other commitments, and mobilize a range of skills and contacts that will be essential in the steps ahead. One of the hazards of student farms is that they can become magnets for idealism, expected to serve too many worthy objectives at once, so try to be as specific as possible in articulating your shared vision.

2. IDENTIFY YOUR ALLIES. Once you have your core group, start thinking about whom you need to convince and who can help you. Faculty members, deans, provosts, the president? Alumni? Student organizations? Someone in the facilities department or in buildings and grounds? Get acquainted with the organization of your school so that you can understand who reports to whom. Most important, consider all the disciplines: there may be someone in the business school or the engineering department who has a keen interest or deep background in farming and can offer you expertise and support.

3. HUNT FOR LAND. Walk or cycle around campus and consider possible open patches of land, small or large. Study local maps. Find out the names of the best agricultural soils in your area, what they look like, and where they can be found. If you think you may have found a possible site, remain skeptical. Think about how easy it is to get to without a car, whether there's water for irrigation available, whether there's storage and electricity nearby. Think about drainage and slope and aspect and shade, not just now, but throughout the year.

Think, too, about history: What did your campus look like fifty years ago? A century ago? Where were the farms in this area? What were they known for? Are there any signs of them remaining — barns, shed, farmhouses, fruit trees? History can be useful for uncovering possible problems (contamination, compaction, flooding) as well as for understanding the potential of a given soil or field. Some student farms are suggested by the existence of an old farm property within the current campus boundaries, in which case a new farm enterprise can also serve a historic preservation function. Many land-grant institutions are rich in underutilized agricultural experiment station land and/or greenhouses.

You may be able to barter space in exchange for providing educational and outreach opportunities later on.

4. DO YOUR HOMEWORK. This step applies to the entire process, of course, but it's also a step in its own right. Many student farms have gotten their start as a class project of some kind and/or have evolved as a series of class or individual student projects. You might start with a simple mission statement or a full-blown feasibility study, including, for instance, a site plan, a business plan, a marketing plan, and field plans. Later projects may include designs for individual buildings or other facilities such as root cellars, hoop houses, greenhouses, biodiesel facilities, wind towers, composting toilets, or photovoltaic arrays.

There are lots of great resources available on all these topics — the websites for the Sustainable Agriculture Research & Education program within the USDA (sare.org) and ATTRA, the National Sustainable Agriculture Information Service (attra.ncat.org), are a good place to start. At a large university, doing your homework can also mean simply getting acquainted with what's going on in different parts of the institution. What challenges does your school face? What new initiatives are in the works? How many different ways can you add academic rigor to your work?

5. SEEK FUNDING. Alas, these are tough economic times, and grant funding can be hard to come by. The good news is that projects have gotten under way and even expanded with widely varying amounts of financial support. Some kind of financial commitment from the institution will be critical for the stability of the farm, but it's important to recognize that this can take many forms — land, buildings, vehicles, utilities, personnel, work-study allocations, compost — and to acknowledge the value of the sale of farm products alone, especially in your first few seasons. Even well established, thriving student farms typically cover only operating expenses. Finally, be frugal with the funds you have. Solicit donations, whether in cash or in kind. Welcome volunteers. Bargain hunt. Shop for tools at yard sales. Recycle. Reuse. Scavenge.

6. START SMALL. If key resources — especially farming expertise — are in short supply, don't hesitate to start your farm as a garden, even a small garden. A small garden well stewarded is going to be worth more to your cause than several acres planted and overgrown (see step 7). In the same vein, limit crops and varieties to a manageable number. If things go well, you can expand and diversify next year and again the year after that. This bit of advice applies to infrastructure projects as well. As Tim Crews puts it, "At the end of the term, a simple manageable initiative brought to completion is infinitely more appealing than a few odd parts of a grandiose vision."

7. KEEP IT WEEDED. The importance of this step cannot be overemphasized. Aesthetics matter, especially if you're in a highly visible location. And, if you want good yields — which you should — weeds will likely be your most important obstacle. Sure, there are insects and diseases to manage, but, if you're using organic methods, aggressive weeds will be your greatest pest challenge.

>>

Use mulches to suppress weeds, and walk your gardens or fields often to see what's going on. Use stakes and string and tape measures if you want your beds and rows straight and even. Clean your tools when you are done with them and put them away where they belong. Mow. Turn the compost, and cover it to keep odors from offending passersby. Don't let piles of plastic mulch or other debris stack up in the corner of some field. Plant flowers, both annuals and perennials. Wash out the harvest buckets at the end of the day, and set them to dry. A well-kept farm is not only more appealing to outsiders; it's also usually a safer and more pleasant place to work. Above all, it demonstrates a sense of commitment.

8. READ. A key rationale for student farming is that book learning and hands-on learning are complementary. If you don't have assigned reading as part of a course or courses associated with the student farm, come up with your own reading list or form a reading group with some friends or colleagues. Troll the stacks of your school's library, poke around in secondhand bookshops, ask older farmers what sources they have found most valuable over the years. Organic and sustainable farming reconsiders traditional farming practices and finds new ways to mix old wisdom with new technologies. An outstanding portal for relevant resources both old and new is the Alternative Farming Systems Information Center housed at the National Agricultural Library (afsic.nal.usda.gov).

9. WRITE. This applies not just to the early, planning stages of the student farm (see step 4) but to its later, everyday functioning as well. Committing what you've done and what you plan to do to paper on a regular basis will help you develop your ideas, facilitate communication among current student farmworkers, and provide an indispensable record of what worked, what didn't, and how much it all cost for student farmers in years to come. Good record-keeping is essential for organic certification and makes it possible to analyze and assess the value — both budgetary and otherwise — of different farm enterprises from season to season.

Note that writing can take many forms, from blogs, e-newsletters, and Twitter updates to personal journals, financial accounts, yield records, and academic papers. Many student farms find it useful to keep a whiteboard list of fieldwork chores or items to harvest so that anyone arriving at the farm with an odd hour to work will know where to start. Others maintain an online or hard-copy farm handbook to keep track of favorite varieties, planting schedules, and other accumulated bits of local knowledge.

10. THINK VERY CAREFULLY before adding livestock. Animals are great, but they require an entirely different order of care than plants: daily attention regardless of whatever else is going on in your life, and, if they pine and die, everyone is going to feel horrible. They require water and food and shelter (including fencing); water that is heavy, food that can quickly become expensive, and shelter and fencing that require maintenance. Above all, animals are time-consuming, easily eating up two to three hours of someone's day, every day.

11. CULTIVATE PARTNERS and supporters beyond campus. Student farms can be terrific venues for improving town-gown relations. Remember that you have as much to gain as to offer in these relationships. Also keep in mind that farmers in your area may see you as a competition for their business, particularly if you sell your produce at the local farmers' market or start a CSA. Get to know your local organic sustainable farming community if you don't already: its members will constitute one of your most valuable resources. This point connects to steps 2 and 4 above as well: get input from multiple stakeholders, and think about how you can work together. The more people you have on your team, the more you'll be able to do in the long run.

12. DON'T FORGET TO SOCIALIZE. Last but not least, enjoy the rewards of what you are doing, and share them. This takes many forms. In the early days of the UC Santa Cruz Farm and Garden, Alan Chadwick and his apprentices used to make bouquets of flowers and put them out in buckets in a central spot on campus for passersby to take. You may be focused on immediate profitability, but generosity can be an excellent long-term investment. Ideally, your farm will have a kitchen, even if it's an outdoor kitchen, so you can cook and share what you have grown. You'll have an easier time attracting and keeping workers if the farm is a place where people enjoy spending time. Hosting events where you invite others to the farm — potluck suppers, harvest festivals, open houses, summer barbecues, commencement celebrations — is also key to the life and continued survival of the farm.

— Excerpted with permission from Laura Sayre and Sean Clark, eds., *Fields of Learning: The Student Farm Movement in North America.* If you are interested in campus farms, be sure to read the whole book!

>⟩⟨⟨

JOIN THE FOOD REVOLUTION

Whatever Jamie Oliver does, he does it large. He is an international superstar with boundless energy, good humor, and a love of food. Good food, too — from English roasts to American burgers and specialties from all countries in between. He's authored over a dozen cookbooks, created a few apps, and launched his own Food Tube channel on YouTube. Whether he's teaching about food and how to cook or demonstrating how much sugar the average American eats in a year (about a truckload), his affable personality captivates.

In the United States, Oliver and his Food Revolution Community have made strong collaborative efforts with the Center for Science in the Public Interest (CSPI) and ChangeLab to make free tool kits available for you to download off the web. To find what you need, Google "Jamie Oliver, Food Revolution, tool kits."

Food Revolution tool kits and support tools:

» Get the Facts
» Find Support
» Start a Campaign
» School Food Basics

» School Food Charter
» School Food Audit
» Decision Makers
» Parents' Bill of Rights

» Milk Fact Sheet
» Obesity & Diabetes
» School Food Presentation

Some of the suggestions and support in the tool kits may appear to be easy and obvious, but even the smallest change may sometimes be a challenge. What's great about the Food Revolution site and the community is the sense of belonging and inclusiveness he creates. For example, find the Food Revolution Community's Facebook fan page and you'll see posts from all over the world. According to that page, there were 9,100 events held in 121 countries to celebrate Food Revolution Day on May 16, 2014. It's encouraging to be part of a larger whole that is doing something fun. As the saying goes, many hands make light work. For advocates and activists, Jamie provides a refreshing voice (with a British accent) and enthusiasm that's enlivening when we activists are face-down in dealing with an adversarial, dysfunctional government or corporate food interests. So enjoy, have some fun, take part, and cook! Jamie's recipes are very well written. It's a good revolution to be part of.

>><<

THE BIG RIG

All Over California

Jamie Oliver's foundation partnered with the California Endowment and together dispatched the Big Rig mobile kitchen classroom for a 40-week tour, providing free home-cooking classes, good food education, and tons of smiles for folks of all ages in underserved communities. While out on tour, the Big Rig connects with local chefs and food educators from San Diego to Sacramento and points between. With classes like Risotto Rules, Fajita Fiesta, The Best Party Food, A Taste of Japan, All About Eggs, Perfect Pancakes, and Fast Food at Home, the teaching, learning, and cooking never stops, even after the Big Rig rolls on down the road to its next venue.

YOU CAN DO THIS

CELEBRATE FOOD DAY

October 24. Every year. Mark your calendars today! Food Day is a national event. It is one day to focus on good food policies and raising awareness about healthy food choices. Food Day's partners list reads like a who's who of good food. The list is as long as it is broad in scope. Partners include the Center for Science in the Public Interest, STOP Foodborne Illness, the Physicians Committee for Responsible Medicine, the National Black Child Development Institute, Jamie Oliver's Food Foundation, Jewish Community Centers, the Farmers Market Coalition, the Farm Animal Rights Movement, American Farmland Trust, and Farm Aid. With many more national as well as state and local partners, there's no way to list them all.

This day is as American as a home-baked heirloom apple pie made with a pasture-raised lard and Turkey hard red winter wheat crust, topped with fair trade organic sugar and a dollop of thick, locally sourced whipped cream. The bonus? According to the Food Day website (foodday.org): *Food Day does not accept funding from government or industry.*

>×<

CHAPTER 3

Build

T HE WORD "COMMUNITY" may mean different things to different people. Are you working toward building a stronger local or regional food community, with and for specific self-identified groups? For example, if you're organizing around farmers, what does that mean to you? Is that every farmer within a certain geographical range? Or only those farmers who practice a certain method? Are they immigrant farmers, beginning farmers, established farmers, and/or people who grow their own food for their own use? Whom do you truly include in your community, and how are you going to do that? There are no right answers here. These are your paths to choose. In order to make real transformative change, however, it is critical to understand for whom you're building, how you are organizing, and if they (in this case, farmers) are all in. Otherwise it's easy to fall prey to favoritism, cliques, discrimination, elitism, and self-interest.

Build with wisdom. Build your program, policy, law, or infrastructure to respect all people, all members of your community, the environment, and food.

Good processes will strengthen your work (see Ask What *Is* Working, page 68). Build on a foundation of strength, respect, and transparency (see Wholesome Wave's organizational values, page 78; Implement a Conflict-of-Interest Policy, page 80; A Donor Bill of Rights, page 81; and Learn from Those Who Came before You, page 108). Creating transparency about what we envision our work to be early on in the development of a project, program, business, or nonprofit will help establish a vital baseline: consensus of definition(s) and hence the articulation of vision, mission, goals, and objectives from which priorities can be determined. Whether that work involves a farmers' market (page 94), a permit program for produce cart vendors (page 98), or a local humane slaughterhouse (page 104), you will have a much better chance at being understood, functional, strategic, and sustainable when your project is built from the ground up with wisdom and respect.

YOU CAN DO THIS

ASK WHAT *IS* WORKING

Words matter. The language we use matters when we talk about people, food, communities, stories, barriers, issues, and solutions. Grantors often want their potential grantees to identify what's broken and then to outline how to fix it. But when you focus on what's wrong or broken, people get defensive. People shut down. They stop talking, then pull up their bridges.

So what if, as potential grantees and activists, we asked instead: What is working well, and how can we do more of it? What do we love about where we live, what we eat, what we grow, what we teach, who is in our community, and what resources we have? You feel a shift, don't you? Immediately the energy moves toward the positive. And once it does, we'll do more of what we're doing right, and with inclusion.

I wish I'd been aware of this process, called appreciative inquiry (AI), when I first starting working as a food activist in a nonprofit. I see in retrospect that this kind of approach (developed by David L. Cooperrider and Diana Whitney and outlined in their book *Appreciative Inquiry: A Positive Revolution in Change*) would've fundamentally shifted our mission statement, visioning, planning, and execution. I think it would have been easier and more inviting for more eaters to get involved. We would've looked at our community in different ways. Also, as a taxpayer who is actively seeking change in our food systems, I see how some nonprofits remain stuck in self-fulfilling prophecies *because their existence is based on what's broken*; that is, when a nonprofit is awarded grants or donations from the government or philanthropists to fix what's broken in a food system, there's an inherent contradiction. If they fixed the problem, they'd also make themselves obsolete, lose their funding, and close their doors. Success would (and should) mean they run themselves out of business. Most don't want to do that.

My goals are to have us really look at the language we use, then shift dialogue and energy away from finger-pointing, defensiveness, and divisiveness. Away from self-righteous indignation, judgment, knowing better, and the savior complex — all of which are exhausting and unproductive. Instead, let's find out what's right. What's good. People know. Just ask them. Start with appreciation.

>><<

PRACTICE THE FOUNDATIONS
OF JUST FOOD SYSTEMS

At the Institute for Agriculture and Trade Policy (IATP) Food + Justice = Democracy Conference, held in September 2012 in Minneapolis, good food activists from a variety of nonprofits, from the Rural Coalition to Slow Food, came up with a draft of six principles of food justice. As we work to build a more just and equitable food system, these ideas will help us be both clear and broad-thinking in our aims.

These principles are in draft form, because "food justice" is a phrase that's open to interpretation, reflecting time, place, and culture. You'll see reflected in the different styles for each of these six principles the voices and concerns of the activists who gathered in each committee. Use these principles as a starting point to discuss the issues and solutions you want to pursue. Use them as building blocks to include everyone. Use them as pillars in whatever you build because good food is not just for a few, but for everyone. Good, healthy, fresh food is a right.

1. HISTORICAL TRAUMA

AT THE HOUSEHOLD LEVEL, we need to practice awareness of how our meal choices may help us practice the values of a just food system. May every family take note of and deepen the practice of food justice every day.

ACKNOWLEDGE as fundamental in our consideration of food justice that we cannot deliver food justice without addressing historical trauma.

FOOD INJUSTICE creates and reinforces health disparities, land loss, historical trauma, cultural genocide, and structural racism, classism, and sexism.

THE INTERDEPENDENCE PRINCIPLE: Everything is interrelated. We must break down barriers that isolate us and reinforce a segregated worldview. We must put policy and practice in place that help us move to understanding and interdependence.

STRUGGLE around meaning and understandings as part of our core work. An aspect of historical trauma is "divide and conquer," and we cannot allow that pattern in our movement(s).

>>

2. LOCAL FOOD SYSTEM, COMMUNITY DEVELOPMENT, AND PUBLIC INVESTMENT

Good, healthy food and community well-being are basic human rights. *Food justice* is the right of communities everywhere to produce, process, distribute, access, and eat good food regardless of race, class, gender, ethnicity, citizenship, ability, religion, or community. *Food sovereignty* is the right of people to define their own food, agriculture, livestock, and fisheries systems. This means recognizing people's rights. *Community food security* is the condition in which all people at all times have access to fresh, healthy, affordable, and culturally appropriate food, outside emergency food situations. Consider the following:

FREEDOM from exploitation

FAIR labor practices

RESPECT, empathy, pluralism, valuing knowledge

RACIAL JUSTICE: dismantling of racism and white privilege

GENDER equity

ENVIRONMENTAL stewardship

INDIGENOUS rights to lands, territory, and resources

Recognize people's rights:

TO SUSTAINABLE livelihoods

TO CONSUME, barter, keep, donate, gift, process, distribute, grow, and sell food

TO LOCAL OWNERSHIP of all aspects of the community food value chain

3. HUNGER RELIEF, HEALTH DISPARITIES, AND THE INDUSTRIAL FOOD SYSTEM

The emergency food system perpetuates food insecurity and health disparities. It is sustained by the corporate food industry. Reforming that system means:

ELIMINATING institutional racism

ENGAGED communities reclaiming, in a democratic process, local and regional food systems

FOCUSING health-care reform on prevention and nutrition

COMMUNITIES caring for one another and themselves

4. LAND

In a fair, just, and sustainable food system:

1. All people recognize themselves as part of the Land, Air, Water, and Sky (LAWS), and uphold the rights of nature to exist, persist, maintain, and regenerate (as per 2008 Constitution of Ecuador, Chapter 7, Article 31).

2. All people have access to places to produce or procure their own food, and the means (knowledge and physical resources) to do so.

3. Control of land is not used to exploit or oppress people, including migrant peoples; it is used to enhance the health, wealth, and dignity of all living beings.

4. Decisions about land use are made at the local level/by the people who are most affected, through transparent, equitable processes, to uphold principles 1, 2, and 3.

5. LABOR AND IMMIGRATION

Because the majority of food chain workers are immigrants and people of color; and because structural racism and inequality in the food system means these communities are disproportionately targeted and impacted; and because of corporate consolidation and the need to bring sustainable food supply chains to scale:

We commit to building a food system that shifts the dominant narrative in a manner that prioritizes the rights of food chain workers, including the right to organize a path to legalization for undocumented workers and a living wage for all workers, farmers, and fisherfolk.

6. TOXIC-FREE AND CLIMATE-JUST FOOD SYSTEM

A just food and water system works to reverse climate change by becoming agro-ecologically independent of fossil fuels while adapting to climate change in ways that address its inequities. A just food and water system is predicated on public policy processes in which communities make free and informed decisions to protect and affirm the interdependent web of life.

IN a just food and water system, communities, farmers, and workers thrive in a healthy environment that is free of toxic chemicals.

IN a just food and water system, corporations are not persons; are banned from using their money for lobbying and political campaigns; and the revolving door is closed.

— Excerpted with permission from the Institute for Agriculture and Trade Policy (IATP), Draft Principles of Food Justice (iatp.org/documents/draft-principles-of-food-justice#sthash.ou5MUf6h.dpuf)

>×<

WE SEE WHAT WE'RE WILLING TO SEE

Where I live, there are some bucolic farms with fields of corn and grand old trees that grace their borders. Sheep and cows graze on green pastures. When I see land like this, I envision a scenario of a peaceable kingdom: fertile lands producing good food for all; equanimity, access, balance, and respect between people, animals, land, and cultivation. But as my friend the author Alice Randall pointed out, we all see things through the lens of our personal histories. My great-great-grandparents were German immigrants who moved to the Midwest, bought land, then worked the land they owned. My relationship to the landscape that I've inherited is different from that of some of my African-American friends and colleagues like Alice. I think it's safe to say that most of their ancestors did not own the land they worked. When Alice looks at those same cornfields, grand old trees, and pastures, she may not envision a peaceable kingdom but rather one of terror, violence, and oppression.

These landscapes endure. They outlast generations, yet they do not reveal their history easily. We must therefore tread gently. When Alice's lens and my own lens come together, we can acknowledge our different scenarios and see a more true history of our country's agriculture, in spite of the pain it may cause.

It is up to all of us to collectively learn with keen eyes, open ears, and compassionate hearts. When it comes to people, places, and history, ignorance is no longer acceptable as we work onward in feeding our communities.

"History, despite its wrenching pain, cannot be unlived, but if faced with courage, need not be lived again." — Maya Angelou

LEARN YOUR HISTORY

The draft principles developed out of the Food + Justice = Democracy conference of the Institute for Agriculture and Trade Policy (IATP) remind us that making an effort to understand the history of the food system we are part of is an important action. Here are some places to look for your local food history.

» State historical societies

» Libraries

» The Agricultural History Society (aghistorysociety.org)

» Museums, including "living" museums

» Seminars, workshops, and classes at local colleges and universities

» Oral histories

» Elders

CAMPAIGN FOR AGRICULTURAL WORKERS' RIGHTS

The best defense is a good offense, or so the saying goes. Here, it's totally applicable. As an eater, a business owner, a farmer, or a producer — whether you buy food at the grocery store or buy in bulk from a wholesaler for your restaurant, hotel, or cafeteria — what you buy makes a difference in campaigning for agricultural workers' rights.

Rule of thumb: buy from local and regional farms and producers first, from people and businesses that treat their workers well, pay them respectable wages, and have them work in safe environments. If that's not possible (for foods that don't grow in the United States, such as coffee, chocolate, and bananas), GRACE Communications Foundation's website Sustainable Table (sustainabletable .org) suggests you look for certified products with labels from Fair Trade USA, the Rainforest Alliance, or United Farm Workers. These certification programs ensure that farmworkers are treated fairly, work in safe environments, and are paid a decent-to-fair wage.

Need Help Finding or Sourcing Products?

The Rainforest Alliance's website (rainforest-alliance.org) has a "Find Certified Products" locator. Just fill in your country and state, then select the types of products you want to find, and it will search its database of Rainforest Alliance Certified™ products. If you're a business and want to source Rainforest Alliance Certified forest products (wood, paper), or food, drinks, and other farm products, you can explore the options under the "Engage Your Business" tab on the home page.

Participate in a Fair Food Program

The Coalition of Immokalee Workers (CIW), based in Immokalee, Florida, has initiated an innovative, highly successful farmworkers' rights campaign and a powerful partnership between farmworkers, Florida tomato growers, and buyers called the Fair Food Program (FFP). Participating buyers pay an extra "penny per pound" premium for their tomatoes, and the growers pass that on as a bonus to workers. The CIW says that between January 2011 and May 2014, over $14 million in premiums was paid.

When Walmart signed on to the FFP in January 2014, it agreed to "work over time to expand the Fair Food Program to other crops beyond tomatoes in its produce supply chain." This agreement has great implications for farmworkers on other large-scale agricultural enterprises that grow crops such as onions, peppers, broccoli, fruits, and nuts.

The FFP is overseen by an independent nonprofit organization called the Fair Food Standards Council (FFSC). According to the CIW, the six main elements of the FFP, which the United Nations Working Group on Business and Human Rights pointed out "could serve as a model elsewhere," are as follows:

A PAY INCREASE supported by the "penny per pound" paid by participating buyers, such as Taco Bell, Whole Foods, and Walmart

COMPLIANCE with the Code of Conduct, including zero tolerance for forced labor and sexual assault

WORKER-TO-WORKER education sessions carried out by the CIW on the farms and on company time to ensure that workers understand their new rights and responsibilities

A WORKER-TRIGGERED complaint resolution mechanism (including a 24-hour hotline staffed by the FFSC) leading to complaint investigation, corrective action plans, and, if necessary, suspension of a farm's Participating Grower status, and thereby its ability to sell to Participating Buyers

HEALTH AND SAFETY committees on every farm to give workers a structured voice in the shape of their work environment

ONGOING AUDITING of the farms to ensure compliance with each element of the FFP

As consumers, we can ratchet up our conscious buying power. Follow and join the CIW to expand the implementation of the FFP. To date, Wendy's and Publix have yet to sign on.

— Excerpted with permission from the Coalition of Immokalee Workers, Fair Food Program (ciw-online.org/fair-food-program)

>><<

CARLOS MARENTES

Executive Director
Centro de los Trabajadores Agrícolas Fronterizos

There are three cups of coffee between me, Carlos Marentes, and my son, Elijah. The dinner in the cafeteria this afternoon is cigar-thin burritos — flour tortillas, refried beans, some meat and cheese. Carlos decides to tell us a story.

"I go to my friend's house to visit," he begins. "We are in his kitchen. He wants to give me something to eat. So my friend washes an apple. Taking care to clean it, he then hands it to me. A red, juicy apple.

"'Thank you,' I say. And then, 'Why did you wash the apple before giving it to me?'

"'So it is good enough for you to eat,' my friend answers. 'To clean it of the chemicals, the pesticides. You never know who touched it or where it has been. You know why, Carlos. A child would, too.'

"'Thank you,' I say again, accepting his answer and the piece of fruit."

As Carlos leans in closer, he continues this story while workers shuffle in and out, picking up a burrito or three for dinner from the cafeteria ladies, respectfully greeting Carlos and us as they do. "But then I asked my friend another question, and now I am going to ask you the same thing." He gazes at Elijah and me across the table that separates us, his eyes dry and clear with birthright, indignation, and wisdom. His words are careful, insistent, barely above a whisper.

"What do you do to care for food like that apple? Just wash it? Food is sacred, isn't it? A right. What do you do for the farmers and the farmworkers who planted, grew, and harvested it? The land, air, and water it needs to grow. The people — like these people — and the children like their children." Carlos looks to Elijah. "Children like you.

"Who should be able to eat good food like that beautiful, fresh apple? *Who* gets to eat *that* food? You see," he says, tapping the table emphatically, "washing the apple was about him, my friend. Nothing else. Nothing." He shakes his head. "What about everything else? What about *everyone else*?"

Carlos Marentes is a practical man. He saw a need in his community and did something about it. As he tells it, he was handing pamphlets out to some farmworkers on a cold El Paso night before they boarded the buses that would take them to the fields. He wanted to talk to the men about organizing around labor issues.

One fellow told him yes, that would be good, to one day be organized. But what would be really nice was a cup of hot coffee and a warm place to sleep so that he didn't have to sleep on cardboard on the sidewalk. So Carlos and his wife, Alicia, led the way to building Centro de los Trabajadores Agrícolas Fronterizos (Border Farmworker Center) on the U.S.–Mexico border, directly across the street from the border control station and the bridge between our two countries. It took the leaders and founders of Sin Fronteras Organizing Project about 10 years to complete the center, together with the city of El Paso, and today it stands — an 8,000-square-foot building.

There is dignity and respect in this place where farmworkers can get that cup of coffee and a burrito made from scratch by the warmhearted cafeteria ladies. It's a place where people can get their mail and leave their things. There are English and art classes for both children and adults, and a food garden is in the works.

Now Carlos can do what he originally set out to do, which is to help workers organize. Carlos is a very practical man.

BUILD A HEALTHY ORGANIZATION

If we're going to be building more resilient, equitable, and just community food systems and working for wholesome food for people — in the myriad ways we can do that — the organizations we build should not only be run ethically and transparently but also provide safe working environments and fair living wages to their staff members. Otherwise, quite frankly, how can you look your community and your board in the eye? Organizations are echoes of the people who work in them, their missions, and what they do. If they're not built on strong, healthy foundations, how does it all square up? Who and what are we, really? Consider Wholesome Wave's organizational values. What are yours?

>><<

WHOLESOME WAVE
Bridgeport, Connecticut

Wholesome Wave (wholesomewave.org) is a Connecticut-based nonprofit headed up by the James Beard Award–winning chef Michel Nischan. Developed out of a commitment to food justice, Wholesome Wave's goals revolve around increasing access and affordability to fresh, healthy, local foods, in both rural and urban areas. Wholesome Wave's bench-mark initiative, the Double Value Coupon Program, doubles the value of SNAP benefits when used at the farmers' market to buy fresh foods. A similar program involves providing individuals affected with a diet-related disease with a prescription for fruits and vegetables at the local market. Their programming has extended to 25 states and the District of Columbia, and they are tirelessly working at the policy level to improve food security for families across the United States. See Wholesome Wave's organizational values (opposite page).

BUILDING STRONG NONPROFITS

The local food movement has given birth to many nonprofit offspring. And many of us who are involved don't have previous experience in nonprofit organizations. Or perhaps because we have the proclivity to be rabble-rousers, any history with processes such as Robert's Rules of Order might have left a bad taste. Or as a worst-case scenario, some of us have experienced how destructive and damaging a dysfunctional organization can be.

Building strong foundations in your organizations will help them function better, treat people more fairly, and flourish over time. Nonprofits take a lot of time and work; they should be run not only like a business with a bottom line but also like an ethical, transparent, and respectful one at that. If you want to rebuild our food systems into something that's fair, just, and equitable, pay your people a fair, living wage; ensure medical coverage; and offer maternity/paternity leave. Try to reflect your mission and values in every way. (See Noli's essay on page 52.)

>⬦<

IMPLEMENT A
CONFLICT-OF-INTEREST POLICY

Small communities are rife with potential conflicts of interest. It may seem as though the same people are always raising their hands to help out, to be on boards. So it's even more important to be proactive and transparent to ensure your organization has a conflict-of-interest policy and that you check in on it at least once a year, with staff and board members, and more frequently as needed with changes in leadership. Like luggage in overhead bins on an airplane, things may have shifted while in flight. Here's some advice on the topic from the National Council of Nonprofits.

A policy governing conflicts of interests is perhaps the most important policy a nonprofit board can adopt. To have the most impact, the policy should be in writing and the board (and staff) should review the policy regularly. Often people are unaware that their activities are in conflict with the best interests of the nonprofit, so a goal for many organizations is to simply raise awareness and cultivate a "culture of candor." It is helpful to take time at a board meeting annually to discuss the types of situations that could result in a conflict between the best interests of the nonprofit — and the self-interest of a staff member or board member.

A conflict-of-interest policy should (a) require those with a conflict (or who think they may have a conflict) to disclose the conflict/potential conflict, and (b) prohibit interested board members from voting on any matter that gives rise to a conflict between their personal interests and the nonprofit's interests. Beyond those two basics, it is helpful for each nonprofit to determine how conflicts at the board and staff level will be managed. Keep in mind that the revised [IRS informational tax form] 990 asks not only about whether the nonprofit has a written conflict-of-interest policy, but also about the process that a nonprofit uses to manage conflicts as well as how the nonprofit determines whether board members have a conflict of interest.

MINUTES of board meetings should reflect when a board member discloses that s/he has a conflict of interests and how the conflict was managed, such as that there was a discussion on the matter without the board member in the room, and that a vote was taken but that the "interested" board member abstained (board members with a conflict are "interested" — board members without a conflict are "disinterested").

A PROCESS used by many nonprofits to find out whether any board member (or staff member) has a conflict of interest, is to circulate an annual "conflict disclosure questionnaire" that asks board and staff members to disclose existing conflicts and reminds them to disclose any that may evolve in the future.

— Excerpted with permission from the National Council of Nonprofits website (councilofnonprofits.org)

A DONOR BILL OF RIGHTS

PHILANTHROPY is based on voluntary action for the common good. It is a tradition of giving and sharing that is primary to the quality of life. To ensure that philanthropy merits the respect and trust of the general public, and that donors and prospective donors can have full confidence in the not-for-profit organizations and causes they are asked to support, we declare that all donors have these rights:

I. To be informed of the organization's mission, of the way the organization intends to use donated resources, and of its capacity to use donations effectively for their intended purposes.

II. To be informed of the identity of those serving on the organization's governing board, and to expect the board to exercise prudent judgment in its stewardship responsibilities.

III. To have access to the organization's most recent financial statements.

IV. To be assured their gifts will be used for the purposes for which they were given.

V. To receive appropriate acknowledgment and recognition.

VI. To be assured that information about their donations is handled with respect and with confidentiality to the extent provided by law.

VII. To expect that all relationships with individuals representing organizations of interest to the donor will be professional in nature.

VIII. To be informed whether those seeking donations are volunteers, employees of the organization, or hired solicitors.

IX. To have the opportunity for their names to be deleted from mailing lists that an organization may intend to share.

X. To feel free to ask questions when making a donation and to receive prompt, truthful, and forthright answers.

— Excerpted with permission from the Association of Fundraising Professionals (AFP) and others, 2013

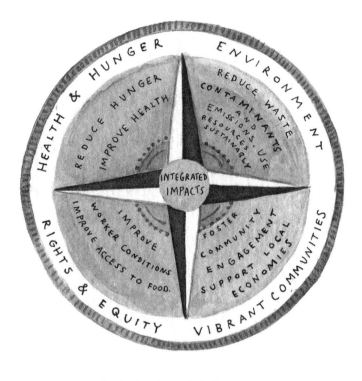

FOOD FUNDER COMPASS

"Donors get pitched a lot," reads the website of the Center for High Impact Philanthropy, which operates out of the School of Social Policy & Practice at the University of Pennsylvania. To help "clarify" the "complicated space" of food-related funding, the center has developed its Food Funder Compass, which "identifies the four primary social impact areas where donors seek change: Health & Hunger; Environment; Vibrant Communities; and Rights & Equity." For anyone who is able to donate money to help build a stronger food community, the center offers a document that lays out a rationale for donor investment; one case example to illustrate how philanthropic funds can produce change; and additional promising approaches, as well as examples of organizations implementing those approaches.

— Excerpted with permission from the Center for High Impact Philanthropy, School of Social Policy & Practice, University of Pennsylvania (impact.upenn.edu)

MOVING THE FEDERAL GOVERNMENT

Gridlocked federal government is generally not a reliable source of funds, especially funds that might lead the way to help create access to healthy foods. It's often up to states, towns, cities, and grassroots organizations. There is a bottom-up aspect to this revolution. But we need a top-down as well.

» Campaign to raise the minimum wage (page 248)

» Let's tax unhealthy "food" and sugary drinks to subsidize fresh food (page 249)

» #VoteFood (page 303)

ASK FOR MONEY (AND USE IT WELL)

It's critically important to your organization's good reputation and function that you ask for and use money ethically and transparently. Beware of mission creep — either moving too quickly, without checking in, or taking on too much — which can lead to using money in ways donors didn't intend. Here's a summary of good advice from the Association of Fundraising Professionals (AFP).

MAKE SURE all solicitation and communication materials are accurate and correctly reflect the organization's mission and use of solicited funds.

ENSURE that donors receive informed, accurate, and ethical advice about the value and tax implications of contributions.

USE ALL CONTRIBUTIONS in accordance with donors' intentions.

ENSURE PROPER STEWARDSHIP of all revenue sources, including timely reports on the use and management of such funds.

OBTAIN the explicit consent by donors before altering the conditions of financial transactions.

— Excerpted with permission from "Solicitation and Use of Philanthropic Funds," Association of Fundraising Professionals

DEAR DONORS

There are many great organizations out there. Look to fund programs that are happy and striving to work their way out of existence and into "planned obsolescence" as Noli Taylor of Island Grown Schools puts it, because they've been so successful at addressing the issues that the problems have all been solved. Obviously this is a highly idealized version of an organization, but use the gist of it. Fund the programs and the people that work.

As it's said that most of an iceberg is underwater, dive below the surface and do research before you fund a seemingly new program. Make sure that it's not redundant. That would be a shame and a waste of your money. In my opinion, solid programs and organizations build upon preexisting work in innovative ways, and they are transparent about it. That said, if it is seed money a new program needs to get on its feet, make sure the leadership is strong, the broader community necessity is great (and replication is avoided), community demand and support already exist, and the newbie has a solid plan.

There's an excellent resource for donors who are specifically interested in sustainable agriculture called the Sustainable Agriculture & Food Systems Funders (safsf.org), and for donors interested in the public health sector, check out the Health & Environmental Funders Network (hefn.org).

This advice goes for nonprofits doing the asking, too. Take the time to do your homework before you ask for funding. Are there other organizations that have done, or are doing, what you're proposing? Research like-minded nonprofits, even if they're out of your geographical zone, to find out whether useful information, strategies, tools, surveys, or data already exist. Usually, organizations are open to sharing the information they've developed. (This book is chock-full of such generosities.) Most times, organizations will only ask for credit where credit is due. Your research should help you ask appropriately for funds to finance true and real needs.

KEEP YOUR GOOD NAME

. . . .

Patti Smith, the godmother of punk, once said, "Build a good name. Keep your name clean. Don't make compromises. . . . Be concerned about doing good work. Protect your work and if you build a good name, eventually that name will be its own currency."

This advice is as useful for nonprofits as it is for artists. You represent your organization when you're out to dinner, at the ballpark, on a bus. And the people who surround you, and whom you hire, are part of the team. Keep your good name.

>><<

A CAUTIONARY TALE ABOUT PUBLIC RELATIONS

She was insistent in her pitch. Instead of responding to our assistant editor's polite "Now's not a good time," the young public relations agent kept pushing, insistent on pitching her story. Our magazine, *Edible Vineyard*, was on deadline to go to press. I said I would get back to her the next week. But for whatever reason, she e-mailed me directly anyway. Something to the effect of: Had I ever heard of Island Grown Schools? They're serving organic school lunches — they're *your* community's farm to school program. A perfect match for *Edible Vineyard*. So many stories to tell.

She was pitching the program I helped launch. She hadn't done her homework. *Edible Vineyard* had already run numerous stories about school food and Island Grown Schools (IGS). We had also donated significant ad space to promote the program, including the coveted back cover.

I felt damn surly about that pitch, so beyond letting that PR rep know that without doing her homework she was doing harm to IGS, I also let the IGS coordinators know that their PR agent was stepping in it big-time by insulting one of their benefactors.

So be sure that anyone who might be speaking on behalf of your organization in any context knows the facts and history. And remember: gifts in kind, such as advertising, computers, graphic design, and lawyers' fees, are all donations and should be treated as such.

>><<

WHAT IS A FOOD HUB?

According to the U.S. Department of Agriculture (USDA), a food hub is "a centrally located facility with a business management structure facilitating the aggregation, storage, processing, distribution, and/or marketing of locally/regionally produced food products."

As much as that definition is official, there remains debate and discussion about the term, and the attempt to define such a dynamic system. Krysten Aguilar, of the Dona Ana County Food Policy Council and La Semilla Food Center in Anthony, New Mexico, explained further:

> A food hub is not simply a facility but a business model that is designed to aid farmers with support and infrastructure. The types of existing food hubs across the country vary greatly, as they should. The key words to consider are "local" and "regional"; there is great diversity across this country in climate, growing seasons, city and town size, and demographic makeup. By considering an area's particular assets and challenges, a food system can be created that effectively serves members of the community, both the suppliers and the buyers.

"Value chains are supply chains that begin on the farm and end at the consumer's table, and which promote values of health, fairness, and sustainability."

— Anthony Flaccavento of the Appalachian Sustainable Development

TIP

The University of Vermont (uvm.edu) recently launched its low-residency "Food Hub Management Certificate Program," the first of its kind in the country, available to anyone interested in a career in food systems

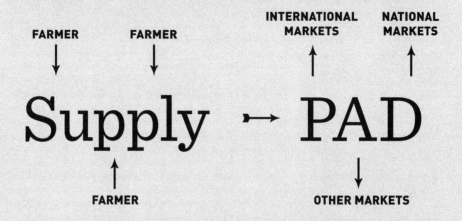

Conventional Supply Chain

FARMER → Supply ← FARMER
FARMER ↑ Supply

Supply ⤑ PAD

INTERNATIONAL MARKETS ↑ PAD
NATIONAL MARKETS ↑ PAD
PAD ↓ OTHER MARKETS

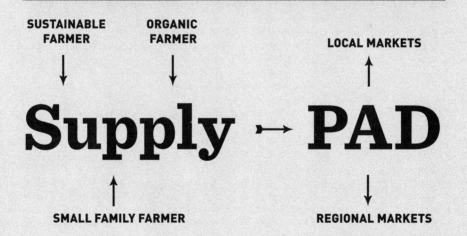

Value Supply Chain

SUSTAINABLE FARMER ↓ Supply
ORGANIC FARMER ↓ Supply
SMALL FAMILY FARMER ↑ Supply

Supply ⤑ PAD

LOCAL MARKETS ↑ PAD
PAD ↓ REGIONAL MARKETS

PAD = PROCESSING, AGGREGATION, AND DISTRIBUTION

— From *Creating a Regional Food Hub: Assessments and Recommendations for Dona Ana County,*
prepared by Krysten Aguilar with La Semilla Food Center.

CREATE A FOOD HUB

La Semilla Food Center is a nonprofit in Anthony, New Mexico, a town in the Paso del Norte region near El Paso, Texas. In order to develop a stronger food system, the center's members started by asking the community questions. Local youths took questionnaires out into the neighborhoods, and that sent a powerful, inclusive message about the future: young people care. La Semilla has generously shared its questionnaire, reprinted here, and you can adapt it to fit the needs of your own community. To build a healthy food hub, first ask your community questions.

Producer Survey Questions

1. What products do you currently grow or produce for sale?

2. How much land do you currently use to grow or raise food for sale (owned or leased)?

3. Where do you normally sell your products? (specify locations)

4. Are there other specific local markets where you would like to be able to sell your products? (please specify)

5. What financial, policy, or labor challenges do you have selling your products at local markets (e.g., lack of access to land or water, difficulty obtaining small loans, high insurance premiums, barriers selling to school)?

6. What infrastructure challenges do you have selling your product at local markets (transportation, storage, etc.)?

7. How interested would you be in the following (i.e., currently participate, very interested, somewhat interested, not interested, unsure):

- Central aggregation facility to combine produce with that of other growers to meet restaurant, store, or institutional demand

- A community kitchen in which you could prepare value-added products to sell at farmers' markets, grocery stores, and other local markets

- Accessing resources to expand your production in order to produce year-round

- A microloan program

- Selling directly to schools and local institutions

- Peer-to-peer learning

- Joining a growers' cooperative to help with marketing, aggregation, and distribution

- Offering a community supported agriculture program

- Participating in a Food Policy Council

- A farm link program to connect young farmers seeking farmland with retiring farmers and/or individuals willing to rent/lease farmland

- Partnering with other landowners to expand production

- A local small farm processing facility to wash, cut, store, and distribute products

- Mentoring young adults interested in agricultural production as a career

- Interest in networking with food buyers

- Interest in having a chef visit your operation

- Food safety, good agricultural practices, organic, or similar trainings and certifications

8. What kind of sustainable practices do you use on your farm (e.g., water usage, biodynamic/permaculture, minimize chemical inputs, non-GMO seeds, certified organic)?

9. Would you like to be included in a database of producers who sell locally?

>>

TIP

Build good relationships with regulators as you build your community's food system. For example, host a food safety workshop on your farm or with your farm-based education organization.

Assess the Value Chain

The scale at which to operate a value chain is critically important if it is to be financially viable for all parties: buyers; producers; and processors, aggregators, and distributors. Local conditions of markets, farmers, and facilities will all play roles in determining at what scale a value chain should operate in a specific area. Asking the following questions will aid you in discovering the appropriate scale of a local and regional value chain to fit your area:

1. How large is the unmet demand for local foods? Can it be met by an expansion of direct market options, such as farmers' markets and CSAs?

2. Who and where are the market drivers for local foods (public schools, colleges, retailers)?

3. What is the estimated total demand, and for what products? Is there a minimum demand that must be met?

4. Roughly how many farms/acres are necessary to meet the demand?

5. Is there enough interest among farmers to meet demand? If so, how much assistance and support is needed in terms of training, financing, and materials?

6. Why are these markets beneficial to farmers? Do they reduce costs, improve prices, or provide easier market access?

7. How many producers will be needed to meet minimum demands? How close are these farmers to one another?

8. What infrastructure is needed to link the desired products to the markets? Does any of it currently exist?

9. What will it cost to build or access the needed infrastructure? What form of funding is available?

10. Is there a local organization or business willing and able to launch the value chain, and to manage it if necessary? It is essential to research each aspect of the value chain through research and experimentation. This will help focus efforts and plans, and should answer the basics:

WHAT farmers are now raising, or could be raising, that can be sold in substantial quantities, and produced profitably and sustainably

WHO is likely to buy these products, where they are located, and what are their essential requirements

WHAT systems and/or infrastructure will be needed to connect area farmers with those buyers, and which parts of this infrastructure need to be developed

— Excerpted with permission from *Creating a Regional Food Hub: Assessments and Recommendations for Dona Ana County*, prepared by Krysten Aguilar with La Semilla Food Center. The section about assessing value chains is based on the work of Appalachian Sustainable Development. (This is one nifty example of how doing your research like La Semilla did, and giving credit where credit's due, benefits all involved. Thanks, Appalachian Sustainable Development and La Semilla!)

>✕<

MAKE A MAP
. . . .

The original mission of Island Grown Initiative (IGI), the nonprofit
that grew out of that first Potluck with a Purpose in 2005 (page 23),
was to support farmers on the 100-square-mile island of Martha's
Vineyard, off the coast of southern Massachusetts. Before the group
even had a name, it had determined one actionable goal by the end
of that dinner: to draw a map. It was a project that had a beginning, a
middle, and an end. We enlisted the skills of a local graphic designer,
and the Martha's Vineyard Commission supported the map with its
geographic information system (GIS) services (see page 92). Getting
the farms' data up-to-date required a lot of phone calls, e-mails, and
face-to-face meetings to explain what we were trying to do and why.

A farm map serves multiple functions: First, it increases awareness of the local
farming scene and encourages consumers to buy direct from the source. Second,
it is a useful resource for zoning agriculture bylaws and right-to-farm designa-
tions in municipalities. And finally, it serves as the basis for redrawing wholesale food distribution routes to supermarkets, restaurants, food banks, and
institutions such as schools and hospitals.

For an island that has a reputation of being all beaches and famous people
on vacation, Martha's Vineyard has more than 25 diversified family farms.
Farmers are raising meat animals, poultry, and shellfish. They are producing
fruits, vegetables, fungi, raw and pasteurized milk, cheese and yogurt, wool, and
sea salt. Because we're surrounded by water, we included shellfish aquaculture
farms on our map.

With no middleman in the mix, farmers would make more money. The map
included a listing of what, in general, the farmers sold and how it was for sale —
whether through their own farm stands, at farmers' markets, or by appointment
only. This worked. Anecdotal evidence offered by our local Cronig's Market,
a supporter of the farm map and the Island Grown Initiative, suggested that
Cronig's actually lost thousands of dollars in sales the first year the map was
out, because people were buying direct from the farmers.

>>

We decided to make the map free and available to the public at farm stands, feed stores, and supermarkets. It was a very persuasive promotional piece. After it was printed, some folks from the map's working group wanted to do more. The map set us on our path. It proved that there were energetic allies and local resources. It also made us proud of our place and the farmers in it. People, we the eaters, were ready to do something about supporting a healthier community food system as opposed to feeling paralyzed by the problems.

GEOGRAPHIC INFORMATION SYSTEMS (GIS)

In order to get our map drawn, we went to our community development agency, the Martha's Vineyard Commission, to enlist the help of their geographic information systems (GIS) specialist. I'm no expert in drawing maps, but I can say that GIS is a powerhouse. It allows maps to be drawn in layers by building up data, and data is what you want to make informed decisions.

Let's say you are in a town or city looking to build an urban agriculture project or a new farmers' market — you'll want information about zoning, roads, types of existing businesses, public office buildings, schools, and public bus routes. Or let's say you're a nonprofit looking to connect land to farmers — with the aid of GIS you can see what's in conservation already, who owns it, and even what soil types there are. It's possible to scale, to layer, to peel away those layers, and to make really cool, very helpful, dynamic maps. Unlike a paper map, a GIS map allows you to select what you want to see; you can add and subtract according to the types of data it is built with.

Check with your city or county government to see whether they have a GIS specialist or share one with another town. The international company Esri (esri .com), headquartered in Redlands, California, is a major supplier of GIS software.

USE MAPMAKING SOFTWARE

Consider this: You're in a neighborhood association and you want to map vacant lots, or maybe open rooftops, for potential community gardens. You're going to need to find out who owns them. Maybe you'll want data about where food is already available in the area, such as restaurants, fast-food joints, corner stores, community centers, schools, farmers' markets, and supermarkets, to help in determining what the need is and whether people are really going to want to grow their own food.

Additional useful data for your map may be how close the gardens are to transportation routes and/or parking lots so community members can get to them. If you're considering the gardens as potentially commercial enterprises, maybe you want to map existing processors, aggregators, and distributors to determine the conventional supply chain or value chain (see page 87). Information is power. GIS is very powerful.

There are any number of online mapmaking tools. At BatchGeo (batchgeo .com), you can copy and paste your addresses (directly from a spreadsheet if you have one) and create a coded, dimensional map. If you're looking for distribution information (say you're a co-op, a farm, a CSA, or a new farmers' market), you could collect physical addresses of grocers, farmers' markets, corner stores, restaurants, food banks, public schools, hospitals, and public transportation stations to see how accessible food outlets are in whatever geographical area you determine.

Check out the blog *Mapgiving* (mapgiving.blogspot.com), which describes itself as "a meeting space for non-profits and cartographers." Or simply go to Google Maps (maps.google.com). Or do your own search: "Best online mapmaking tools."

ORGANIZE A FARMERS' MARKET

My own big sister, Ann Bliss, was the founding chair of the Cobblestone Farmers Markets in Winston-Salem, North Carolina. She also worked as an attorney and as a judicial officer in the Wisconsin court system before moving to North Carolina. She has provided the following advice for farmers' market organizers. Also see page 97, where she gives more specific advice to growers and vendors who participate in farmers' markets.

Network

It's as critical a part of your infrastructure as signboards, washing stations, and portable toilets. This means building relationships with folks at city hall, county government, community and school groups, businesses, and other markets.

Write Clear Market Rules

Vendor qualifications, attendance, advertising (as in product labeling), and standards of conduct for all market participants should be addressed. Create an internal process for review and revision, and rewrite the rules as needed. Give every vendor a copy, and keep a copy on-site during market hours. Enforce them, gently but firmly.

Build Credibility

For the public, that means continuity: market days, hours, and location are reliable, and every market offers a safe, enjoyable, high-quality environment. For growers, funders, and supporters, credibility is an earned reputation for an ongoing commitment to compliance and accountability. Have a budget, and keep accurate, detailed financial records for every item of income and expense associated with market operations, including in-kind contributions from volunteers.

Avoid Mission Creep

The evil twin of genuine enthusiasm, mission creep results in taking on too many projects, saying yes every time someone starts a sentence with "Let's ...," and forgetting that other people's time and energy are not infinitely expendable or available on demand.

Watch out, too, for the belief that great ideals and a good cause excuse bad behavior and wrongful acts. This devil lurks in each and every detail of your market operations. One wink, and the hours and hours you've invested in networking and building credibility will go up in smoke.

Caution!

Don't fail to distinguish between community outreach and education and advertising. Both are important. Neither can fully substitute for the other. Community outreach and education is labor intensive and builds market participation over time. Advertising tends to be expensive and can fade quickly, but it is critical to shopper attendance and market "brand" recognition.

Be clear about whether your organization is a qualified tax-exempt entity.

Don't ignore the demands of sound business practice as defined by the contemporary American legal and regulatory environment. This means permits, insurance, taxes (sales tax, too), health and sanitation compliance, and security, to name just a few. Be wary of the common adage, "It's easier to get forgiveness than to get permission."

START A MARKET AT A REST STOP

The Massachusetts Department of Transportation has begun a Farmers' Market Program in which farmers are invited to use free space at all 18 of the service plazas on Massachusetts highways. Eleven of those plazas are on the Mass Pike, the big highway that crosses Massachusetts from east to west, connecting with I-90 in New York. Drivers can shop at farmers' markets right across from the plazas' donut shops and fast-food joints. If you want to start a farmers' market at a rest stop in your state, start by enquiring at the department of transportation.

THE FARMERS MARKET COALITION
Iowa

The mission of the Farmers Market Coalition (farmersmarketcoalition
.org) is to "to strengthen farmers markets for the benefit of farmers, consumers, and communities." The coalition runs an electronic mailing list
(a.k.a. a Listserv), provides a list of resources, offers information about
the Farmers Market Promotion Program (FMPP), holds webinars, and
hosts events. Find these good guys!

Here is what they are working to do, their priorities in their own words:

TO SERVE as an information center for farmers markets.

TO BE A VOICE for North American farmers market advocacy.

TO FOSTER strong state and regional farmers market associations.

TO BRING private and public support to the table to sustain farmers markets in
the long term, for the benefit of farmers, consumers, and communities.

TO PROMOTE farmers markets to the public.

TO DEVELOP and provide educational programming and networking opportunities for farmers market managers and farmers market vendors.

— List excerpted from Farmers Market Coalition (farmersmarketcoalition.org)

KNOW YOUR LAW

Law and food share an inextricable relationship. There are multiple laws and
regulations affecting every bite we take, every seed we plant, every piece of meat
we grill, and every pint of ice cream that's shipped. The kind of laws I'm talking
about in this book were not handed down at Mount Sinai. So they can be exam-
ined, rewritten, and implemented to reflect the scalability — from industrial
agribusinesses to small growers and producers, from international food systems
to local food systems — and the reforms that must be made to support greater
access to healthy food for everyone. It's very possible that your town, village, or
city doesn't have the permits or regulations that encourage small business owners to open up shop and start selling healthy whole foods, whether out of trucks,
parking lots, or farms. But you can change that and much, much more once you
have the right guides, tools, and information to give you support.

ANN BLISS

For farmers at a market.

PARTICIPATE in the development of written market rules, and honor them.

STAFF BOOTHS with workers who have good people skills. On peak days or when "hot" items like strawberries come in, staff up. What you might save in wages or time will be lost in wasted, unsalable product if you cannot keep customers flowing.

SUPPORT your market staff with recipes, know-how, and information about how to cook with the fruits, veggies, cuts of meat, fish, and dairy products that you sell.

INVEST in safe, solid canopy or tenting equipment and attractive display arrangements. Smile. You are good.

Look Out For . . .

FARMERS' MARKETS that do not have rules or don't have a will to enforce them.

SHOPPERS who want you to break the rules for them, for any reason or for just this once. It hurts the market as a whole and turns a positive community initiative into an exclusive private party.

MARKETS that do not recruit, or at least welcome, vendor representation in their organizational structure. Or markets that have no structure, or no organization.

Never . . .

MISREPRESENT your product as to either origin or method of production, either by implication, evasion, or outright misinformation.

BREAK THE RULES of your market. For anyone, for any reason, even just this once. Even if it means losing a sale. If it's hard for you to say no, ask other vendors for phrases and strategies to use when you are pressed. Your market colleagues will respect you, and you will have modeled what it takes to contribute to the success of the market as a whole, rather than just getting yours and getting out.

FAIL to keep accurate, complete, detailed financial records. The fact that most market vendors transact in cash is not unknown to the IRS.

FORGET that cleanliness counts when selling to the public.

CREATE A PERMIT PROGRAM
FOR PRODUCE CART VENDORS

Mobile food vendors can travel deep into the neighborhoods most in need of fresh produce, and unlike supermarkets, they don't require large capital investments to start operations. Mobile vendors can also adjust their inventory quickly to fit the unique cultural demands of the community. Establishing a permit program for these vendors may also have economic benefits, providing local entrepreneurs with small business opportunities and contributing to neighborhood economic development by revitalizing the street scene. In some places, produce cart vending might even be an avenue to promote agritourism by highlighting the unique offerings of the local agriculture to attract outside consumers.

How the Ordinance Works

The National Policy & Legal Analysis Network to Prevent Childhood Obesity's (NPLAN) model ordinance creates a streamlined permit program for "produce cart vendors," retailers who sell only fresh, uncut fruits and vegetables from a mobile cart, much like a produce stand on wheels. The ordinance sets forth the requirements for vendors, the rules for vending, and a range of incentives a local government may provide to encourage vendors to sell in neighborhoods that lack other sources of fresh produce. Giving vendors priority consideration when applying for a permit, discount rates on permit fees, access to small business loans with low interest rates, and small business counseling and technical assistance are some of the incentives suggested in the model ordinance.

Why Only Fresh, Whole Produce?

In most communities, state law regulates the health and sanitation requirements for most types of food sales, including mobile food vending. But in many states, the retail food code regulations exempt the sale of whole fresh produce from produce stands.

NPLAN designed its Model Produce Cart Ordinance (available for download at nplan.org) to take advantage of this exemption, by limiting sales to whole fresh produce so that communities in those states simply need to implement the local ordinance. Because state law varies, it is important for individual communities to review their state retail food code before enacting the model ordinance to determine whether and how state law regulates whole fresh produce vending. By establishing a streamlined permit program for produce cart vendors, communities can make it easier for residents to buy fresh fruits and vegetables for their families. NPLAN's Model Produce Cart Ordinance is a simple, cost-effective way for local government to make fresh produce — and the corresponding benefits of a healthy diet—more accessible.

— Reprinted with permission from ChangeLab Solutions, changelabsolutions.org (see page 293)

JOIN FARM HACK

Farm Hack (farmhack.net) is an "open source community for resilient agriculture." Calling itself a "farmer-driven" organization, Farm Hack focuses on improving farm tools. Its success is made by its members, who come together in person and online to design and build farming equipment that is affordable, adaptable, and easy to fix. They're talking cover-crop rollers, laydown weeders, multi-dibblers (rolling tools for marking seedbeds), oat and grain dehullers, and even things like record-keeping and profitability analysis tools. Farm Hack is all about innovation, community-driven design, and mutual aid.

>×<

WHAT'S GOING ON

FOOD + TECH CONNECT
New York, New York

Food + Tech Connect (foodtechconnect.com) is a media and research company building "a network for innovators transforming the business of food." See its website for news about all manner of food and technology topics, such as crowdfunding for food start-ups, ways to meet other innovators from across the food supply chain, the latest infographics, marketing, and more.

TAINTED PIG

It all went terribly wrong that gray autumn afternoon. The lack of planning, the late start. The woodman's ax, the piercing screams of the pig, blood pooling on hard, merciless ground. The men chased the frightened, injured animal and delivered inept blows until it finally succumbed to a painful death.

Despite my best efforts to know my food and look dinner in the eye — I'd helped feed and care for that pig — in *its* end, I turned my back, covered my ears, and squeezed shut my eyes. With bile and adrenaline on my tongue, it was all too late, too much, and all too little. To fight or fly — my body shook in the in-betweens. This slaughter was all wrong, and it couldn't be stopped or undone.

Years later I still wonder: What was I thinking? Does "connecting" to my food equate the necessity to bloody my hands and take part in an animal's slaughter and butchering? Though I had no business doing what I'd taken on — I was no farmer then and am still not one now — I'd set out for the experience of raising and slaughtering an animal to feed my family. In retrospect it was complete foolishness. Yet it's an intention that I see too many backyard growers devise today, in the name of local food. I had neither the knowledge nor the skills to take on that complex relationship and the responsibilities between human, animal, and meat. Especially the specific skills of slaughter — safely, humanely.

That night, I came home in the dark, mute, dirty, and smelling of death. The shower couldn't have been hot enough, the scrub brush not wire enough, the soap not lye enough.

What I thought I'd chosen was a conscientious path, the result of soul-searching and seeking beyond the plastic-wrapped boneless, skinless cuts of protein from factory farms, on sale cheap for my budget and my convenience. I had wanted to be actively engaged: to work, to see, then to do.

That tainted pork sat in our freezer for what felt like years. With pain and fear frozen in its every cell — to eat it or to feed it to others would've been the antithesis of sustenance, for it was toxic. I couldn't do it. I finally gave my freezer-burned transgressions a burial in an unmarked grave, deep enough so that even the raccoons or my dog could not dig it up.

Quitting meat would've seemed to be a normal, highly justified reaction to that night, but I didn't. I am not a vegetarian; my body needs animal protein, still. So I stand today, back in the kitchen. Ready to do something of worth to help ensure that no one, no animal, goes through what we did that sad night. Indelibly I remain a conspirator, witness, and perpetrator. Pig blood figuratively stains my feet, hands, and eyes; my memory; and now my actions. To take that memory and to do something with it is all I can do to honor that poor, innocent, pitiable animal and the meals it never became.

>×<

SUPPORT HUMANE SLAUGHTER

If animals are going to be raised for our sustenance, humane slaughter is a mandate. I've been sickened to come across videos online supposedly championing local food and small, diversified family farms yet showing sadistic behavior toward animals. Abuse is abuse whether it happens on a bucolic farm or in a corporate, industrial-sized slaughter and processing plant. If you see examples of such abuse, don't turn a blind eye. Instead, act by speaking out. And most important, do not purchase or be served meat from inhumane slaughters even if the farm is "local" or the animal was "sustainably raised." Inhumane slaughter is totally unacceptable and preventable. You can find people who care enough to slaughter meat animals properly. Check out the following resources.

Animal Welfare Approved

The Animal Welfare Institute (awionline.org), a nonprofit organization founded in 1951, began its Animal Welfare Approved (AWA) standards program (animal welfareapproved.org) in 2006. The program establishes basic standards for how animals should be treated. I wonder how many local or small-scale slaughters of local four-legged livestock like sheep, pigs, goats, or cows wouldn't meet basic AWA standards. Here is a list of prohibited actions, which AWA considers cruelty to animals:

SHACKLING, dragging, hanging, cutting, bleeding, or dressing any sensible animal

BEATING or striking any animal

INTENTIONAL electrical prodding or poking of an animal in a sensitive area such as the anus, the eyes, or the genitals

PICKING up or throwing a sheep by its wool

INTENTIONALLY driving animals over an animal that has fallen or will not move

ANY other action that causes intentional harm to an animal

Customers, look to buy meat from sources with AWA certification. Folks raising livestock, check out the institute's resources for helping you raise and slaughter animals humanely.

5-Step Animal Welfare Rating Standards

Maybe you've seen meat labeled with the Global Animal Partnership's 5-Step Animal Welfare Rating Standards (globalanimalpartnership.org/the-5-step-program). The supermarket chain Whole Foods Market has adopted this ranking system, which shows consumers a range from step 1, which prohibits crates and cages, to step 5+, which says that the entire life of the animal was spent on an integrated farm.

Auditing Welfare in Slaughter Plants, Beef Feed Lots, and Dairies

These days in Temple Grandin's career, she is more on the road with her work about autism than she is discussing humane livestock handling systems. Nevertheless, her website (www.grandin.com) is an important resource for people concerned with animal welfare: the width and breadth of Grandin's expertise and her generosity in sharing observations are unparalleled. Check out her guidelines for audits of slaughter plants, building plans, and critical control points (CCPs) of humane slaughter, and much more.

BACON & EGGS

The chicken contributes,
But the pig gives his all.

— Howard Nemerov

>×<

BUILD A LOCAL SLAUGHTERHOUSE

Somebody's got to do it. It's a noble and connected thing to slaughter your own animals for your own consumption. But the acts of slaughtering and processing are not for everyone. What if you put your focus and energy into building a humane slaughterhouse for many, as opposed to humanely slaughtering for one? I have yet to slaughter a chicken, though I helped build and support our community's mobile poultry slaughterhouse.

The lack of access to small-scale, size-appropriate humane slaughterhouses is a barrier to small family farmers who might otherwise raise chicken and turkeys, or even diversify their enterprise with four-legged livestock: pigs, sheep, goats, and cattle. "Mobile slaughter is crucial" to building local and regional food systems, U.S. Secretary of Agriculture Tom Vilsack said in a Bloomberg News interview in July 2014. Mobile slaughterhouses for poultry and four-legged animals are making an impact in communities they serve. But as with any enterprise, the building and implementing of any slaughter option will only be as good as the people who run it and the careful plans they've made before purchasing equipment or drawing up a building plan.

On Martha's Vineyard, we started a poultry-slaughtering program and built a mobile poultry-processing trailer because the investment was relatively small, for both our nonprofit and for the farmers. (See my book *The Mobile Poultry Slaughterhouse: Building a Humane Chicken Processing Unit to Strengthen Your Local Food System*.) If we couldn't come through, we hadn't wasted a farmer's longer investment in raising pigs or cattle, for example. Chickens are gateway livestock in many small farming enterprises, and the number of backyard growers is on the rise. Both commercial and noncommercial growers are potential customers for a mobile poultry-processing trailer. Regulations are different in each state, but poultry exemptions do exist, which means you should be able to turn a gray area into an opportunity. To learn about your state's regulations, go to the Niche Meat Processor Assistance Network's website (nichemeatprocessing.org).

>><<

JEFFERSON MUNROE

Here's what Martha's Vineyard farmer Jefferson Munroe, of The GOOD Farm, has to say about running a mobile poultry-processing trailer (MPPT):

1. Processing is a customer service industry — remember that the farmer is a customer.

2. If the equipment depreciates faster than it pays for itself, then your MPPT isn't a workable model. It should at least be forecast to pay for itself within three years.

3. Pricing will give farmers different incentives for how many birds to grow. If you give them a flat rental fee, they will raise as many birds as possible for each processing. If you charge per bird, they'll raise many fewer. And if you charge both, you can gently steer to the number of birds you as a processor want to charge for in a day.

"It's the little details that are vital. Little things make big things happen." — John Wooden, basketball player and coach

SLAUGHTERHOUSES ON FARMS
Whatcom County, Washington

What if counties took up the challenge of facing down zoning barriers to slaughterhouses so that small family farms finally had access to infrastructure without the cost and stress of transporting live animals great distances? The answer: Farmers in the region would most likely begin to raise more livestock and, consequently, produce healthier, higher-quality meat.

In September 2013, Whatcom County in Washington State voted (narrowly) to allow slaughterhouses of less than 7,000 square feet with just a building permit and the proper permits for waste handling and right to water. Larger slaughterhouses (up to 20,000 square feet) would still have to face a public hearing.

FIND A POLICY GEEK (OR BECOME ONE)

I have a mentor who has been doing agriculture policy work in Washington, D.C., for decades. Now in her early 60s, she's weary of the many and constant challenges in food policy today: having to do more with less money; struggling with the insider political nature of the grant processes; seeing industry, corporate, political, and status quo interests held above farmers' interests. She's especially tired of a history and culture of chauvinism and racism, both overt and implied. These days, as we finish up one of our conversations, she always ends with, "You should be doing this work. They listen to people like you, and they're tired of me." That's about my "white American privilege" as opposed to her brown immigrant status.

But her plea also speaks to how urgently we need help in this regard. Are you interested in the details and struggles of such work? Or do you know someone who might be? Here are some good places to start to look at what advocacy work is being done now, and where you might find comrades.

The Rural Coalitio/Coalición Rural

According to its website, The Rural Coalition/Coalición Rural (ruralco.org) links over 90 grassroots member organizations "to serve as a critical advocacy voice of African-American, American-Indian, Asian-American, Euro-American, Latino, and women farmers, ranchers, farmworkers, and rural communities throughout the U.S."

The National Sustainable Agriculture Coalition

The National Sustainable Agriculture Coalition (NSAC) is, according to its website (sustainableagriculture.net), an "alliance of grassroots organizations that advocates for federal policy reform to advance the sustainability of agriculture, food systems, natural resources, and rural communities." Check out its lists of board members and supporting organizations to learn who's who in your region and what they are doing.

BECOME AN INTERPRETER

If you can speak, read, or write in more than one language, consider becoming an interpreter for a food-based organization. As an interpreter, you can reach out to community members, immigrants, and the press. Blain Snipstal, a farmer and agroecology organizer, is one of the Rural Coalition's (see opposite page) representatives to La Via Campesina (www.viacampesina.org) and its North American region. He tweeted, "Without translators there can be no revolution!"

REGIONAL ENVIRONMENTAL COUNCIL
Worcester, Massachusetts

The Regional Environmental Council in Worcester, Massachusetts (recworcester.org), prints brochures for its community farmers' market and schedules for its mobile farmers' market in 11 (at last count) different languages, from Albanian to Arabic. The schedules are distributed at family health centers; Special Supplemental Nutrition Program for Women, Infants, and Children (WIC) offices; and low-income and elderly housing units.

LEARN FROM THOSE WHO CAME BEFORE YOU

I want to close this chapter with some words of wisdom from Don Ralston and Marty Strange, the founders of the Center for Rural Affairs (cfra.org), a nonprofit that started in 1973 and remains based in the town of Lyons, Nebraska (population 851). The center is grounded in a sense of place and committed to the rural. Their work includes developing advocates (see Speak, page 188), affordable health care for farmers, federal policy review and action items, and small business support.

In his August 2014 *New York Times* op-ed, "Don't Let Your Children Become Farmers," Bren Smith wrote that "it's time for farmers to shape our own agenda."

> We need to fight for loan forgiveness for college grads who pursue agriculture; programs to turn farmers from tenants into landowners; guaranteed affordable health care; and shifting subsidies from factory farms to family farms. We need to take the lead in shaping a new food economy by building our own production hubs and distribution systems. And we need to support workers up and down the supply chain who are fighting for better wages so that their families can afford to buy the food we grow.

"None of these demands will be met," Smith concluded, "until we start our own organizations — as in generations past — and shape a vision of a new food economy that ensures that growing good food also means making a good living."

The Center for Rural Affairs is one of those organizations that closes the gap of "generations past" because not only are they doing the work of supporting farmers, but they have been doing it for over 30 years and they are still standing strong. Here, then, are some of their lessons learned, from all those years of fighting the good fight.

>>

Shine the light on others. Share the spotlight and recognize those whose shoulders upon which we all stand.

TEN QUICK THOUGHTS (IN NO PARTICULAR ORDER) ABOUT SOME LESSONS WE HAVE LEARNED

1. There is no work you will ever do that pays better than doing what you believe in every day. Doing what you believe in often requires financial sacrifice, but you won't notice it if you are being fulfilled. If you are keeping score, however, you are losing.

2. Rural organizations not rooted in rural places are easily distracted, often shallow, and usually ineffective. Loving rural places enough to criticize them and to know their strengths when you see them requires being there.

3. Do not take yourself too seriously. People who do not have fun, who cannot laugh at themselves, who carry the weight of the world on their shoulders and anguish over every negative turn of events don't last long in this business, drain energy from others, and can't see the forest for the trees.

4. The most important decisions are hiring decisions. Hire good people and give them lots of room to do their thing. If you don't, you spend all your time cleaning up messes.

5. Take care of each other. Whether it is the way you run meetings, the way you allocate salaries, or the fringe benefits you provide, mutuality is the most valuable source of good morale.

6. Don't let the staff get out in front of the board. If the board is not leading, it cannot or will not play its most important role: protecting the integrity of the organization, establishing its political independence, and defending it from its critics.

7. Conduct yourself with honor and integrity and courage. Make the issues, don't become the issue.

8. You cannot invent too many ways to reward sharing and to encourage sacrifice. People who are not expected to share will hoard, and hoarding is the bane of good resource management in a small organization.

9. Listen to those with whom you disagree. Especially, understand the other side's argument in a political debate better than they do. Know it so well that you know what it is about their own arguments they don't really believe. There is nothing more demoralizing than being confronted with your own doubts.

10. Manage your resources prudently, conserve everything, especially time, and never cut cord. You might need it.

— Excerpted with permission from Don Ralston and Marty Strange, "The Center for Rural Affairs in the First 20 Years: A Short Memoir, Mostly More or Less True"

>×<

CHAPTER 4

Grow

THERE ARE SQUASHES coming up in the 12' x 12' plot in which the pigs used to dig and fertilize the soil. Those vegetables are the herds' growing legacy since they left for the slaughterhouse last fall. Two small hoop houses are abuzz with bees, pollinating the tomato plants. Sweet pea tendrils spiral up and out the deer fencing that encloses this garden. Some will become deer's graze, but that's the way it is. Every creature has to eat, and Daniele Dominick, the owner of this garden/mini-farm behind the Scottish Bakehouse restaurant in Vineyard Haven, Massachusetts, knows this very well.

Years ago, this land used to be the restaurant's back parking lot. But Daniele built it up slowly, starting by composting organic material such as coffee grounds and eggshells, which reduced her waste management costs and now provides nutrients to the soil for the restaurant's kale, carrots, onions, and herbs that were planted for the cooks. This garden is also a surrogate for people like me who can't, or don't, garden. A few picnic tables line the perimeter, providing peace and sanctuary. If and when people want to dig in, get their hands dirty, or soak in some of that transformative calm that is gardening, the gate is always open.

To grow is to change — a strange and wonderful perpetual impermanence in our daily and seasonal rhythms — yet this remains largely invisible in the big picture of the circumstances and chain of events that it takes to get a seed from harvest to plate. My hope is to shed some light and hope on growing food we get to eat — or, as is the case for the 26.5 million Americans who live in food deserts, not to eat.

Ron Finley, a guerrilla gardener in South Central Los Angeles, poetically said, "To change the community, you have to change the composition of the soil. We are the soil." Finley's legacy is in a city that owns 26 square miles of vacant lots and where, he said in a 2013 TED talk, "the drive-thrus are killing more people than the drive-bys" because people are dying from diseases like obesity and diabetes that grow out of terrible diets.

What we grow and how we grow impacts us today and for generations to come. What if we grew as if seven generations of life depended on it?

Save farmland by developing a succession plan (page 113). Diversify the crops you plant (page 119). Grow lightly with great returns, as in aquaponics (page 121). Plan community gardens (page 131). Grow free food for more people (page 143), as does the eloquent Finley. Think very local and create a kitchen garden (page 151). Every day, we grow a little bit. Some days — if and when we're lucky — we grow more than others.

A FARM RECLAIMED

It took 16 years for Krishana Collins to be able to unpack, settle down, and have a farm she could call her own. Now she has a 75-year lease on Tea Lane Farm in Chilmark, Massachusetts. "When I tell people about it, they're like, 'The town sold you the buildings for one dollar and gave you the land to farm for how long?'

"Yes," this sprightly nymph answers. "And I hope other towns will look around and see if this is a solution for their farming community one day."

Tea Lane Farm, an old dairy farm located in the agricultural heart of Martha's Vineyard, had fallen into disrepair. The town and the family who owned the farm agreed on a selling price; the town and the Martha's Vineyard Land Bank (a conservation organization established in 1986 by the voters) then split the responsibilities of use and caretaking between themselves, signing an agreement that would allow for a "tenant farmer" who could lease three acres to farm for a one-time payment of $20,000 for a 75-year lease. The town also sold the four buildings (a 1755 house and three outbuildings) to the farmer for $1. In exchange, the farmer committed to living on the property for at least 11 months a year and submitting to an annual performance review. The town of Chilmark put out a request for proposals for use of the Active Farming Area, and interested parties submitted their farm plans for the buildings and land, which were reviewed by the town's special Farm Committee.

Chilmark received at least six proposals from area farmers. As a bystander, I found it gut wrenching to watch, because we live in a small community where farms are scarce and land values extraordinarily high. To have friends and neighbors compete for such high stakes was trying for me, but I know not as difficult as for the farmers who were competing against each other. Because this particular property evoked so much emotion from the community, people had very strong opinions and a sense of ownership about it.

But what ultimately kept the community together was that no one wanted the property to be developed. The town and the MV Land Bank collaboration protected the land from being developed into another McMansion, a second or third or fourth vacation home.

Krishana won the bid with a solid business plan, her established flower business, and a livestock proposal to raise sheep and cattle herds in the effort to improve the farm's soil. A committee member was quoted in the local press as saying, "She seemed like she was determined, that's what sold me." At her presentation in front of the town's Farm Committee, Krishana said, "I've been farming for 20 years and I've never given up and I've persevered on borrowed land and . . . I know I can carry it to Tea Lane Farm. I want people to drive by and be proud." Krishana has finally unpacked, and she is going to be farming for a while now.

>×<

MAKE A FARM SUCCESSION PLAN

When I drive south out of my hometown, Madison, Wisconsin, on U.S. 151 through Fitchburg to Verona, I cuss a lot. Because along that old familiar route, there used to be acres of fertile farmland. Working open spaces, dairy farms, local life, and culture. Now it's housing developments. Suburban sprawl. One municipality dissolves into the next in rote houses, slick tarmac roads, and mini strip malls. I know people need and deserve decent houses to live in, and we also need land to farm for food security and food sovereignty. Smart development includes wise and thoughtful farm transfers, the succession of farmland from one generation to the next, whether it stays in the family or not. A farm succession plan helps current landowners plan for their retirement. Land For Good (landforgood .org) has several useful, free downloadable guides. Here's a summary of its Farm Succession Guide. Start here to save farmland.

Know Your Goals and Current Situation

Farm owners: What are your hopes and dreams? Your goals? What do you want your farm legacy to be?

Who has a stake in the farm? Identify family, nonfamily, CSA members, and neighbors.

If you know whom to transfer the farm to, identify advisers such as a lawyer, accountant, lender, and Extension agent, and prepare the documents for the transfer.

What do you need to consider regarding financial needs, time lines, heirs, successor, tax implications, and affordability for the next owner?

Next Steps

Estimate retirement needs; inventory farm assets; talk to family members; update business plan; learn about easements, leases, and other creative transfer tools.

— Excerpted with permission from Land For Good

A FARM TRANSFER PLAN

ASSET TRANSFER: Spell out how farmland, buildings, and other assets are conveyed from one party to another.

GOAL SETTING & FAMILY COMMUNICATION: Set forth personal, family, and business goals, as well as ways to ensure constructive communication among all involved.

MANAGEMENT TRANSFER: Lay out how management tasks, responsibilities, and income shift over time from one farm operator to another.

BUSINESS PLAN: Set out strategies for farm operations, personnel, marketing, finance, and business entity formation.

ESTATE: Direct the eventual transfer of assets, usually with the goal of preserving as much of the estate value as possible for the beneficiaries.

LAND USE: Map out land use options that address agriculture, forestry, and recreation uses as well as conservation and development.

RETIREMENT: Address how and where the retiring person(s) want to live, their anticipated income, and health-care costs.

"Two out of three farms will likely change hands in the next 20 years. Ninety percent do not have an exit plan."

— Land For Good (landforgood.org)

LAND FOR GOOD

Keene, New Hampshire

Land For Good (landforgood.org), whose slogan is "Gaining Ground for Farmers," is a nonprofit that connects land and farmers in New England. It offers help for farmers like Krishana (page 112) who need land, landowners who are seeking to transfer and preserve land for agricultural use, farm families who are interested in turning over farms to the next generation, and concerned communities.

Kathryn Z. Ruhf, the executive director, said in an informational YouTube video about her organization that it "is one of the few organizations nationally that focuses on the issues of land access, farm transfer, management of working lands, land tenure, and really helping at a project level, including individual clients. So it is a very unique niche." Farm seekers, farm families, landowners, and communities are the recipients of the organization's help. But truly, that is all of us, because we're all part of a community somewhere, and we all have to eat. Though this organization is based in New England, the information and advice it provides are important and applicable across the country.

KATHRYN Z. RUHF

Town, village, and city decision makers, public officials and civic leaders — here are some suggestions about how to support farmers in your community.

1. Make sure that farmland access, secure tenure, and farm succession are addressed in town plans and ordinances.

2. Promote use of town land for farming uses.

3. Offer rental agreements that consider farmers' need for security and affordability.

4. Encourage landowners to make their land available for farming.

5. Identify, prioritize, and protect significant agricultural parcels in town.

YOU CAN DO THIS

GREEN YOUR CITY SPACES

Do you live in a city with vacant lots, boarded buildings, and stretches of urban wasteland? Perhaps no American city more than Detroit has seen itself so gutted by the boom and bust cycles of capitalism. That ravaging included a drastic reduction of the city's trees, too. According to the website of the nonprofit Greening of Detroit (greeningofdetroit.com), in the three decades between 1950 and 1980, approximately 500,000 trees in the city were lost to urban expansion, attrition, and Dutch elm disease. By the end of the 1980s, the city was losing "an average of four trees for every one planted."

The Greening of Detroit set out to reverse this trend and make good use of the city's abundance of vacant land, which was estimated to be about 20 square miles. Its mission is to inspire "sustainable growth of a healthy urban community through trees, green spaces, food, education, training and job opportunities." Look to their experience for ideas of your own, in your own place.

>×<

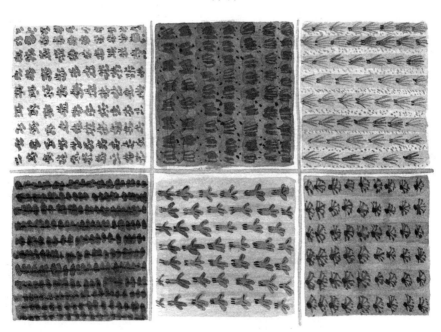

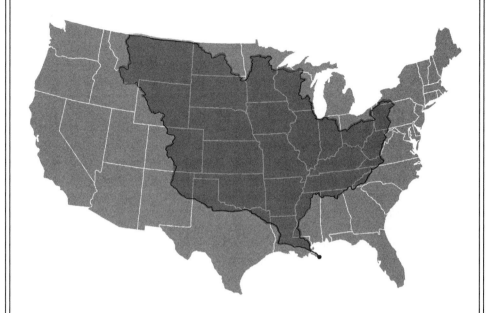

FOLLOW THE RIVERS

Local growing practices have implications beyond the farm, as a group of Iowa farmers fishing in the warm waters of the Gulf of Mexico discovered. Their vacation fishing showed them that their own pollution was deadening the miles and depths of the formerly most fertile waters in North America, and they returned home determined to figure out how to send clean water down the Mississippi River and into the delta. This story is covered in Green Fire Productions' series of films, *Ocean Frontiers* (ocean-frontiers.org). The series seeks to address the question of how to "meet our ever-expanding demands on the ocean without destroying it." Watch these films; screen them in your communities, and see how collaboration between states, farmers, and fishermen works in this massive effort to fix an environmental disaster, both on the land and in the sea.

NEW CROPS AT THE AG FAIR

Imagine growing up in the United States, then moving to a place where you couldn't grow sweet corn. Or tomatoes. Or collards. Now imagine that you are from the region of Minas Gerais, in southeastern Brazil, and have moved to the United States; you'd miss taioba (*Xanthosoma sagittifolium*) the way an American would miss the common vegetables grown here.

There were big smiles and lots of gesticulating when I popped open my trunk to display the taioba plants I was driving to different gardeners. The guys in the van next to me were on their way to work when I pointed to the plants in my car. "Taioba!" I said, but they shook their heads. "Not here!" It turns out, taioba *can* grow in Massachusetts, just not year-round. Though this staple grows in a rainforest, during the summer on Martha's Vineyard, the climate is similar enough.

Island Grown Initiative collaborated with the UMass Ethnic Crops Program to support local farmers in diversifying their crops to meet the demands of a growing local immigrant population of Brazilians. In 2006, there were an estimated 3,000 Brazilians living and working on Martha's Vineyard. That's a big potential market for farmers, and especially for a crop that evokes home for so many.

UMass did the science in figuring out how to grow crops from Brazil (as well as Honduras and Ecuador, because of additional large immigrant populations in Massachusetts from those countries) in New England. Island Grown Initiative did community outreach in both English and Portuguese with help from the Vineyard Health Care Access Program. Elio Silva, a local Brazilian businessman, helped connect the crops, the visiting UMass graduate students, and the farmers to eaters. Taste tests were held at the local grocery store, and a few chefs incorporated the produce in their menus. If you can get people to taste something new and show them how to cook with it, you will help drive the market. Best of all: to see the joy on people's faces when they saw their beloved taioba again.

>×<

In the summer of 2008, taioba (along with jiló and maxixe) found its way onto the Martha's Vineyard Agricultural Fair's list for the first time in its 130-plus-year history, and local growers scooped up some red, white, and blue ribbons.

DIVERSIFY WITH ETHNIC CROPS

The number of immigrants in the United States — in 2009, 12.5 percent of the total U.S. population, or 38.5 million people — provides an opportunity for farmers to diversify their crops. Many crops grown in other parts of the world can also be grown in the United States; it just takes research to figure out how. Farmers in communities with large populations of immigrant groups, be they Hmong, Iraqi, or Jamaican, can profit from providing something for these varied culinary preferences.

The National Agricultural Library of the U.S. Department of Agriculture coordinates the Alternative Farming Systems Information Center (afsic.nal.usda .gov), which gathers information about growing ethnic vegetables. In addition to the University of Massachusetts Ethnic Crops Program, the University of Kentucky, the University of Maryland World Farmers, and Rutgers all address the burgeoning popularity of ethnic vegetables.

WHAT'S GOING ON

WORLD FARMERS
Lancaster, Massachusetts

Flats Mentor Farm is a program of the nonprofit World Farmers (worldfarmers.org). Their CSA pledges to its members "an array of ethnic vegetables that would otherwise not be found . . . without traveling to Laos, Kenya, and Brazil." Flats Mentor Farm supports immigrant farmers with land, infrastructure, and technical and marketing assistance. In July of 2014, Fabiola Nizigiyimana, a refugee from Burundi, a single mother of five, and a farmer at the Flats, was honored as one of America's Champions of Change in Agriculture at the White House, for her efforts in founding a farmer co-op for 230 farmers (from countries including Tanzania, Nigeria, Uganda, Kenya, Laos, and Haiti) on the 40 acres of river bottom that is the farm. It's like a United Nations of small, sustainable agriculture.

MARIA MOREIRA

Moreira, as the executive director of World Farmers, has particular insight and expertise in working with immigrants. She is herself from the Azores, and a farmer as well. At Flats Mentor Farm, she started a CSA as a transitional mode to help build the capacity of the farmers, while they met and worked on developing a co-op for themselves. The CSA, supported by mentoring, helped farmers at Flats learn about harvesting, quality control, food safety, and marketing. And it fed people. Here's her advice.

ASSESS CAPACITY. Capacity in this sense means not only the farmers' ability to farm, but also to handle food safely and market it after the harvest. In the case of a multicultural, multi-language farming community that includes a wide variety of agricultural backgrounds, the challenges of communication, definitions, and establishing a common ground are of major importance in this first step.

MENTOR. Connecting more experienced farmers with less experienced farmers is a way to "provide technical assistance" (a grant proposal term), with less money, in a human way that also builds relationships and community. "Mentoring is not about a classroom somewhere, away from the farm. It's a training system that is cooperative and educational, in order to build the production capacity of farmers," explained Maria.

COLLABORATION. Vet any collaborations or partnerships in grants on how well potential collaborators treat their farmers. "Go to the farms, go see if food is really being grown, if communities are being positively affected, if peoples' freezers are getting full. Speak to the farmers and find out how they are being treated, fairly or not."

HAVE A PLAN A, B, AND C. When the Market Basket chain of independent grocers closed temporarily in Massachusetts, it left a large hole in market opportunities for local farmers. When you diversify, then if (or when!) an account is lost, you won't get stuck. Plan B or C means it's time to get creative. Use that mailing list of customers you've been collecting to send out an e-mail update about what you've got ready and ripe to sell. Post on social media, "Fresh tomatoes now at the farm stand!" Or maybe it's time to pay a visit to the local cafeteria directors or restaurants (see pages 58 and 282). Inquire at your local farmers' market, to see if they've any spots open, even if it's midseason. Connect with a local/regional food processor — artisan — small batch may be your out with those tomatoes. Eaters want fresh food. Find a way to let them know you've got it and get it to them.

BUILD INDEPENDENCE. A cooperative is one strategy in a farmers' business plan, but they cannot be dependent on only one. "Farmers need to know the math and understand the system so they can make their own decisions and create the co-op that they want, before they can decide if they want to use the co-op as part of their business strategy."

AQUAPONICS

John Pade, a fourth-generation dairy farmer and the cofounder and owner, with Rebecca Nelson, of Nelson and Pade Inc., remembers picking rocks out of the fields with his grandfather and father on their Wisconsin dairy farm. "Every spring they'd look up at the sky and say, 'If only we could control the weather we could make a living farming.' That's why I got so interested in aquaponics. For the last 20 years, we've been working to reinvent the family farm. One where you can grow good food for your family and community *and* put your kids through college."

All year long, it is a perfect summer-solstice day in Nelson and Pade's aquaponic greenhouse in Montello, Wisconsin. And every day of the year, clean, fresh food is harvested from their greenhouse and sold at a price they determine — to schools, restaurants, and grocery stores as well as direct from their farm stand. Dinosaur kale, Swiss chard, heirloom tomatoes, beets, carrots, herbs, brussels spouts, onions, salad greens, sweet corn, even dwarf fruit trees such as lemon, banana, and pomegranate — just about anything can grow in an aquaponics system. It mostly depends on what you're trying to do. And then there's the protein: freshwater fish, in this case tilapia.

There's no dirt under an aquaponics farmer's fingernails, yet the food is as organic as organic gets. The fish and plants are about the least stressed around because they live and grow in ideal conditions. Moreover, there's minimal potential for *E. coli* and other foodborne pathogens because in this system, *E. coli* doesn't exist. It's not there because fish, unlike warm-blooded livestock, don't carry the bacteria in their guts.

Clean and alive, this farm is permeated by a Zen calm. It smells healthy but not stagnant or fishy. It's warm but not too hot or sweaty. This is no test-tube sterile chemistry lab with weird clones and Frankenfish. The tilapia swim against an unpolluted current and are fed a healthy diet three times a day. Unlike farmed salmon, tilapia require very little protein in their diet, since they're primarily herbivores.

The plants' root systems, compared to that of their soil-sisters, are small because the plants don't need to search for nutrients to photosynthesize. The roots are constantly bathed in aerated nutrients, and once they've taken up what they need, which is effectively everything, the naturally cleaned water is circulated back into the fish tanks. You couldn't spray the plants with pesticides if you wanted to, or you'd kill your fish crop. Everything is interconnected, in the most efficient ways possible.

>>

Aquaponics is an example of controlled-environment agriculture (CEA), in which the grower establishes an ideal environment for the chosen crops. In CEA, every living thing grows at its optimal level, from the fish population density to the temperature of the water. Nothing is exposed to pollutants such as acid rain or oil spills. The "fields" where the crops grow and "streams" where the fish thrive do not fall to the mercy of unpredictable or severe weather patterns and events such as hail, unseasonable cold or hot spells, drought, and flooding. And the farmers get to enjoy ambient growing weather year-round, whether it's a blowing 30-degrees-below-zero Wisconsin winter or a humid Midwestern summer day. Rebecca planted a patch of sweet corn in February, to harvest in March for fun and to accompany the Nelson and Pade's staff feast, because, well, she could. "Harvesting and eating sweet corn in March. That was pretty cool," she said.

"When people walk in here they can't believe how clean it is. They can see themselves living in their greenhouse. For a developing country or an NGO, the fish and vegetable combination seals the deal for communities and governments interested in food sovereignty and biosecurity," explained Pade the day we walked through their 5,000-square-foot greenhouse.

Indeed, Nelson and Pade work all over the world, in 40 countries, including various locations in the United States and countries with vastly different challenges: Haiti, Costa Rica, Australia, Botswana, and Thailand. As arable land and clean water are diminishing and weather patterns are changing dramatically due to climate change, highly tuned agricultural innovations are an excellent alternative. "When you can control the environment, and not use any mined or manufactured inputs like fertilizers, it's a highly desirable way for a community, a town, a government, to secure food for its people," explained Pade.

REBECCA NELSON

There are three key points Rebecca Nelson wants you to know about science-based commercial food production in aquaponics:

1. You can feed a community: schools, restaurants, farm stands.

2. It's every day. It's more similar to being a dairyman than a soil farmer. If you want to take a day off or a vacation, you need to have someone there to step in.

3. It's not backbreaking work. There's not a lot of heavy lifting required.

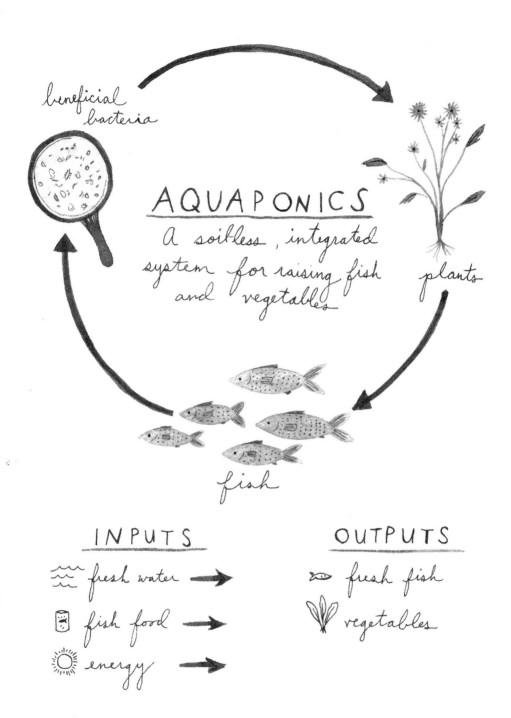

beneficial bacteria

AQUAPONICS

A soilless, integrated system for raising fish and vegetables

plants

fish

INPUTS

~~~ fresh water →

🥫 fish food →

☀ energy →

OUTPUTS

🐟 fresh fish

🌱 vegetables

TIP : Give guided tours of your greenhouse. Hold them on a regular day and time, so it's easier for schools, hospitals, locals, or anyone else to come and learn what you are doing and how.

SEEK FUNDING FOR COMMERCIAL AQUAPONICS

There is a misconception perpetuated online that you can start an aquaponics business without a significant monetary investment. Yes, you can build a system in your basement for a few hundred bucks and you will harvest some lettuce and veggies and some fish. For home food production, this is a great setup. But a basement or hobby system will not scale up to the needs of a commercial grower. Commercial growers need proven efficiencies, consistent and high-quality products, repeatable systems and processes, and, most important, food safety protocols and biosecurity procedures.

If you want to grow on a commercial scale, you need to treat an aquaponics business like any other start-up. You need a well-thought-out, well-written business plan; adequate start-up and first-year operational funding; proven equipment; a properly designed controlled-environment greenhouse or other structure; proper training and long-term support; and good management and marketing. And of course, there is a cost to all of this. Most commercial projects that we see move forward are funded by someone who has the means to do it as opposed to someone who is seeking grants.

The good news is that as awareness of aquaponics grows, so does the number of successful models out there, which increases the number of farms that will get funded from more traditional sources like banks and private investors.

We have growers who have gotten low-interest loans and USDA-backed loans from the state and federal government, economic development groups, and other agencies that are supportive of sustainable agriculture and local food.

There have been some aquaponic farms that have failed, and if you look back, they typically had a design that just didn't work, a lack of proper environmental control, and/or insufficient funding.

The successful aquaponic farms emulate the path of other successes, treating a commercial aquaponic farm as a business and not as an overgrown hobby.

Aquaponic growers fall under all kinds of regulatory umbrellas that were never intended to prohibit aquaponic farming, but often they do. Or at least, getting started is complicated and costly.

Departments of health, agriculture, fisheries, and natural resources of cities, counties, states, and the federal government all can have regulations that might affect an aquaponic grower. And the regulations vary in each location, so there is no clear road map we can provide showing where to go for what permits. And then there are zoning and building permits that have to do with establishing and running your business in a particular location.

It sounds intimidating, but growers find their way through it every day by educating the decision makers about what aquaponics is and how an aquaponic farm benefits a community. As an example, when we moved back to Wisconsin, there were nine permits/licenses that we needed to build our first greenhouse, and it took about six months to get it all done. Over the years, we have spent a great deal of time working with state officials, regulators, and representatives of the Department of Agriculture Trade and Consumer Protection (DATCP) and the Department of Natural Resources (DNR). We have also collaborated with the Wisconsin Aquaculture Association and University of Wisconsin system to help get the word out. Now, it takes two to four weeks and half the number of permits to start an aquaponics business in Wisconsin. In fact, the DNR has hired someone specifically to help businesses like ours get through any regulatory hurdles. As a note, most of the regulation you deal with has to do with either building the greenhouse or moving and holding live fish.

For prospective aquaponic growers, it is important to do your homework, both on the funding and business planning side and the regulatory side. There are excellent resources out there that can help, and likely someone nearby has already been through the process who might be able to offer some guidance.

—Rebecca Nelson, of Nelson and Pade Inc., adjunct instructor at University of Wisconsin–Stevens Point

>×<

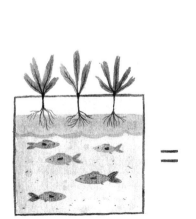

=

COMMERCIAL AQUAPONIC FARMS

Here are a few successful models of aquaponic farms, suggested by Rebecca Nelson.

Greens & Gills (Chicago, Illinois)

There is a lot of talk about urban agriculture. With Greens & Gills (greensandgills.com), it is more than talk. This organization runs a profitable urban farm without government help or grants. It produces fresh fish and veggies efficiently and supplies local markets in Chicago. At the time its founders were planning their business, it was illegal to do aquaponics within the Chicago city limits because no livestock was allowed in the city, and fish were considered livestock. A few years ago Mayor Rahm Emanuel signed a law allowing aquaponics, and then it took another year to get through all of the other regulations related to growing and selling food in the city. Through great persistence and determination, Greens & Gills became the first legally operating commercial aquaponics farm in Chicago.

Northstar Homestead Farms (Hayward, Wisconsin)

The founders of Northstar Homestead Farms (northstarhomestead.com /farm-aquaponics.php) are three of the hardest-working, most creative, and most innovative women I know. They have embraced aquaponics and have integrated the operation and production of their aquaponics green-house with that of their all-natural farm. The aquaponics allows them to provide year-round fresh veggies and fish to their CSA customers.

Early Morning Harvest (Panora, Iowa)

As traditional farmers, the members of the Hafner family were seeking alternative methods of agriculture that were more environmentally friendly and easier than what they had been doing. In 2000, the Hafners transitioned their farmland and cattle to organic and continued pursuing new and innovative methods that they could use on their farm, Early Morning Harvest (earlymorningharvest.com). Adding aquaponics was a way to keep the farm interesting and profitable, and something that would help keep the next generation interested in farming. Keeping the next generation on the farm is a very important component to keep farms farming, especially the good ones!

NATIONAL SECURITY STARTS
WITH FOOD SECURITY

Food security is foundational to a country's national security. When people have access to healthy food and their nutritional needs are met, they can learn, work, function, and be productive members of any society. This is what it means to feed human capital in a secure and affordable way. "Someone asked Rebecca what the goal of our aquaponics system is," recounted John Pade. "She answered, 'I want to see aquaponics feeding people around the world.' They thought she was joking, but she's not."

Rebecca Nelson is serious when she says aquaponics done properly can "feed the world," and she's also not chiming in for Monsanto or Big Ag when she says it. "What kind of seeds people plant in their aquaponics greenhouse is up to them," she explains. "It's the same deal as any farm. What we show here, season in and season out — because it's all really just one long continuous season — is the optimization of science-based food production that doesn't beholden any farmer to any one input from any one specific company, over and over again. You can grow what you want and it's beyond organic, naturally. Because if it's not good for the fish, you can forget about enjoying your Friday Night Fry."

Aquaponics is a natural system, like a lake system, just optimized. "The Aztecs built rafts, put their crops into them, drifted them out on lakes, brought them back, and harvested the food," Rebecca says. "We didn't invent aquaponics, but we perfected it." While this may sound like hubris, the efficiencies of energy inputs to pounds of food are undeniable.

>⟨⟨

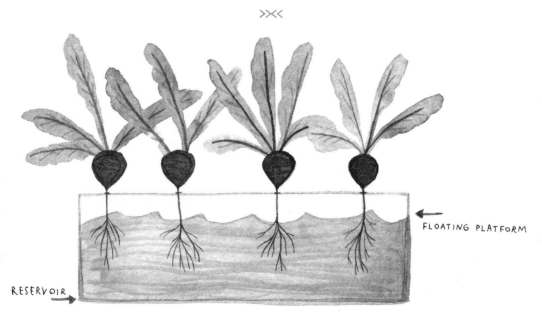

FLOATING PLATFORM

RESERVOIR

REBECCA NELSON

"In the field in Arizona, one of the biggest lettuce-producing areas in the United States, they typically plant two lettuce crops per year and grow 60,000 to 80,000 heads per acre combined in those two crops. In our aquaponic systems, we grow about 500,000 heads per year per acre, plus about 40,000 pounds of fish, with continuous production and substantially less water. So, we are growing six times more lettuce per acre using one-sixth of the water. Though this production is from our science-based, highly efficient systems and is not typical of all aquaponic systems.

"When you look at energy inputs for that field production, you need to consider: energy for irrigation pumps (lots), fuel for the tractors, plows, transportation of farmworkers and the energy used in manufacturing those tractors, plows, etc., and then include the fuel for moving that lettuce to markets across the United States.

"What aquaponics can do is provide both a protein crop [the fish] and a variety of fresh vegetables. From a nutritional standpoint, that is about as good as it gets, and this makes aquaponics an excellent method of making nutritious food accessible to people around the world. Plus, there are no pesticides, herbicides, or chemical fertilizers used on the plants and no antibiotics or growth hormones used on the fish. From a global perspective, I think there is great potential for aquaponics to have an impact on hunger and improve the availability of fresh and nutritional food choices to people, even in the most remote areas and regions that do not have arable farmland.

"So, even though we have heat and electrical usage in a concentrated space, we're still using less energy per head of lettuce that goes to a consumer's plate because we continuously grow so much in a small space.

"Another factor to consider is that modern greenhouses are much more energy efficient than they used to be. We incorporate dual-layer plastics which provide insulation; energy shields to reduce solar radiation in the summer and maintain heat in the winter; energy-efficient heaters; and, often in cold climates, heat sources that include wood, wood waste, or waste heat. Our greenhouse here in Wisconsin uses about half the total energy as those we had in California, even though it is a much colder climate. This is due to improvements in energy efficiency."

SAVE SEEDS

Saving seeds is a revolutionary act. As chemical companies buy up seed stock, it's vitally important to maintain genetic diversity in food crops. Moreover, saving seeds is a crucial aspect of food sovereignty. When we practice seed saving, we are practicing independence from corporate control. And when we choose open-pollinated seeds — seeds that pollinate naturally by wind or water, by animals like birds and insects and humans — those seeds adapt to changes in the environment and climate and locale, over time. That's genetic diversity and resiliency, in a seed. When saving seeds, it's wise to keep an eye on quality. Below are some basic guidelines suggested by Native Seeds/SEARCH (Southwestern Endangered Aridland Resources Clearing House, nativeseeds.org) to consider when saving seeds.

CHOOSE healthy, undamaged seeds.

DO NOT keep seeds from diseased plants: some viruses are transmitted through seeds.

SAVE SEEDS from as many plants as possible and enough seeds for next year's planting.

BE SURE seeds are clean of unwanted sticks, chaff, seedpods, and so on. This will reduce the bulk that is stored, as well as the threat of some possible pests and diseases.

GOOD RECORD KEEPING about your garden and seeds is key.

STORE SEEDS in a dry, cool (not freezing) place.

>×<

"When you plant a seed, you choose an entire agricultural system." — Ken Greene, cofounder of the Hudson Valley Seed Library

START A PUBLIC SEED LIBRARY

According to the Richmond Grows Seed Lending Library in Richmond, California, there are over 300 seed-lending libraries across the United States and in 15 other countries. Seed libraries operate on basic shared principles, encouraging people to grow food, preserve genetic diversity, and develop and support food sovereignty. Seed libraries can also provide the impetus to share and preserve local history and stories.

START by adapting the potluck (page 23) to identify your collaborators. Reach out to gardeners, garden clubs, independent farmers, librarians, information data specialists, graphic designers, lawyers, community organizers, farm to school coordinators, local historical societies and oral historians, and museum curators.

SCREEN A FILM about seeds and seed saving (page 173).

ENCOURAGE seed savers to get their soil tested.

DETERMINE seed-saving protocols and seed-returning guidelines. There are examples of these online in English and Spanish at richmondgrowsseeds.org.

FIGURE OUT your space. Do you want to start simply? See Share Seeds at Eating In Public (for examples of small wall-mount seed swap stations, and download their free DIY building instructions. So cool! nomoola.com).

WANT to go big? Is there a public library, community center, or Grange hall that is willing to be host to your library?

IDENTIFY funds, gifts, and in-kind donations to help support acquiring storage and office supplies like cabinets, a computer, and signage.

VISIT a seed library or reach out to the community of seed libraries for a sister library or a mentor. SeedLibrarian.com maintains an international seed library locator.

CHECK OUT the Seed Library Social Network (seedlibraries.org) for inspiring photos and examples of existing seed libraries and seed libraries in the news. It's also a place to find information about your local collections and keep up with announcements about workshops and summits.

ATTEND a seed-saving school to keep abreast of the latest news in biotechnology, hone seed-saving skills, and network with the country's leading seed mavericks! (nativeseeds.org)

>×<

BUILD A COMMUNITY GARDEN

Community food gardens provide land to people who don't have access to it otherwise. They are no small undertaking, but the payoffs are big in terms of bringing people together, saving money on food expenses, and sharing costs for infrastructure items such as tools and fencing. Start small, and be well organized, engaging families right from the start as you plan for the long term. This detailed checklist was developed in part by University of California master gardener volunteers under the auspices of the UC Cooperative Extension. You'll find some of the steps particularly relevant to urban areas. As with everything else in this book, adapt it to your place as needed.

1. Get Your Neighbors Involved

There is a lot of work involved in starting a new garden. Make sure you have several people who will help you. Over the years, our experience indicates that there should be at least ten interested families to create and sustain a garden project. Survey the residents of your neighborhood to see if they are interested and would participate. Hold monthly meetings of the interested group to develop and initiate plans, keep people posted on the garden's progress, and keep them involved in the process from day one.

2. Form a Garden Club

A garden club is a way of formally organizing your new group. It helps you make decisions and divide up the work effectively. It also ensures that everyone has a vested interest in the garden and can contribute to its design, development, and maintenance.

It can be formed at any time during the process of starting a community garden; however, it's wise to do so early on. This way, club members can share in the many tasks of establishing the new garden.

>>

The typical garden club will have many functions, including:

ESTABLISHING garden rules

ACCEPTING and reviewing garden applications

MAKING plot assignments

COLLECTING garden dues (if any)

PAYING water bills

RESOLVING conflicts

The typical garden club has at least two officers: a president and a treasurer, although your garden club may have more if necessary. Elections for garden officers usually are held annually.

3. Find Land

Look around your neighborhood for a vacant lot that gets plenty of sun (at least six to eight hours each day). A garden site should be relatively flat (although slight slopes can be terraced). It should be relatively free of large pieces of concrete left behind from demolition of structures. Any rubble or debris should be manageable: that is, it can be removed by volunteers clearing the lot with trash bags, wheelbarrows, and pickup trucks. Ideally, it should have a fence around it with a gate wide enough for a vehicle to enter. It is possible to work with a site that is paved with concrete or asphalt by building raised beds that sit on the surface or by using containers. You can also remove the asphalt or concrete to create areas for gardens, but such a garden will be much more difficult, expensive, and time-consuming to start. A site without paving, and soil relatively free of trash and debris, is best.

The potential garden site should be within walking distance, or no more than a short drive from you and the neighbors who have expressed interest in participating. If the lot is not already being used, make sure the community supports establishing a garden there. It's best to select three potential sites in your neighborhood and write down their address and nearest cross streets. If you don't know the address of a vacant lot, get the addresses of the properties on both sides of the lot; this will give you the ability to make an educated guess on the address of the site.

It is illegal to use land without obtaining the owner's permission. In order to obtain permission, you must first find out who owns the land. Take the information you have written down about the location of the sites in step 3 to your county's tax assessor's office. Or go to a branch office listed in the white pages of the telephone directory. At this office, you will look through the map books to get the names and addresses of the owners of the sites you are interested in.

4. Find Out If Your Proposed Site Has Water

While you are researching site ownership, contact the water service provider in your area to find out if your potential site has an existing water meter to hook in to. Call your water provider's customer service department, and ask them to conduct a site investigation. They will need the same location information that you took with you to the tax assessor's office. Existing access to water will make a critical difference in the expense of getting your project started.

Depending on the size of your garden site, you will need a ½-inch to 1-inch water meter. If there has been water service to the site in the past, it is relatively inexpensive to get a new water meter installed, if necessary. If there has never been water service to that site, it might cost much more for your water provider to install a lateral line from the street main to the site and install your new meter.

5. Contact the Landowner

Once you have determined that your potential site is feasible, write a letter to the landowner asking for permission to use the property for a community garden. Be sure to mention to the landowner the value of the garden to the community and the fact that the gardeners will be responsible for keeping the site clean and weed-free (this saves landowners from maintaining the site or paying city weed abatement fees). Establish a term for use of the site, and prepare and negotiate a lease. Typically, groups lease garden sites from landowners for $1 per year. You should attempt to negotiate a lease for at least three years (or longer if the property owner is agreeable). Many landowners are worried about their liability for injuries that might occur at the garden. Therefore, you should include a simple "hold harmless" waiver in the lease and in gardener agreement forms. For more information on the lease, and the hold harmless waiver, see step 7, Leases and Liability.

Be prepared to purchase liability insurance to protect further the property owner (and yourself) should an accident occur at the garden. For more information on the liability insurance, see step 7.

6. Get Your Soil Tested

It might be advisable to have the soil at the site tested for fertility pH and presence of heavy metals. Unfortunately there's no national database of soil testing labs. (Want to start one?) So it's best to contact your state's agricultural Extension office for information about getting it done.

>>

7. Leases and Liability

Landowners of potential garden sites might be concerned about their liability should someone be injured while working in the garden. Your group should be prepared to offer the landowner a lease with a "hold harmless" waiver. This "hold harmless" waiver can simply state that should one of the gardeners be injured as a result of negligence on the part of another gardener, the landowner is "held harmless" and will not be sued. Each gardener should be made aware of this waiver and should be required to sign an agreement in order to obtain a plot in the community garden. Landowners may also require that your group purchase liability insurance. (Note: if you affiliated with an organization, explore the opportunity of getting insurance through them.)

8. Planning the Garden

Community members should be involved in the planning, design, and setup of the garden. Before the design process begins, you should measure your site and make a simple, to-scale site map. Hold two or three garden design meetings at times when interested participants can attend. Make sure that group decisions are recorded in official minutes, or that someone takes accurate notes. This ensures that decisions made can be communicated to others, and progress will not be slowed. A great way to generate ideas and visualize the design is to use simple drawings or photos cut from garden magazines representing the different garden components — flower beds, compost bins, pathways, arbors, and so on — that can be moved around on the map as the group discusses layout.

BASIC ELEMENTS OF A COMMUNITY GARDEN

Although there are exceptions to every rule, community gardens should almost always include:

AT LEAST 15 PLOTS assigned to community members. These should be placed in the sunniest part of the garden. Without plots for individual participation, it is very difficult to achieve long-term community involvement. Raised bed plots, which are more expensive, should be no more than 4 feet wide (to facilitate access to plants from the sides without stepping into the bed), and between 8 and 12 feet long (it is advisable to construct your raised beds in sizes that are found in readily available lumber, or that can be cut without too much waste). In-ground plots can be from 10 x 10 up to 20 x 20 feet. Pathways between beds and plots should be least 3 to 4 feet wide to allow space for wheelbarrows. The soil in both raised bed and in-ground plots should be amended with aged compost or manure to improve its fertility and increase its organic matter content.

A SIMPLE IRRIGATION SYSTEM with one hose bib or faucet for every four plots. Hand watering with a hose is the most practical and affordable for individual plots (and it's almost a necessity when you start plants from seed). Drip and soaker-hose irrigation can be used in all areas of the garden for transplanted and established plants, but especially for deep-rooted fruit trees and ornamentals. If no one in your group is knowledgeable about irrigation, seek out a landscape contractor or nursery or garden center professional to help you develop a basic layout and materials list.

AN 8-FOOT FENCE around the perimeter with a drive-through gate. In our experience, this is a key element of success. Don't count on eliminating all acts of vandalism or theft, but fencing will help to keep these to tolerably low levels.

A TOOL SHED or other structure for storing tools, supplies, and materials. Recycled metal shipping containers make excellent storage sheds and are almost vandal-proof. Contact the port authority in your area for leads on where to find them.

A BENCH or picnic table where gardeners can sit, relax, and take a break, preferably in shade. If there are no shade trees on the site, a simple arbor can be constructed from wood or pipe, and planted with chayote squash, bougainvillea, grapes, kiwis, or some other vine.

A SIGN with the garden's name, sponsors, and a contact person's phone number for more information. If your community is bilingual, include information in two languages.

A SHARED COMPOSTING AREA for the community gardeners. Wood pallets are easy to come by and (when stood on end, attached in a U-shape, and the inside covered with galvanized rabbit wire) make excellent compost bins.

>>

NICE ADDITIONS TO YOUR GARDEN PLAN

A SMALL FRUIT TREE ORCHARD, whose care and harvest can be shared by all the members. The orchard can also create shade for people as well as shade-loving plants.

A WATER FOUNTAIN. This can be a simple drinking fountain attachment to a hose bib (or faucet) you can purchase at a hardware store.

PERIMETER LANDSCAPING, which can focus on low-maintenance flowers and shrubs, plants that attract butterflies and hummingbirds, or roses and other flowers suitable for cutting bouquets. Herbs are also well suited to perimeter landscaping and help to create barriers to unwanted pest insects who do not like the smell of their essential oils.

A CHILDREN'S AREA, which can include special small plots for children, a sandbox, and play equipment.

A MEETING AREA, which could range from a semicircle of hay bales or tree stumps, to a simple amphitheater built of recycled broken concrete. Building a shade structure would be beneficial as well.

A COMMUNITY BULLETIN BOARD where rules, meeting notices, and other important information can be posted.

CREATING A GARDEN BUDGET. Use your design to develop a materials list and cost out the project. You will need to call around to get prices on fencing and other items. You might be surprised at the cost. A community garden with just the basic elements listed above typically costs between $2,500 and $5,000. At this point, your group might decide to scale back your initial plans and save some design ideas for a "Phase Two" of the garden.

9. Where to Get Materials and Money

While some start-up funds will be needed, you can also obtain donations of materials for your project. Community businesses might assist and provide anything from fencing to lumber to plants. The important thing is to ask.

Develop a letter that tells merchants about your project and why it's important to the community. Attach your wish list, but be reasonable. Try to personalize this letter for each business you approach. Drop it off personally with the store manager, preferably with a couple of cute gardening kids in tow! Then, follow up by phone. Be patient, persistent, and polite. Your efforts will pay off with at least some of the businesses you approach.

Be sure to thank these key supporters and recognize them on your garden sign, at a garden grand opening, or other special event.

Money can be obtained through community fund-raisers such as car washes, craft and rummage sales, pancake breakfasts, and bake sales. They can also be obtained by writing grants, but be aware grant-writing efforts can take six months or longer to yield results, and you must have a fiscal sponsor or agent with tax-exempt 501(c)(3) status (such as a church or nonprofit corporation) that agrees to administer the funds.

10. Make Sure Your Garden Infrastructure Is in Place

If you have not yet formed a garden club, now is the time to do so. It's also time to establish garden rules, develop a garden application form for those who wish to participate, set up a bank account, and determine what garden dues will be if these things have not already been done. This is also the time to begin having monthly meetings if you have not already done so. Also, if you haven't already contacted your city councilperson, he or she can be helpful in many ways, including helping your group obtain city services such as trash pickup. Their staff can also help you with community organizing and soliciting for material donations.

11. Get Growing!

Many new garden groups make the mistake of remaining in the planning, design, and fund-raising stage for an extended period of time. There is a fine line between planning well and overplanning. After several months of the initial research, designing, planning, and outreach efforts, group members will very likely be feeling frustrated and will begin to wonder if all their efforts will ever result in a garden. That's why it's important to plant something on your site as soon as possible. People need to see visible results or they will begin to lose interest. To keep the momentum going, initiate the following steps even if you are still seeking donations and funds for your project (but not until you have signed a lease and obtained insurance).

CLEAN UP THE SITE. Schedule community workdays to clean up the site. How many workdays you need will depend on the size of the site and how much and what kind of debris are on-site.

INSTALL THE IRRIGATION SYSTEM. Without water, you can't grow anything. So get this key element in place as soon as possible. There are plenty of opportunities for community involvement, from digging trenches to laying PVC pipes.

>>

PLANT SOMETHING. Once you have water, there are many options for in-garden action. Stake out beds and pathways by marking them with stakes and twine. Mulch pathways. If your fence isn't in yet, some people might still want to accept the risk of vandalism and get their plots started. You can also plant shade and fruit trees and begin to landscape the site. If you do not yet have a source of donated plants, or don't wish to risk having them vandalized, plant annual flower seeds that will grow quickly and can be replaced later. (Note: Seeds for community and school gardens may be obtained through local gardening programs, feed stores, gardening stores. Look for heirloom varieties. Check with seedsavers.org.)

CONTINUE TO BUILD. Continually improve the garden as materials and funds become available.

12. Celebrate!

Have a grand opening, barbecue, or some other fun event to give everyone who helped to make this happen a special thank-you. This is the time to give all those who gave donated materials or time a special certificate, bouquet, or other form of recognition.

13. Troubleshooting

All community gardens will experience problems somewhere along the way. Don't get discouraged — get organized. The key to success for community gardens is not only preventing problems from ever occurring, but also working together to solve them when they do inevitably occur. In our experience, these are some of the most common problems that crop up in community gardens.

VANDALISM. Most gardens experience occasional vandalism. The best action you can take is to replant immediately. Generally the vandals become bored after a while and stop. Good community outreach, especially to youth and the garden's immediate neighbors, is also important. *Don't get too discouraged.* It happens. Get over it and keep going. What about barbed wire or razor wire to make the garden more secure? Our advice: don't. It's bad for community relations, looks awful, and is sometimes illegal to install without a permit. If you need more physical deterrents to keep vandals out, plant bougainvillea or pyracantha along your fence and let their thorns do the trick!

SECURITY. Invite the community officer from your local precinct to a garden meeting to get his or her suggestions on making the garden more secure. Community officers can also be a great help in solving problems with garden vandalism and dealing with drug dealers and gang members in the area.

COMMUNICATION. Clear and well-enforced garden rules and a strong garden president can go a long way toward minimizing misunderstandings in the garden. But communication problems do arise. It's the job of the garden club to resolve those issues. If something is not clearly spelled out in the rules, the membership can take a vote to add new rules or make modifications to existing rules. Language barriers are a very common source of misunderstandings. Garden club leadership should make every effort to have a translator at garden meetings where participants are bilingual. Perhaps a family member of one of the garden members who speaks the language will offer to help.

TRASH. It's important to get your compost system going right away and get some training for gardeners on how to use it. If gardeners don't compost, large quantities of waste will begin to build up and create an eyesore and could hurt your relationships with neighbors and the property owner. Waste can also become a fire hazard. Make sure gardeners know how to sort trash properly, what to compost, and what to recycle. Trash cans placed in accessible areas are helpful to keep a neat and tidy garden.

GARDENER DROPOUT. There has been, and probably always will be, a high rate of turnover in community gardens. Often, people sign up for plots, then don't follow through. Remember, gardening is hard work for some people, especially in the heat of summer. Have a clause in your gardener agreement that states gardeners forfeit their right to their plot if they don't plant it within one month, or if they don't maintain it. While gardeners should be given every opportunity to follow through, if after several reminders nothing changes, it is time for the club to reassign the plot. Every year, the leadership should conduct a renewed community outreach campaign by contacting churches and other groups in the neighborhood to let them know about the garden and plots available.

WEEDS. Gardeners tend to visit their plots less during the wintertime, and lower participation, combined with rain, tends to create a huge weed problem in January, February, and March. [Author note: Bear in mind that these suggestions were gleaned from a Los Angeles community garden group! Take this occasion to think about the geography-dependent seasonal challenges your garden might face.] Remember, part of your agreement with the landowner is that you will maintain the lot and keep weeds from taking over. In the late summer/early fall, provide gardeners with a workshop or printed material about what can be grown in a fall and winter garden. Also, schedule well in advance garden workdays for early spring, since you know you'll need them at the end of winter. If you anticipate that plots will be untended during the winter, apply a thick layer of mulch or hay to the beds and paths.

Good luck with your community garden project!

— These steps were inspired by and adapted with permission from *Community Garden Start-Up Guide,* by Rachel Surls, University of California Cooperative Extension (UCCE) County Director, with the help of Chris Braswell and Laura Harris, Los Angeles Conservation Corps, updated March 2001 by Yvonne Savio, Common Ground Garden Program Manager, UCCE, © Regents of the University of California. Used by permission.

COMPOST COMMUNITY
Tallahassee, Florida

Community composting at a community garden is one aspect to reducing waste and costs at a garden. But what if you're throwing organic waste into your household or business trash cans? Waste removal costs money, and it really is the definition of waste because all that potential is lost when that organic material is thrown into a landfill.

Some local food system entrepreneurs are digging the potential and making a buck doing it. Compost Community of Tallahassee is doing just that. According to its website (compostcommunity.org), for a nominal monthly fee, this organization will pick up organic waste from households or businesses; cultivate it into "the microbial life that will make it what it will be," as Sundiata Ameh El, the owner/operator of Community Compost, puts it; and about six months later, nutrient-rich, beautiful compost is returned to those who participate. A win-win!

FOOD FOREST

Austin, Texas

Check out the sketch below of the proposed East Feast Festival Beach Food Forest pilot project in Austin, Texas. Modeled after the Beacon Food Forest in Seattle, the proposal would see a little over two acres of land turned into an edible landscape, with fruit trees, a butterfly garden, kids' play structures, a stormwater wetland filtration system, and other features.

GROW FREE FOOD

Be a guerrilla gardener. Plant food in public spaces. A row of kale along the library. Climbing peas at the base of trees along the sidewalk. Grow food in that narrow piece of sad ground that's between your lawn and the street, called the parkway, usually owned by the city. An act of art and rebellion, guerrilla gardening is not just about food to harvest. It's about people. Community. Transform food and farming from the ordinary into the extraordinary.

Plant food gardens and fruit or nut trees in front of public buildings such as libraries, fire stations, and school administration buildings. Or work with local businesses to convert their grassy yards into rows of edible food. Food, not lawns (foodnotlawns.com).

>×<

"Gardening is the most therapeutic and defiant act you can do, especially in the inner city. Plus you get strawberries."

— Ron Finley (see page 111)

WHAT IS AGROECOLOGY?

Miguel A. Altieri, of the University of California, Berkeley, Department of Environmental Science, Policy, and Management (ESPM), gives the following definition:

> Agroecology is a scientific discipline that uses ecological theory to study, design, manage and evaluate agricultural systems that are productive but also resource conserving. Agroecological research considers interactions of all important biophysical, technical and socioeconomic components of farming systems and regards these systems as the fundamental units of study, where mineral cycles, energy transformations, biological processes and socioeconomic relationships are analyzed as a whole in an interdisciplinary fashion.

— "What Is Agroecology?," Agroecology in Action (agroeco.org)

SHELLFISH AQUACULTURE
Martha's Vineyard, Massachusetts

With some salvaged building materials from the dump, a bunch of volunteers built a pilot shellfish aquaculture site in the late 1970s on the brackish shore of Lagoon Pond on Martha's Vineyard. The innovation — to hire a biologist who would provide technical support to manage local shellfish stocks and develop shellfish aquaculture — was rallied around by the local shellfish constables. The nonprofit MV Shellfish Group (mvshellfishgroup.org) became the first public solar shellfish hatchery in the country in 1980 and has since spawned gazillions of shellfish, from oysters to sea scallops, quahogs, mussels, and the coveted bay scallop.

Shellfish, the "Vacuum Cleaners of the Sea" (to quote one of the group's older posters), help clean the brackish waters of the degradations of development such as fertilizers, pesticides, and bacterial containments. And we eaters love our fresh oysters, steamers, and fried clams. Farming the sea, shellfish aquaculture, is an outstanding green local industry, providing jobs, cleaner water, and a culturally appropriate, delicious, fresh, whole food to the region. The MV Shellfish Group has also provided retraining for fishermen to transition into shellfishing and has worked on developing projects in other regions of the world, such as Zanzibar. And whenever the MV Shellfish Group holds a fundraiser, there are lines out the door. These folks bring the best raw bar, and you'll never beat them in a shucking contest.

KEEP BEES
. . . .

For one out of every three bites of food we eat, we have pollinators such as honeybees to thank. And now more than ever we need healthy honeybee colonies.

HOLD A HONEYBEE COMMUNITY MEETING. Invite beekeepers and want-to-be beekeepers. In every group of beekeepers there's probably at least three answers to every question, but it's important to share info about your specific locale.

INVEST IN AN OBSERVATION HIVE. It's a great demonstration tool that can be, with care, taken to living local fests, agricultural fairs, and school classrooms.

START A POLLINATION PROGRAM to complete a community garden, a farm, or a school garden, or just because you want good local, raw honey to eat. See Hold a Potluck with a Purpose (page 23) for tips on finding your people and gathering to organize.

FIND EACH OTHER! Urban, rural, suburban farmers and beekeepers: you need each other. Farmers need healthy pollinators for crops, and beekeepers need land to set up hives or expand territories. To search, start with your nearest and dearest Extension agent(s). Go to the U.S. Department of Agriculture's website (usda.gov). Search "Cooperative Extension System Office," then search their map. Every state and territory has an Extension agent.

PLANT YOUR GARDEN with medicinal and culinary herbs, edible flowers, and produce that bees will love. Here's a list to get you curious. Grow in succession to keep bees happy all season long. Grow what you like to eat and what works in your plant zone.

» Lavender	» Nasturtiums	» Violet
» Society garlic	» Common yarrow	» Squash
» Marshmallow	» Dill	» Pumpkin
» Anise hyssop	» Borage	» Raspberry
» Bergamot	» Hibiscus	» Blueberry
» Garlic chives	» Okra	» Blackberry
» Dandelions	» Thyme	» Strawberry

>✕<

ALETHEA MORRISON

Alethea is the author, with her husband, Mars, of *Homegrown Honey Bees*. Here is some of her excellent advice for would-be home-hivers. (For more, read the whole book!)

GET ONLINE. Beesource.com is an active online community where people post information and have conversations about every beekeeping topic imaginable. It can be a great place to ask questions and get feedback.

TAKE A WORKSHOP. Many beginning beekeepers take workshops before setting up their first hives. Those can be a great introduction to beekeeping or can reinforce and help you absorb the information you are gathering.

Local bee associations often offer these classes.

JOIN THE CLUB. Books and online forums are great, but there is no substitute for folks living nearby who can give you information about beekeeping in your specific area and help you out in person when you need it. Beekeepers love what they do, and many of them are happy to share their wisdom with someone as inexperienced but enthusiastic as you!

— Excerpted with permission from *Homegrown Honey Bees* (Storey Publishing, 2012) by Alethea Morrison and Mars Vilaubi

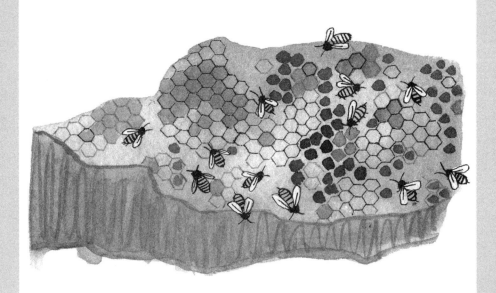

ZONING FOR BEEKEEPING

Before you even think about keeping bees in a densely populated neighborhood, determine your zoning district and ordinances and permitting requirements. These vary widely from town, to city, to state, so it's really up to you to determine what you can and cannot do. If the cannots overwhelm, maybe you'll be inspired to join a planning board to try to change things (page 293)!

According to an article by Kristen M. Ploetz, Esq., in *Modern Farmer* magazine, some or all of the following are regulated by many zoning ordinances:

MINIMUM LOT SIZE required for keeping bees

SITING OF HIVES and minimum setbacks to property lines and adjacent structures

PERMISSIBLE TYPES of hives and bee species (i.e., gentle stock or no Africanized bees)

MAXIMUM NUMBER of hives/swarms

WHETHER ENCLOSURES, fencing, or hedges (flyaway barriers) are required

REQUIREMENTS for on-site water sources (to minimize drift onto adjacent properties with standing water sources such as pools)

— Excerpted with permission from *Modern Farmer,* "Dear Modern Farmer, How Do I Legally Start an Urban Bee Hive?"

WHAT'S GOING ON

BACKWARDS BEEKEEPERS
Los Angeles, California

Laura Stewart, Max Wong, Sue Talbot, and Roberta Kato are friends, neighbors, and fellow associates in Backwards Beekeepers, an organization committed to taking beekeeping back to basics. Renouncing treatments of any kind and most management practices, such as feeding, requeening, and using foundation instead of letting the bees build natural comb, their motto is "Let the bees be bees!" This maxim expresses a strategy of letting colonies alone and the strongest will survive.

A key to the group's success is that they capture native colonies of feral bees, which they've found to be more disease- and pest-resistant than commercial packages. Their bee-rescue hotline offers local residents and businesses a welcome service for capturing swarms that land on their property, and it provides an ample resource of free bees for people who want to start beekeeping or expand their apiaries.

— Excerpted with permission from *Homegrown Honey Bees* (Storey Publishing, 2012) by Alethea Morrison and Mars Vilaubi

MELINDA RABBITT DEFEO
How to Introduce a Honeybee Observation Hive in the Classroom

Melinda Rabbitt DeFeo is an agriculture educator extraordinaire. She helped usher in Island Grown Schools from its inception and was the first IGS school coordinator to make the crucial leap from the nonprofit sector into the public school system as a paid educator — an outstanding sign that farm to school education had come a long way. She organizes and hosts the Edgartown School's annual Garden Celebration Day, where she's found that the observation beehive is the most requested activity by both kids and teachers.

I asked Melinda to share her advice and experience about how to introduce a live honeybee observation hive in the classroom. Here, in her own words, is her advice.

ACKNOWLEDGE that there can be a lot of perceived danger. If your lead administrator has an overactive fear of bees or insects you may need to work a lot harder in the beginning to gain trust and the support you will need to develop a meaningful program using the hive.

UNDERSTAND the difference between a standard hive and an observation hive. I have a long-term dream of having a full-blown hive at school, but the controlled environment of an observation hive is the way to go until others catch up with your enthusiasm for teaching real skills hands-on and gain enough awareness regarding the importance of pollinators.

TEACH. Both adults and children are fascinated with bees and will stay engaged when given an opportunity to observe them up close with someone to teach them about what they are seeing.

CONNECT with an experienced beekeeper (apiarist) or seek out a beekeepers association. In general, associations have a mission to educate and want to provide material support and resources. Some even have loaner hives or are willing to help build one for your program. A big thank-you goes to Tim Colon, a professional beekeeper in our community, who held my hand in 2013 to get it up and running.

ATTEND bee school! My own learning received a giant boost when I made the decision to start my own hive and attend bee school, but it still took a lot to gain the confidence to actually get a hive installed in the seventh grade science lab at Edgartown School. So I'm pleased to say that, for the past two years, the observation hive has taken up residency for five to seven weeks as a full-blown science unit!

THINK special event. Having a hive visit for a limited time allows others to get comfortable with the idea.

TRAIN bee ambassadors. My seventh grade students have become Bee Ambassadors during our Garden Celebration Day and are part of the teaching team at the bee station. It is sweet to see them patiently answer questions from kindergarteners on up, fly around in bee costumes, and assist in the tasting of delicious local honey.

SHARE resources. An observation hive can travel. Ours has gone to the Chilmark School a few times as part of their Science Friday program.

BEFRIEND the school nurse. In the school world of health and safety, this is the go-to person for assessing risk. My principal replied to my proposal only to say to check in with the nurse regarding allergies and risk, then go from there. When I approached her, I found we had no known bee allergies, and since the nurse and I already had a working relationship, she asked what I thought. I was able to reassure her that the bees would be 100 percent secure inside the hive (we have small locks on all the latches) and the hive would arrive loaded and ready to roll. And away we go . . .

— Melinda Rabbitt DeFeo, sustainable agriculture educator

WHAT'S GOING ON

CLASSROOM HIVES
Boston, Massachusetts

For more information about keeping an observation hive in a classroom, visit this nonprofit, Classroom Hives (classroomhives.org), formed by a group of educators who were so inspired by the Museum of Science's observation hive that they not only introduced these types of hives into their classrooms but went on to develop this site to share their passion and experiences to inspire you to go out and safely introduce the fascinating world of beekeeping into schools. One of their best resources? The FAQ section that includes costs and how to maintain a hive in the summer vacation months. A must-read before you go to your administrators!

"Avoid insecticides that contain neonicotinoids, which potentially negatively affect honeybees and other pollinators."

— Recommendation from *A Review of Research into the Effects of Neonicotinoid Insecticides on Bees, with Recommendations for Action* by Jennifer Hopwood, Mace Vaughan, Matthew Shepherd, David Biddinger, Eric Mader, Scott Hoffman Black, and Celeste Mazzacano

THE XERCES SOCIETY
Portland, Oregon

The nonprofit Xerces Society protects wildlife through the conservation of invertebrates and their habitat. Established in 1971, the society is at the forefront of invertebrate protection worldwide, harnessing the knowledge of scientists and the enthusiasm of citizens to implement conservation programs. Its resources include information about how to manage pesticides to protect bees, plant lists, and the Pollinator Conservation Resource Center — an interactive map to help you find resources specific to your geographic region.

Pollinators are essential to our environment. The ecological service they provide is necessary for the reproduction of over 85 percent of the world's flowering plants, including more than two-thirds of the world's crop species. The United States alone grows more than one hundred crops that either need or benefit from pollinators, and the economic value of these native pollinators is estimated at $3 billion per year.

— The Xerces Society (xerces.org)

VERTICAL GARDENS
Chicago, Illinois

Chicago's O'Hare Airport planted a towerlike aeroponic system. Greens, herbs, and berries grow supported in towers, similarly to hydroponically grown plants except that the roots are misted rather than bathed in nutrient-rich water.

GROW A KITCHEN GARDEN

Roger Doiron is the founder and director of Kitchen Gardeners International (KGI), a Maine-based nonprofit network of over 30,000 individuals from 100 countries who are taking a hands-on approach to relocalizing the food supply. Here, Doiron goes through the basics of starting a kitchen garden of your own.

In its simplest form, a kitchen garden produces fresh fruits, vegetables, and herbs for delicious, healthy meals. A kitchen garden doesn't have to be right outside the kitchen door, but the closer it is, the better. Think about it this way: the easier it is for you to get into the garden, the more likely it is that you will get tasty things out of it. Did you forget to add the chopped dill on your boiled red-skinned potatoes? No problem — it's just steps away.

Starting a Kitchen Garden

If you have to choose between a sunny spot or a close one, pick the sunny one. The best location for a new garden is one receiving full sun (at least six hours of direct sunlight per day), and one where the soil drains well. If no puddles remain a few hours after a good rain, you know your site drains well.

After you've figured out where the sun shines longest and strongest, your next task will be to define your kitchen garden goals. My first recommendation for new gardeners is to start small, tuck a few successes under your belt in year one, and scale up little by little.

But what if you're really fired up about it? Even in year one, you may be able to meet a big chunk of your family's produce needs. In the case of my garden in Scarborough, Maine, we have 1,500 square feet under cultivation, which yields enough to meet nearly half of my family of five's produce needs for the year. When you do the garden math, it comes out to 300 square feet per person. More talented gardeners with more generous soils and climates are able to produce more food in less space, but maximizing production is not our only goal. We're also trying to maximize pleasure and health, both our own and that of the garden. Kitchen gardens and gardeners thrive because of positive feedback loops. If your garden harvests taste good and make you feel good, you will feel more motivated to keep on growing.

>>

Preparing the Garden Site

If you're starting your kitchen garden on a patch of lawn, you can build up from the ground with raised beds, or plant directly in the ground. Building raised beds is a good idea if your soil is poor or doesn't drain well, and you like the look of containers made from wood, stone, or corrugated metal. This approach is usually more expensive, however, and requires more initial work than planting in the ground.

Whether you're going with raised beds or planting directly in the ground, you'll need to decide what to do with the sod. You can remove it and compost it, which is hard work, but ensures that you won't have grass and weeds coming up in your garden. If you're looking to start a small or medium-sized garden, it's possible to cut and remove sod in neat strips using nothing more than a sharp spade and some back muscle. For removing grass from a larger area, consider renting a sod cutter.

Choosing Garden Crops

The most important recommendation after "start small" is "start with what you like to eat." This may go without saying, but I have seen first-year gardens that don't reflect the eating habits of their growers — a recipe for disappointment. That said, I believe in experimenting with one or two new crops per year that aren't necessarily favorites for the sake of having diversity in the garden and on our plates.

One of the easiest and most rewarding kitchen gardens is a simple salad garden. Lettuces and other greens don't require much space or maintenance, and grow quickly. Consequently, they can produce multiple harvests in most parts of the country. If you plant a "cut-and-come-again" salad mix, you can grow 5 to 10 different salad varieties in a single row. And if you construct a cold frame (which can be cheap and easy if you use salvaged storm windows), you can grow some hearty salad greens year-round.

When it comes to natural flavor enhancers, nothing beats culinary herbs. Every year I grow standbys such as parsley, chives, sage, basil, tarragon, mint, rosemary, and thyme, but I also make an effort to try one or two new ones. One consequence of this approach is that I end up expanding my garden a little bit each year, but that's okay, because my skills and gastronomy are expanding in equal measure, as are my sense of satisfaction and food security.

Planting a Garden: Where, When, and How

Next, sketch out a garden plan of what will be planted where, when, and how. To do this, you need to get familiar with the various edible crops and what they like in terms of space, water, soil fertility, and soil temperatures. KGI also has a new, interactive Vegetable Garden Planner that makes it super simple and fun to handle planning a kitchen garden.

Starting from Seeds or Transplants?

When the time comes to plant your kitchen garden, you'll need to decide which plants to start from seed and which to buy as transplants. Many gardeners choose to plant all of their crops from seed for a variety of reasons, including lower costs, greater selection, and the challenge and satisfaction of seeing a plant go from seed to soup bowl. But whether you're a greenhorn or a green thumb, there's no shame in buying seedlings. Doing so increases your chances of success, especially with crops such as eggplants, peppers, and tomatoes that require a long growing season.

Much Ado about Mulch

After you've sown your seeds or planted your plants, introduce yourself to the kitchen gardener's best friend, Mr. Mulch. Just about any organic matter you can get your hands on — straw, grass clippings, pine needles, shredded leaves, dead weeds that haven't gone to seed — can be used as mulch. I bring in mulch from neighbors who would otherwise throw it away. Mulch plays three main roles: It deters weeds, helps retain moisture, and adds organic matter to the soil as it decays. I apply it to the pathways between my beds and around all of my plants.

KEN GREENE

Greene, cofounder of the Hudson Valley Seed Library, advises asking this question of your retail seed company: Can my seed dollars be traced back to biotech or pharmaceutical corporations? (Note, for example, that seeds from Seminis [seminis.com] are from Monsanto.)

When and How Much to Water Your Garden

Fruits and vegetables are made mostly of water, so you'll need to make sure your plants are getting enough to drink. This is especially important for seedlings that haven't developed a deep root structure. You'll want to water them lightly every day or two. Once the crops are maturing, they need about an inch of water per week, and more in sandy soils or hot regions. If Mother Nature isn't providing that amount of rain, you'll need to water manually or with a drip irrigation system.

Garden Maintenance

Sun and rain willing, fast growers such as radishes and salad greens will begin to produce crops as early as 20 to 30 days after planting. Check on them regularly so you get to harvest them before someone else does. In my garden, those "someones" include everything from the tiniest of bacteria to the largest of raccoons. Various protective barriers and organic products can deter pests and diseases, and if you have trouble with rabbits, deer, or other four-legged critters, your best defense may be a garden fence.

Succession Planting: Plant Now and Later

Getting the most pleasure and production from your garden comes from learning the beauty of succession planting. Rather than trying to "get your garden in" during one busy weekend, space your planting out over the course of several weeks by using short rows. Every time you harvest a row or pull one out that has stopped producing, try to plant a new one. Succession plantings lead to succession harvests spread out over several months — one of the key characteristics of a kitchen garden.

As you gain new confidence and skills, you can look for ways to incorporate perennials including asparagus and rhubarb into your edible landscape. And no discussion of kitchen gardens would be complete without mentioning flowers, which should be added from the start. Flowers add beauty and color to the garden and the kitchen table. They also attract beneficial insects while, in some cases, repelling undesirable ones.

— Excerpted with permission from Roger Doiron, Kitchen Gardeners International (kgi.org)

>><<

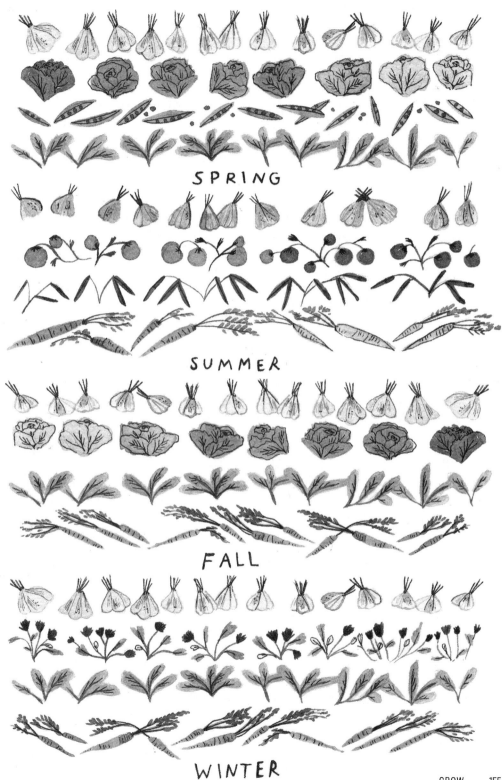

SPRING

SUMMER

FALL

WINTER

YOU CAN DO THIS

ORGANIZE A WORKPLACE CSA

At my publisher, Storey Publishing, in North Adams, Massachusetts, employees regularly enjoy deliveries of bread, pizza, and cookies from a local bakery, as well as eggs, chickens, honey, and a variety of fruits from other producers. Workplace CSAs — in which nearby farms make an agreement to make deliveries to a workplace in exchange for a certain number of employees making a commitment to participate — can be a great deal for all involved. Farmers can have a lot of sales in one place, and employees don't have to shop somewhere else after work.

Do you know local farmers, growers, and artisans who have goods to offer that would appeal to you and your co-workers? Usually it makes sense to take an informal poll among your co-workers, then approach the local farmer with a query. Could you bring 100 pounds of apples to our office next week? There are many ways to spin this: Maybe you'd like simply a one-off holiday pie delivery from a local bakery. Or maybe your workplace could sustain a regular weekly CSA delivery of a full range of veggies and fruits all year long.

You may want to check out these two farms, which have formal workplace CSA programs: Katchkie Farm, in Kinderhook, New York (katchkiefarm.com), and Cedarville Farm, in Bellingham, Washington (cedarvillefarm.com).

TIPS

BE CLEAR on all sides what responsibilities and commitments you are making, how money will be collected, and how the goods will be distributed.

WHERE at your company will the distribution happen? Make sure to clear this with all relevant parties. Boss? Custodian? Scheduler of the conference room?

IS THERE A PLACE in the refrigerator for all those chickens until the day ends?

DOES EVERYONE have a bag to carry away his or her loot?

DOES the farmer need help unloading?

>×<

STATE-SPONSORED CSAs

What if a state helped to offset costs for its employees to join CSAs? In 2013, building on a successful pilot project launched in three counties, Vermont expanded its Workplace Community Supported Agriculture (CSA) Program, which "enables Vermont state employees to conveniently purchase locally grown food and produce at numerous sites around Vermont." According to the state website, nearly 75 percent of the state employees had never previously participated in a CSA, and most planned to re-enroll.

WHO GROWS OUR FOOD?

While this chapter on growing mostly focuses on small-scale farming — on backyard and community gardens and local CSAs — most of our food in this country is grown on a large industrial scale, and with the labor of unprotected migrant workers, many of whom are American citizens and school-age children.

Here are some troubling facts about the human cost behind our diet:

MORE THAN 400,000 CHILDREN work in American fields to harvest the food we all eat.

CHILDREN WORKING in agriculture endure lives of extreme poverty. The average farmworker family makes less than $17,500 a year, well below the poverty level for a family of four.

POVERTY among farmworkers is two times that of workers in other occupations.

INCREASING THE INCOMES of migrant farmworkers by 40 percent would add just $15 to what the average U.S. household spends every year on fruits and vegetables, according to a researcher at the University of California, Davis.

FARMWORKER FAMILIES often cannot afford child care and so have no choice but to bring their children out into the fields.

FARMWORKERS are provided with substandard housing and sanitation facilities. As many as 20 percent of farms lack toilets and drinking water for workers, even though they are required to provide them.

ACCORDING TO Migrant Health Promotion (mhpsalud.org), a non-profit focused on public health, "Seventy-two to 78 percent of farm-workers are uninsured. Over half of the farmworkers surveyed in the National Agricultural Workers Survey said accessing medical care was 'difficult,' and 77 percent cited cost as the major difficulty."

— Information from the film *The Harvest/La Cosecha: The Story of the Children Who Feed America* (theharvestfilm.com)

>✕<

CHILD WORKERS

When you hear the words "farm" and "child," with any luck you'll think of a beautifully green school garden or that new farm to school program in the city down the highway. But the reality is that hundreds of thousands of children have their hands in the soil for more than 12 hours a day, in the occupation that the USDA calls the most hazardous one in existence. U. Roberto Romano's heartrending film *The Harvest/La Cosecha: The Story of the Children Who Feed America,* focuses on the lives of United States citizen child migrant workers, many of whom face great health risks and barriers to an education because of the work they do. These kids drop out of school at four times the national rate. Why? Because we let them. Some facts:

WORKING HOURS outside of school are unlimited in agriculture.

ON AVERAGE, children in agriculture work 30 hours a week, often migrating from May to November, making it exceedingly difficult to succeed in school.

ALMOST 40 PERCENT of farmworkers migrate, and their children suffer the instability of a nomadic lifestyle, potentially working in multiple states in a given season and attending multiple schools, each with a different curriculum and standards.

THE RISK of fatal injuries for children working in agriculture is four times that of other young workers.

CHILD FARMWORKERS are especially vulnerable to repetitive-motion injury.

FARMWORKERS LABOR in extreme temperatures and die from heat exposure at a rate 20 times that of other U.S. workers, and children are significantly more susceptible to heat stress than adults. Heat exposure can lead to temporary illness, brain damage, and death.

ENVIRONMENTAL Protection Agency pesticide regulations are set using a 154-pound adult male as a model. They do not take children or pregnant women into consideration.

RESEARCH indicates that child farmworkers have a much higher rate of acute occupational pesticide-related illness than children in other industries and that there is a strong link between pesticide exposure and developmental disabilities. Long-term exposure in adults is associated with chronic health problems such as cancer, neurologic problems, and reproductive problems.

— *The Harvest/La Cosecha: The Story of the Children Who Feed America* (theharvestfilm.com)

TIP

Screen the film *The Harvest/La Cosecha*. Invite high schools
or college groups, politicians, business owners, and the local
media. For tips on screening a film, go to page 173.

YOU CAN DO THIS

PROTECT MIGRANT WORKERS

There are many organizations dedicated to migrant farmworkers. Get involved!

The Association of Farmworker Opportunity Programs

We provide job training, pesticide safety education, emergency assistance, and an advocacy voice for the people who prepare and harvest our food. Many member organizations operate a variety of programs in addition to the U.S. Department of Labor's National Farmworker Jobs Program, including Head Start, education, and housing counseling.

The AFOP also operates train the trainer pesticide safety programs for farmworkers. Funded by the United States Environmental Protection Agency, AFOP trains outreach workers in member agencies and related organizations in the Worker Protection Standard and in the latest techniques and materials. The trainers at the local level then conduct trainings for groups of farmworkers to help them understand and protect themselves from the dangers of pesticides. The program is now operational in 14 states. It is known as Project HOPE.

— The Association of Farmworker Opportunity Programs (afop.org)

National Center for Farmworker Health

The National Center for Farmworker Health (NCFH) is a private nonprofit corporation, established in 1975, located in Buda, Texas. NCFH provides information services, technical assistance, and training to more than 500 private and federally funded migrant health centers as well as other organizations and individuals serving the farmworker population.

— National Center for Farmworker Health (ncfh.org)

Migrant Legal Action Program

For more than 40 years, the Migrant Legal Action Program (MLAP) has provided legal representation and a national voice for migrant and seasonal farmworkers, the poorest group of working people in the United States.

MLAP works to enforce rights and to improve public policies affecting farmworkers' working and housing conditions, education, health, nutrition, and general welfare. The program works with an extensive network of local service providers.

MLAP staff is actively involved in advocacy, including legislative and administrative representation. MLAP also provides extensive support to local migrant service providers through training, technical assistance, and other services.

— Migrant Legal Action Program (mlap.org)

College Assistance Migrant Program

The College Assistance Migrant Program (CAMP) is a unique federally funded educational support and scholarship program that helps more than 2,000 students annually from migrant and seasonal farmworking backgrounds to reach and succeed in college. Participants receive anywhere from $750 to $4,000 of financial support during their freshman year of college and ongoing academic support until their graduation.

— MigrantStudents.org (migrantstudents.org/scholarshipsources.html)

Student Action with Farmworkers

SAF works with farmworkers, students, and advocates in the Southeast and nationwide to create a more just agricultural system. Since 1992, we have engaged thousands of students, farmworker youth, and community members in the farmworker movement.

— Student Action with Farmworkers (saf-unite.org/node/3)

Food Chain Workers Alliance

The Food Chain Workers Alliance is a coalition of worker-based organizations whose members plant, harvest, process, pack, transport, prepare, serve, and sell food, organizing to improve wages and working conditions for all workers along the food chain.

— Food Chain Workers Alliance (foodchainworkers.org)

CHAPTER 5

Connect

RACE, RELIGION, POLITICS. These are subjects we've been raised not to bring up in polite company, though we food activists tend to have no problem raging over food politics, decrying it daily in the news and social media and on our blogs while many wax poetic and swoon over a fresh leek, a grass-fed hamburger, good Chinese takeout, or fried chicken on Sundays. It's time we taboo the taboo of "polite company" and start talking about the vast and interesting intersection of food, farming, religion, and faith, because, let's face it, polite chit-chat does not transformative change make. Let's start talking to communicate, to learn, and to be understood. Food justice, economics, environment, health, animal welfare, laws — rich topics like these are woven into religious texts, liturgies, and prayers from religions and spiritual traditions around the world.

What religions, spiritual practices, arts, and ideas make up your beautiful, complicated, collective cultural soup? How can you help support the people who partake of it? Who is invited to the table, who isn't, and how can you reach out?

Foster among veterans the slow and safe unshackling of emotional and physical bonds (page 164). Realize the joy and wonder of a cow parade (page 170). Help make punishment bearable and truly rehabilitative (page 176). Honor the spirit of religious congregation (pages 183 and 186). Connect.

Where and when and how do you find your greatest sense of accomplishment? How does this guide you in the work you pursue? Decide what is worth doing and take action from your center, your spirit. To help heal the darknesses, corruptions, and detours of our food systems, like those of my father's diseased heart (page 9), connect.

YOU CAN DO THIS

MENTOR VETERANS

. . . .

In a 2012 TEDxManhattan presentation, Vietnam veteran Howard Hinterthuer talked about the many rehabilitative benefits of engaging vets in gardening, focusing on the Organic Therapy Project, a self-help program of the Center for Veterans Issues in Milwaukee, Wisconsin. Howard described the project as "organic in the sense that we do organic growing. But it's also organic in the sense that the program itself comes from people who've been through traumatic experiences and have found that gardening is very helpful in recovery."

Howard tells of great soldiers coming home only to face the challenges of relearning life after the military. He discusses some of the food-related health issues so many vets deal with, like heart disease, obesity, hypertension, and cancer, and emotional difficulties such as post-traumatic stress disorder (PTSD) and homelessness. He talks about his own experience of finding solace and safety in gardening, the rehabilitative powers of growing food, and the optimism of planting a seed. He explains how gardens are safe places not just for vets but for neighborhoods as well. Howard talks about harvesting green peppers and learning how to eat a more healthful diet. Only in passing does he mention the phrase "peer-to-peer mentoring." To me, "peer-to-peer" sounds like that spark of magic, miracle, and healing that makes a program like the Organic Therapy Project a success. Vets mentoring vets, to help transition to home, whole in health and spirit. This project, founded by veteran William Sims, is part of the Center for Veterans Issues in Milwaukee, Wisconsin (cvivet.org).

HOMEGROWN BY HEROES

Look for this label, a certification offered by the Farmer Veteran Coalition (farmvetco.org), not only to assure consumers of the safety of the food but also to support veteran farmers. As far as eligibility requirements, any veteran or active-duty member of the U.S. military, regardless of age, who produces agricultural products, may apply to use the Homegrown by Heroes label on those goods (hgbh.org).

THE FARMER VETERAN COALITION
Davis, California

The Farmer Veteran Coalition (farmvetco.org) is a California-based non-profit whose programming includes mentorship matching, job and internship opportunities, farmer veteran events and conferences, and farm equipment donations. If you're a farmer or a farm equipment dealer, you can donate new or used equipment through the Farmer Veteran Coalition to reach a farmer veteran. Download the Farmer Veteran Coalition's resource guide, "Veterans Careers in Agriculture," for information about how you or someone else can use the GI Bill or Post-9/11 GI Bill. Here are their guiding principles:

1. We guide the passion of our veterans so that they may earn for themselves a meaningful, financially sustainable place in the agricultural community. This could entail full-time or part-time employment, or a critical supplement to disability-related income.

2. We believe in the meritocracy of American agriculture, where personal responsibility for one's actions and individual initiative in pursuit of one's goals can create personal success. We believe in the fundamental dignity of physical work.

3. We acknowledge the plurality of agricultural crops, practices, scale and markets available to our veterans. We honor, guide, and support the practical farming path chosen by each veteran.

4. We are committed to leveraging our work through a network of partnerships. This allows us to more effectively help a larger number of veterans, particularly those in the onset of their civilian careers.

5. We support all valid national, regional, or crop-specific efforts to connect veterans with agriculture and encourage collaboration with other groups providing services to our nation's veterans.

6. We recognize the range of opportunities for employment throughout the agricultural economy. We sponsor and encourage both employment and self-employment in agriculture, and equally value the contributions made by all members of the agricultural industry who feed America.

7. We are conscious of the high number of veterans that return with both visible and invisible wounds. We respect the privacy of our veterans, and we will provide support to help make them stronger farmers.

8. We recognize the geographic and psychological isolation common to both farmers and veterans. Creating contact between our farmer veterans, and a sense of community among them, is an important part of our mission.

— Reprinted with permission from the Farmer Veteran Coalition (farmvetco.org)

RURAL SOLUTIONS
Ames, Iowa

Rural Solutions is one of many programs under the auspices of Easter Seals Iowa. According to its website (easterseals.com/ia/our-programs /rural-solutions), Rural Solutions provides "agricultural work site and home modification consultations, peer support, services for the family, information and referrals, and medical equipment loan services." Any individual with a disability or farm member with a disability living in a town with a population of less than 2,500 in Iowa is eligible. To find an Easter Seals affiliate in your state or region, visit the national website (easterseals.com) and do a "Connect Locally" search.

> "Only 17 percent of the U.S. population lives in rural areas, but rural residents account for 44 percent of our military. These rural veterans are returning to their farms, ranches, and rural communities with disabilities such as traumatic brain injury and post-traumatic stress disorder at high rates."
>
> — White House Rural Council, Jobs and Economic Security for Rural America, 2011

AGRABILITY

AgrAbility (agrability.org), a national program sponsored by the USDA, came into existence out of the 1990 Farm Bill. Its funding and oversight flows through the National Institute of Food and Agriculture. AgrAbility provides resources for farmers and ranchers who suffer disabilities, whether they've occurred on or off the land or the sea. It offers farm safety trainings and webinars, and it is vested in prevention. Its resources include an extensive database of assistive technologies — tools, equipment, modified work practices, and do-it-yourself solutions — to help people work with more ease and safety in the garden or on the farm. According to the AgrAbility website, migrant and seasonal farmworkers, family members, and noncitizens are all eligible for services. Anyone "engaged in agricultural-related occupations, forestry, fishing, and lawn care will find many of the resources available through AgrAbility applicable to their workplaces."

DISABLED, BUT ABLE TO FARM

This story, by Rob Dillard, was the third report in a series called "Being Physically Disabled in Iowa," from Iowa Public Radio. It aired on December 1, 2011.

Seventy-four-year-old Bill Sandquist has farmed 300 acres southwest of Adel, Iowa, for 54 years. But the last six have been entirely different.

"I used to raise a lot of hogs, used to feed cattle," Sandquist said. "Then in '05, when cancer took my arm, I had to give up the hogs. Basically, we're grain farmers now and partially retired, too."

Sandquist is among the 20 percent of U.S. farmers who work the land with some type of physical disability, according to estimates by the National AgrAbility Project. That's compared to the 6 percent of the overall workforce who are disabled.

And for Sandquist, the transition was sudden.

After he harvested his crops six years ago, Sandquist noticed the muscle in his lower right arm was growing larger. He was diagnosed with sarcoma, a form of cancer that strikes bones and the body's connective tissues. Doctors recommended quick amputation. Bill's wife, Colleen, said, "They had told us chemo won't work, radiation won't work, and it's either a life or a limb."

Surgeons removed Bill Sandquist's right arm to the elbow, and in its place he wears a prosthesis.

"It's not a bionic arm or hand by any means — it's all physical with flexing my shoulder," Sandquist said. "It's pretty simple and I got on to it pretty quick."

By shrugging his shoulder, Sandquist can open and close the metal claw that now serves as his right hand. The fact that he's naturally left-handed has made it slightly easier to adjust to farming with one arm, but he has been forced to adapt pieces of equipment and now operates more things with his feet.

Sandquist's giant combine has undergone a transformation — many of the controls have moved to the floorboard.

"First couple of years I combined, I didn't have the foot controls and I did everything with my prosthesis and my left hand," Sandquist said. "This just made it a lot easier."

For advice on what modifications to make to his farm machinery, Sandquist turned to the Rural Solutions program offered by Easter Seals of Iowa (see page 167). Over the last 25 years, Rural Solutions has helped more than 1,700 disabled Iowa farmers remain close to the land.

"Sometimes, due to the severity of a disability, a farmer may not desire, or it may not be safe, to return to the farming operation, so in some instances we may be just helping them to stay in their home," said Tracy Keninger, the program's director. "Perhaps a person with a high-level spinal cord injury — that may be their goal."

Sandquist's goal was to get back in the field.

"I just like to get up every morning and be part of the farm, part of agriculture, part of my family," Sandquist said.

Farming is a physically demanding occupation and it places strain on Sandquist's prosthesis. Even though it was constructed with a durable leather harness and reinforced cables, he has broken three prosthetic limbs since the amputation. Plus, the job is filled with an endless string of routine repairs that require agility.

"You know one thing I can't do is pound a damn nail," Sandquist said.

He said his greatest fear is losing grip with the prosthesis while climbing out of the combine and tumbling off.

Keninger said it's common for disabled farmers to overcompensate for their disability and injure themselves.

"Despite the fact his prosthetic device operates very effectively for him . . . there's still extra stress and strain on that left hand, the able-body side," Keninger said. "We often see overuse in one portion of the body to compensate for where there may be a limitation."

Keninger grew up on a farm near Ackley in north central Iowa. She decided to dedicate her career to farmers with disabilities after watching her father recover from a serious encounter with some rather large livestock.

Only about 20 percent of farmer disabilities are caused by farm accidents, according to estimates by the National AgrAbility Project. Most cases involve people surviving health conditions such as strokes, cerebral palsy, and muscular dystrophy.

Sandquist said he has adapted pretty well and things are looking up on the farm. Thanks to the long, hot summer, they harvested a bumper crop this fall. And during Sandquist's last semiannual checkup, there was no sign of the cancer that took his arm.

— Excerpted with permission from Iowa Public Radio (iowapublicradio.org)

YOU CAN DO THIS

PARADE COWS DOWN MAIN STREET

The cow parade always gets me. I've done that walk up Main Street in Brattleboro, Vermont, with my eldest son and his classmates from the Putney School a couple of times. And I gotta say, it makes a momma proud to walk with her child and his cow. The wonder of this rite of passage wasn't lost on me, this parade of teenagers and their heifers.

But in the 2012 Strolling of the Heifers, it was the cleanup crew that truly impressed me. They were students from the public high school who were costumed like some sort of genetically modified blackflies crossed with superheroes, and they wielded their wheelbarrows, shavings, shovels, and brooms with purpose. It was their job to clean the cows' poop along the parade route. They were the ones who buzzed in and around the cow parade that hot June day, making nice and fun of a messy, stinky, somebody's-got-to job.

And the pretty heifers, they were all gussied up for the parade, like their handlers. Some were crowned with wreaths of wildflowers, and one beauty even had "Our Family Farms" shaved on its side, a kind of bovine mohawk. What inspired a group of teenagers to join the poop patrol at the Strolling of the Heifers? Because, as one of them explained, they wanted to raise awareness about the homeless veterans in their town. "Huh?" I asked, slow to connect. "We learned about homeless vets from Home At Last. [Home at Last, Inc., is a nonprofit in Brattleboro, Vermont.] They came and spoke at the high school. We don't have cows and aren't farmers, but we do have a social action group and we wanted to be in the parade. So we thought we'd do this," she said, gesturing with mucky shovel in hand. It was impressive, all the way around.

THE STROLLING OF THE HEIFERS
Brattleboro, Vermont

What started in 2002 as a funky parade to support local dairy farmers in southern Vermont has morphed into a community-wide festival with such big-name sponsors as the ice cream giant Ben & Jerry's and the organic and natural meat producer Applegate. Now the Strolling of the Heifers (strollingoftheheifers.com) is a nonprofit organization that hosts days of events, including a Slow Living Summit. It raises money for microloans for farmers and offers small educational grants to local teachers to bring agriculture education into their classrooms. Groups such as regional 4-H dairy clubs, the Putney School, and the nonprofit Farms for City Kids in Reading, Vermont, bring their heifers groomed, prepped, and trained (as much as teenage cows may be trained, that is). But for me, the best part remains the heart and soul of that crazy cow parade up Main Street.

THROW A LIVING LOCAL FEST

"Have some fun." That's Kate Warner's advice. Kate, an architect and the founder of the Vineyard Energy Project, is a self-described avid alternative energy geek. Her work had been very singularly focused on climate change, a topic that can be hard to get people to wrap their heads around because it's so damn depressing. As an antidote, and to reach people beyond the usual choir, she pulled together local partners in land conservation and agriculture to create the Living Local Harvest Fest.

Started in 2007 on Martha's Vineyard, this October festival is one part ag fair, one part re-skilling, and one part local food fair. Local experts hold demonstrations about such things as how to make sauerkraut, press apples, and fillet a fish and freeze it. Presentations and panels discuss the potential of slaughterhouses, community composting programs, food hubs, and solar power. Thanks to business sponsors, the event remains free and open to the public. And that's the point. Everyone is invited. Though the biggest attraction? Morning Glory Farm's pumpkin-tossing trebuchet. There's something spectacularly medieval about watching a 30-pound pumpkin fly through the air over a field the length of a football field. And then learning how to make a pie out of it.

"There is a sense that there is a richness in this world that's enormous fun if you can find it. And it's the kind of fun that you can have while actually making the world a better place for other people, too." — Sherwin Nuland

YOU CAN DO THIS

SCREEN A FILM
. . . .

The initiative Community Cinema (communitycinema.org) promotes
free screenings of PBS Independent Lens films. Recent titles include
The Island President (a documentary on how the Maldives islands
are sinking due to climate change) and *Facing the Storm: Story of
the American Bison* (a historical documentary that also looks at
the current situation of the bison on the Great Plains). Films like
these address issues of cultural identity, food, and climate change.
Educators and students will find downloadable lesson plans for film
modules under Community Cinema's "Community Classroom."

In the film *Soul Food Junkies*, filmmaker Byron Hurt weaves strong visual imagery of American food deserts (urban or rural areas in which people, especially
those without access to cars, have highly limited access to fresh, affordable,
nutritious food), commentaries, and personal stories about the cultural history
and health impacts of soul foods, processed foods, healthy foods, and education.
These are tough and challenging topics to untangle because of racism, shame,
blame, shifting responsibilities, diets that harm, diets that help, cultural identity, generational gaps, marketing, and historical myths. Discussion guides like
the one excerpted here, written specifically for *Soul Food Junkies*, help guide all
of us through these issues with care, integrity, safety, and respect.

For tips on holding a film screening, go to page 210.

>>

DISCUSSION GUIDE FOR *SOUL FOOD JUNKIES*

1. What are some of your memories, feelings, or other associations with food? How do they compare with those expressed in the film?

2. Why are eating habits so hard to break? Do you think it's possible to be addicted to a specific food or to food in general? Explain.

3. Some people feel that using healthy substitutes in soul food (e.g., smoked turkey instead of pork fat to flavor greens, or herbs instead of salt) changes the nature of soul food, making it less authentic, even robbing African-American culture of one of its defining characteristics. How would you respond to this criticism?

4. Is eating just a matter of personal behavior and preference? When do eating habits — or the effects of eating habits and food choices — step over into the public realm?

5. Do governmental or other public agencies have a role in guiding or responsibility to guide what or how people choose to eat? Defend your position. What about public figures, such as Dick Gregory (who appears in the film) or Michelle Obama? How influential can they be in promoting a healthy lifestyle?

6. The film talks about the intersections of food and politics, especially in the 1950s and 1960s. Do you feel that there are connections between food and politics today? How are they connected?

7. Do you feel that food deserts, that is, areas that lack markets selling healthy foods, are responsible for the poor nutrition found among many low-income African Americans? What are some other reasons for their poor nutrition?

8. What can local governments do to create better access to healthy foods for low-income populations? What can residents of a locality do to obtain better food options in their community?

9. How much of a role should schools play in establishing good eating habits?

10. Does your community provide ways for people to learn about good nutrition? If not, how could the community create opportunities for this kind of learning?

— Excerpted with permission from the Community Cinema discussion guide for *Soul Food Junkies* (available at itvs.org/films/soul-food-junkies/engagement-resources)

AGRICULTURAL HISTORY SOCIETY

My father, Paul C. Gartzke, always had Wisconsin State Historical Society journals lying on the coffee table when he worked from home, comfortably seated on the living room couch. The journals never sported color photos, so I wasn't much interested as a kid. But he loved them. He circled passages he liked or disagreed with, and he dog-eared pages to lecture us from when we gathered together at the dinner table at 6:00 p.m. sharp. He loved learning and teaching, though he could be pedantic about it all.

But for me, living in a community shifted the study of history from academic to real life, from pages to people. In my quest to learn more about food and farming, I discovered the Agricultural History Society (aghistory society.org). Founded in 1919 in Washington, D.C., the society started publishing its journal in 1927. Included in the journal are articles and research from all periods of history. A recent call for papers included the topical and timely subject "illicit agriculture," as in the farming of illicit substances, criminal farming sites, and/or illegal or subaltern agriculture activities.

So, you guerrilla gardeners out there who plant food in public spaces (page 143), sounds like this is for you or your next panel discussion! A presentation subject right up your alleys, vacant lots, and parkways . . . There's an article, blog, or paper ripe and ready to publish, along the lines of "Green Zebra Tomatoes, Silver Cloud Cannellini Beans, and Duborskian–South River Rice: The New Illicit Crops, and the Gateway Crops to Good Healthy Food for All."

"A people without a knowledge of their past history, origin, and culture is like a tree without roots." —Marcus Garvey, *What's Going On*

PLANT A GARDEN AT A JAIL

There's always more than one meaning to any one word. Consider "the farm," which can also be slang for jail or prison. In our country, a prison's actual farm connotes exploitive hard labor and dangerous work, sometimes called "rehabilitative," though most likely not. But these are new times or at least a chance at them, one hopes. And this slang usage of "the farm," this duality of meaning, poses a conundrum, a disconnect, for the entire current vernacular and dialogue around the local food movement. Or, maybe a chance to connect?

I thank my friend, esteemed colleague, and kindred soul Alice Randall for bringing this aspect of food activism's language to my white-privileged attention. Consider how the following phrases, on which this book is based, read: farm to school, farm to table, farm to institution, farm to prison. And even the U.S. Department of Agriculture's own "Know Your Farmer, Know Your Food" initiative potentially tumbles deep in this tumult. Language matters. So here we are, learning how we speak to one another in order to be understood whether and wherever it is: on the farm, in the garden, in prisons and jails. In this case, I truly *do* mean connecting farms to farm food, to people who live in jails and prisons.

Work to support good food and good food education in jails, prisons, and halfway houses in your area. Build a food garden. The healing and health and rehabilitative benefits of gardening are proven. Or if you're a farmer, sell your whole, fresh food to the cafeterias (for tips on selling, see pages 48 and 263).

Petition your state's department of agriculture to partner with your state's department of corrections. In January 2014, Washington State announced the launching of its Farm to Prison pilot program, to supply local food to correctional facilities. You can support this process by encouraging the adaptation of established farm-to-institution benefits and guidelines. There is a vast amount of widely available information, advice, and help to be tailored from farm to school (page 34) and farm to hospital programs (page 263).

Get a gleaning program (page 215) connected to the confined citizens and their cafeterias. Develop skilled labor: some inmates in California and Colorado are learning food and farming skills and working in small goat or cow dairies and fisheries.

Or start a culinary arts program. At the Fife and Drum Restaurant inside the Northeastern Correctional Center, a minimum-security prison near Concord, Massachusetts, lunch is made from scratch and served by inmates. It's a good deal, too, at around $3.21.

WHAT'S GOING ON

THE SANDUSKY COUNTY JAIL GARDENING PROGRAM
Fremont, Ohio

Inmates at the Sandusky County Jail tend a 1.5-acre plot and get to eat the benefits, which include their locally raised broilers. Garden overages? Yes: 375 pounds of food was donated to food pantries and soup kitchens in 2010.

THE INSIGHT GARDEN PROGRAM
San Quentin Prison, California

All food harvested from the prison garden at San Quentin, which was featured on *ABC World News*, is given to the community. Go to the Insight Garden Program's website (insightgardenprogram.org) for resources and news about prison farm programs nationwide.

GETTING KIDS BACK TO THEIR ANCESTRAL ROOTS

This essay is by Kathleen Yetman, a FoodCorps fellow (see page 54 for more on FoodCorps). She interviews Gilbert Ivins, a FoodCorps service member.

Cibecue, Arizona, is a community of 1,700 White Mountain Apache tribal members situated among stunning red rock hills, scrub juniper, and sprawling grasslands. It is located on the Fort Apache Indian Reservation in eastern Arizona at the foot of the White Mountains. Cibecue is off the beaten path — an hour's drive from any other town or city — and due to its isolation, food options are limited. There are three convenience stores in Cibecue. Last year, while serving as a FoodCorps service member, I perused the shelves of the largest of the three. There was one cooler in the back of the store sparsely stocked with packaged cucumbers and half-ripe tomatoes, and a couple of heads of iceberg lettuce. These were the only vegetables for sale in the community. In one of the other stores, with a growling stomach, I searched for the healthiest item, and after settling on a 16-ounce block of cheddar cheese, discovered that it cost $7. In that same store, one can buy 308 ounces of soda for the same price.

Most Cibecue families make a weekly trip 48 miles to Walmart, where food is cheaper and there is a greater variety. You can imagine what families are left to purchase if they can't make that weekly trek. So it's not all that surprising that kids growing up there may have never seen a real carrot. In 2010, FoodCorps partnered with the Johns Hopkins Center for American Indian Health (JHCAIH) and beginning last year placed two FoodCorps service members on the reservation to teach gardening and nutrition to kids at Dischii'bikoh (Cibecue) Community School. Through the Edible School Garden program, third, fourth, and fifth graders learn about the plant life cycle, tools to help them choose healthier foods, and about the wild foods their ancestors used to eat.

This year, we are fortunate to have Gilbert Ivins as our service member in Cibecue. Gilbert is a member of the White Mountain Apache Tribe and has lived in Cibecue his whole life. Prior to FoodCorps, he worked as an emergency medical technician and firefighter in his community. Last week I sat down with Gilbert to hear about his service.

GILBERT: Being a FoodCorps service member is really cool because I get to be the stepping-stone for many young Native American youth making a positive change toward their health and nutrition. So far this year with the kids from Cibecue Elementary, I have seen that my presence there has made a big difference. I've seen kids try all the vegetables and fruits we brought them. . . . One student told me he wished he could never grow old so he could stay in Edible School Garden and Native Vision forever and that Edible School Garden would continue throughout his time in school all the way up until he graduates. FoodCorps has touched the hearts and souls of the Apache youth in Cibecue.

KATHLEEN: What are some of the challenges you see facing kids in your community?

GILBERT: The gangs and the influences they have on the kids — drugs, alcohol, and violence. Obesity is another issue that comes into play because the parents don't discipline their kids enough to choose healthier products and instead feed them all the nonhealthy food that is easily available at any given moment.

KATHLEEN: How do you see your service addressing all of these challenges?

GILBERT: By teaching and showing these kids healthy from nonhealthy items. I hope that kids take home and share with their parents the information they get from our classes. I hope too that the parents will come to us with questions about healthy eating lifestyles.

— Excerpted with permission from Kathleen Yetman, FoodCorps Fellow, and Gilbert Ivins, FoodCorps service member, January 29, 2013

INDIGENIZE LOCAL FOOD:
WE ARE PLANTING GOOD SEEDS

Elizabeth Hoover, assistant professor of American studies and ethnic studies at Brown University, is spending her sabbatical going across the country, visiting Native American farming/gardening/food sovereignty projects. Here is something of what she's seen.

Kanenhi:io Ionkwaienthon:hakie (Mohawk for "We Are Planting Good Seeds") is a collective of farmers, educators, and entrepreneurs in the Akwesasne Mohawk community, located on the borders of New York, Ontario, and Quebec.

Kanenhi:io collaborates with the Akwesasne Freedom School (AFS), a Mohawk immersion school founded in 1979 by parents who were concerned with the lack of culture and language in the public school systems. The school conducts full-day language immersion classes for students in pre-K to grade 8, with a curriculum based on the Ohen:ton Karihwatehkwen (Thanksgiving Address). The AFS owns the 10.5-acre site where Kanenhi:io has developed the community garden, greenhouse, and cannery. In addition, school staff and parents are partnering with Kanenhi:io group members to involve students in the production of food.

The greenhouse was constructed in 2008, and has provided community members with a place to start seedlings for the community garden and home gardens, as well as to grow warm-weather crops like tomatoes and amaranth. The community cannery was developed between 2011 and 2014, and has provided a place for community members to dehydrate, can, and freeze produce, as well as to press apples into cider. One of Kanenhi:io's goals in the coming year is to expand the offering of food preservation and gardening classes offered at the cannery, as well as expand the video and book library.

In addition to planting market crops in the community garden, Kanenhi:io has been working with seed savers across Haudenosaunee territory to bring back more heritage seed varieties — both to preserve these crops planted by ancestors on this land, and in an effort to work traditional foods back into people's diets.

In addition to the Freedom School students, Kanenhi:io also works with the Ohero:kon rites of passage program, begun by bear clan mother Louise McDonald as a way of educating adolescents about their traditional roles and obligations as they become Mohawk adults. Because horticulture is such an important aspect of Mohawk culture and health, members of Kanenhi:io are working to involve the Ohero:kon adolescents in farming and gardening projects. Part of the Mohawk creation story includes the first garden, which sprang forth from Sky Woman's daughter. As part of the rites of passage ceremony, the youth create a woman out of soil, into which they plant corn, beans, squash and tobacco. Through nurturing the land, as well as the social and cultural relationships that are integral to sustainable food production, Kanenhi:io, the Akwesasne Freedom School, and the Ohero:kon rites of passage are working to make Akwesasne a healthier, more food sovereign community.

— Excerpted with permission by Elizabeth Hoover, From Garden Warriors to Good Seeds (gardenwarriorsgoodseeds.com)

YOU CAN DO THIS

DECOLONIZE YOUR DIET

The Decolonizing Diet Project (DDP), directed by Martin Reinhardt, an Anishinaabe Ojibway and assistant professor of Native American studies at Northern Michigan University, is an ambitious, year-long eating challenge to eat only foods that were in the Great Lakes region before 1602. The aim is to restore the relationship between humans and regional native foods. A few tasty local morsels? Squash, bison, and wild leeks from the region.

The desire to reclaim traditional foods is spreading across the country. Luz Calvo, a professor, gardener, and food activist in Oakland, California, recently began a similar Decolonize Your Diet Project in California, aimed at promoting the "heritage foods of greater Mexico and Central America as a way of improving the physical, emotional, and spiritual health of US Latinos/as."

WHAT'S GOING ON

NATIVE AMERICAN FOOD SOVEREIGNTY ALLIANCE (NAFSA)
Longmont, Colorado

Terrie Bad Hand and Pati Martinson of the Taos County Economic Development Corporation know what it means to support farmers, indigenous local culture, and food entrepreneurs. They manage a commercial incubator kitchen, hold food safety workshops for health regulators, and manage a mobile slaughter and processing unit called the Mobile Mantaza, which they built to support area ranchers. Together with the First Nations Development Institute, they formed NAFSA in 2013, with funding provided by the W. K. Kellogg Foundation. Responding to the imperative and potency of local, sustained food movements in Indian country, NAFSA, according to its website (nativefoodsystems.org), will "be a vehicle to facilitate change in areas of tribal, regional and national policy on issues affecting Native food production and diet and be a support network for grassroots Native efforts as they work to revive tradition and community based food systems."

HOST INTERFAITH DISCUSSIONS
ABOUT FOOD

· · · · · · · · · · · · · · · · · · · ·

The interfaith discussion guidelines excerpted here were made in collaboration with GreenFaith.org and the movie *Fresh*. Though their guide was made with this particular movie in mind, their tips apply to getting together to discuss any movie or book, or simply just a potluck.

DISCUSSION GUIDELINES

1. Seek to learn from others. Good interfaith discussions encourage people to share their own ideas and traditions and explore those of others. Recognize that there is no such thing as a "stupid" question about someone else's religion. If you don't understand something someone says, ask politely for an explanation. Be willing to explain what your tradition means to you.

2. Create an atmosphere of forbearance and mutual respect. Often, we don't know how to ask a question about someone else's religion because we lack understanding of their tradition. We may feel hesitant to ask a question about someone else's religion because we fear that we may give offense. We suggest that the group leader recognize these concerns and encourage participants to ask each other the best way to pose questions about their traditions and give each other advice about good ways to approach sensitive subjects. The purpose of interfaith dialogues such as these is to share and to learn not to pass judgment on others.

3. Be prepared to teach each other about your religion. Most religions have terms for the leaders, sacred writings, or other important aspects of their traditions that can be difficult for others to pronounce or understand. We recommend that members of each religion represented make an effort to teach others the names by which they refer to the divine and other unique terminology. Seek to be a good ambassador and teacher to others about your tradition.

>>

4. Seek common ground; recognize differences respectfully. The world's great religions share many values and common interests. Use your interfaith dialogue as a place to identify these shared values and interests. At the same time, there are legitimate differences between great religions. Often, these differences result from historical circumstances, experiences of suffering, or theological teachings (as compared to moral teachings). Be sensitive to and respectful of these differences. If you follow these guidelines, your interfaith discussion should be a rewarding experience.

5. Invite a member of each religious tradition in attendance to offer a closing prayer or blessing and to describe the meaning of this prayer or blessing within their community.

Think about developing an e-mail or contact list of participants. Interfaith efforts can be difficult to organize and lists such as these can be helpful in identifying participants for future events or for making follow-up from this event easier.

— Excerpted with permission from Interfaith Discussion Guide, produced by GreenFaith (below) and the makers of the movie *Fresh*

WHAT'S GOING ON

GREENFAITH

The interfaith organization GreenFaith (greenfaith.org) offers terrific guides for congregations, houses of worship, households, and individuals to download for free. Their PowerPoint presentation "Food and Faith: Actions within Houses of Worship" asks compelling questions to bring to any congregation, Christian or otherwise. Examples include:

WHY does the food we purchase matter, and how does this tie in with our faith?

WHAT kind of food is served at events and coffee hour?

WHEN can you encourage composting and recycling?

HOW can you make small and big changes, and how will you successfully navigate the barriers?

Also download *Repairing Eden,* a Good Food Toolkit made in conjunction with the Johns Hopkins Center for a Livable Future.

SAMPLE DISCUSSION QUESTIONS FOR *FRESH*

The film *Fresh* shows the ways in which our current food systems harm people, animals, and the whole earth.

WHAT ARE some of the most painful or jarring images from the film? What bothered you the most, or caused you the greatest discomfort? For people? For animals? For the environment? Why?

WHO IS responsible for creating the harmful impacts or systems that *Fresh* describes? What commercial, governmental, and cultural forces are responsible?

ALL RELIGIONS recognize that people act wrongly and need to make reparations for their wrongdoing. How does your tradition refer to this dynamic? What terms or words does it use for this purpose, and what do those terms mean?

HOW CAN YOU imagine your faith community engaging the wrongdoing that *Fresh* reveals and seeking to make it right?

WHAT DOES your religious tradition teach about animals? What moral teachings are supposed to govern our treatment of animals? What stories from sacred texts or religious traditions teach us about animals and the value they hold in the eyes of the Divine?

IS FRESH FOOD a religious issue? What religious teachings support the significance of fresh food?

IN WHAT WAYS is the current food system bad for its workers? For small farmers? For rural communities?

WHICH of the positive examples in *Fresh* struck you most powerfully? Why? What values or virtues from your religious tradition do these positive stories exemplify?

— Excerpted with permission from GreenFaith.org and FRESHthemovie.com.

BRING TOGETHER FOOD AND RELIGION

INVITE farmers to talk at your place of worship. If you're a farmer, connect with your local places of worship, even if they're not of your identified faith.

START an on-site farmers' market, CSA program, or community composting for your congregation.

HOST a community farm-to-table dinner. Encourage guests to cook with at least one local, seasonal ingredient. (Great start: farm-fresh eggs.)

ORGANIZE a CROP Hunger Walk (cropwalk.org). These walks are organized by the Church World Service to raise money to help eradicate hunger around the world. Or simply find the closest one to walk in!

ORGANIZE your congregation to host a film screening, a conference, or a workshop around an issue that is relevant to your community now.

ENCOURAGE fresh, unprocessed, whole foods to be served at community gatherings and coffee hours.

INVESTIGATE whether your existing kitchen can be certified as commercial or whether you want to build a commercial kitchen. Then you may be able to help clean and process gleaned produce or make another value-added product such as cheese, jam, or even beer. (Think like the Trappist monks of St. Joseph's Abbey, in Spencer, Massachusetts, who brew the only Trappist beer outside of Europe.)

Things Clergy Can Do

BRING congregation members together to focus on food and justice.

ARRANGE a special prayer or sermon for Food Day, October 24 every year (foodday.org), or World Food Day, October 16 every year (worldfood dayusa.org).

WEAVE food and faith into your sermons. Host local food activists, farmers, fishermen, or beekeepers (see page 145) to speak to your congregation. Invite a farmers' market manager, farmer, or good food advocate to talk about his or her projects, be they

focused on food insecurity, school food reform infrastructure, policy, or turning lawns into gardens.

START a sustainability committee with a goal of integrating some good food change and action within a year. Compost, build a garden, plant an orchard.

ENGAGE the youth program around food education every day.

PARTNER with other congregations to create a local interfaith lecture/sermon series. Invite the public.

>×<

RAWTOOLS, INC.
Colorado Springs, Colorado

It is a stark video. It may as well be an instructional piece on blacksmithing. The only sounds are the furnace and the rhythmic clank of hammer to anvil with forge-hot steel in between. Leather-gloved hands grip a vise that secures the red-hot barrel of a gun — the object that is being transformed from a weapon into a garden tool. This is a real-life, modern-day take on the biblical passage Isaiah 2:4:

> They will beat their swords into plowshares
> and their spears into pruning hooks.
> Nation will not take up sword against nation,
> nor will they train for war anymore.

The "raw" in RAWtools is "war" spelled backward. This Colorado-based nonprofit is affiliated with Beth-El Mennonite Church in Colorado Springs. Its impetus, though grounded in the Isaiah passage, came from the 9/11 terrorist attacks on the World Trade Center and the Pentagon. When the founder and executive director, Mike Martin and his wife, learned that some of the recovered metal from the twin towers was repurposed into the construction of U.S. warships, they were determined to effect change in the vicious cycle of hate begets hate, terror begets terror. RAWtools' mission, as stated on its website (rawtools.org) is "to repurpose weapons into hand tools to be used in the creation of something new, preventing the weapon's use for violence and creating a cycle of peace." The organization continues to hold repurposing events in conjunction with places of worship, for Martin Luther King Jr. Day celebrations, and at justice conferences.

After forging garden tools and sending them out into the world anew, RAWtools encourages the new owners/gardeners to share their stories of how the tools are used, in whose gardens, and how much food they cultivate. The greatest challenge RAWtools faces is not finding homes for the garden tools but, ironically, securing the legal access to the guns they want to repurpose. By partnering with local police departments, places of worship, and nonprofits, the group hopes that the sounds of anvil, hammer, and hot metal will ring on, in community choruses of "grow food, grow peace."

Look for the YouTube video "Swords to Plows."

— RAWtools

CHAPTER 6

Speak

"Don't forget it. Use your voice."

— Patti Smith at a live performance, Toronto, Ontario, March 7, 2013

ACCORDING TO WEB DESIGNER, speaker, and writer Brad Frost, every day 822,240 websites are created, 499,680 WordPress posts are published, and 144.8 billion e-mails are sent. Four and a half million photographs are uploaded to Flickr, 40 million are uploaded to Instagram, and 300 million posted to Facebook. Five hundred million tweets are tweeted a day. Four billion things are shared on Facebook. And every minute, 72 hours of video are uploaded to YouTube. In 2003, there were 300,000 books, each with a unique International Standard Book Number (ISBN). By 2012, there were 15 million ISBNs. Ten percent of the 130 million books ever made were published in 2012. IBM has stated that 90 percent of the data ever created was created from 2011 to 2013.

It is against this continuous cacophonous barrage and background of information that it's now, more than ever, paramount to develop and support deft and agile storytellers. Storytellers who watch and listen. Who collect and distill the noise into the elements and narratives that connect us.

To effect change around food systems, we need the stories that ignite, cajole, create empathy, and evoke compassion. The "protagonist" locally grown, the "antagonist'" agribusiness, and everything else in the continuum all have direct and indirect consequences on the health of a mind, body, and soul. The story of food can be as provocative and compelling as ancient Greek myths or classics of literature, seductive as Nabokov or Austen. But it needs to be told well and deliberately, so it can be heard, felt, and understood. And in the midst of the cacophony, a story needs good stewardship; otherwise it will get lost.

In conferences about regional food systems, in workshops around the farm bill, in donors' meetings deciding the allocation of funds, there is a call from these places to tell the stories of farmers, ranchers, fishermen, of food systems, of food-related policies and public health. Common and ancient threads of storytelling help connect the cold, hard statistics of food-related diseases and lack of access to fresh, healthy, responsibly raised foods, to reality and to us, the people.

So speak out. Promote good work (page 192), keep informed (page 193), listen (page 194), learn to tell stories (page 198), hold a poetry workshop (page 202), publish your writings (page 204), and use the media (page 208). Stories connect us to our food. Food connects us back toward one another. It is a most delicious dynamic and nurturing relationship. Especially when home-cooked and shared.

WITNESSES TO HUNGER
Philadelphia, Pennsylvania

Mariana Chilton, a professor at the Drexel University School of Public Health, is an antihunger advocate and activist profiled in the documentary films *A Place at the Table* and *The Same Heart.* She appears to have put her master's degree in ethnography to good and practical use in the project Witnesses to Hunger, which puts cameras in the hands of people experiencing hunger. It put a human face on the statistics of hunger and food insecurity for the policymakers in Washington, D.C.

The idea behind this program, which started in Philadelphia in 2008, is that real experts on hunger are the mothers and other caregivers of young children who are in need of food and resources. The Witnesses to Hunger program asks the caregivers to use the cameras to show what is most important to them.

The photographs cannot be denied. They speak directly to the heart and humanity of the disenfranchised, the marginalized, the people we should be taking care of.

Witnesses to Hunger is a project of the Center for Hunger-Free Communities (centerforhungerfreecommunities.org).

"No social movement in history has achieved victory without significant leadership from the people most affected by the problem. There is no way we can end hunger and slash poverty in America unless low-income Americans, who have experienced the problems themselves, play a central role in the movement." — New York City Coalition Against Hunger

YOU CAN DO THIS

BE A WITNESS
....

Read about the Witnesses to Hunger project in Philadelphia. Could you imagine such a project in your own community? Do you have pictures to take, words to share? Do you see others whose voices you'd like to hear? What are you a witness to? How else could you express what you witness? Moreover, how can you include the people who are most affected?

The Hunger-Free Communities Network (hungerfreecommunities.org), hosted and administered by the Alliance to End Hunger (alliancetoendhunger.org), has collected free guides and tool kits from a number of resources. Look for these as leads: "A Positive Partnership: Advice from Witnesses to Hunger on Engaging Your Community In Advocacy" (published by Drexel University for Hunger-Free Communities) and "Stepping Up to the Plate: Healthy Food Access and the Anti-Hunger Community's Response" (published by MAZON: A Jewish Response to Hunger).

WHAT'S GOING ON

HOWCAST

Howcast (howcast.com) produces short, basic instructional videos for everything from how to fix your car radiator to how to play chess to how to visit Vancouver. Its "How to Use Social Media" series explains (especially for those who didn't grow up with it) the basics of how to use social media sites such as YouTube, Twitter, and Facebook. There are also tutorials on using Skype — from setting up an account, to determining your privacy settings, to how to do conference calls, make presentations, and set up chats.

YOU CAN DO THIS

PROMOTE GOOD WORK

Whether it's for an organization you're part of or just an organization whose aims you'd like to help promote, consider these different ways to publicize good work.

USE Facebook, community online calendars, and posters to announce your events. Take photos of your events and post them on your Tumblr, Twitter, Pinterest, or Instagram accounts.

WRITE and send press releases about your event, about two weeks before. Always include place, time, location, and contact person or your spokesperson.

ANNOUNCE your event on community radio, local National Public Radio (NPR) stations, local newspapers, and community television.

INVITE local, regional, or federal politicians to join you.

THANK the people who help you out. Always. Take out an ad in the paper to do it.

>><<

"A nation of sheep will beget a government of wolves."

— Edward R. Murrow, journalist

WHAT'S GOING ON

COOKING UP A STORY

Cooking Up a Story (cookingupastory.com) is an online television show and blog about "organic food, sustainable agriculture, food politics, ranchers, farmers, backyard gardening, cooking, recipes, and more." I troll this site for video stories in the series Food.Farmer.Earth and interviews like the one with the CEO of the Oregon Food Bank, Rachel Bristol. *Cooking Up a Story* also features talks about industrial farming, sustainable fisheries, and more by such dignitaries as Temple Grandin (author and consultant to the livestock industry on animal behavior), Paul Hawken (author and environmentalist), Carlo Petrini (founder of the Slow Food movement), David Korten (author of *Agenda for a New Economy*), and Deborah Madison (cookbook author).

KEEP INFORMED

Create a Google news alert for topics, organizations, and people in the world of food whom you are interested in following. Keeping up-to-date helps inform your own storytelling. Here are few people, podcasts, organizations, and topics that I'm following now:

» Animal Welfare Approved

» Media Voices for Children

» On Being

» Media Action Grassroots Network

» Food Hubs

» #VoteFood

» Seed Saving

» Jeni Britton Bauer

"I'm an artist. Gardening is my graffiti. I grow my art . . . just like a graffiti artist where they beautify walls, me, I beautify lawns and parkways. I use the garden and the soil like a piece of cloth. And the plants and the trees, that's my embellishments for that cloth. You'd be surprised what the soil can do if you let it be your canvas." — Ron Finley (see page 111)

LISTEN

· · · · · · · · · · · ·

"Stop it already. Enough." A farmer I know was letting me have it. "Farming is hard. It sucks, frankly. And you're making it look pretty. You need to stop." Chastened, I listened. He was the one farming, not me. All I did was write about it, and he had a lot to say about that.

His point landed hard. He felt that I, that is, the media, "all of it," romanticized farming. In the magazine I edited and co-own, *Edible Vineyard,* I did my best to take a well-rounded approach to the content. I tried to be unprecious and unpretentious yet authentic in voice. The magazine's aesthetic was to use untouched, unfussy photography. Yet in that farmer's view, it still created too much pretty attention, putting farmers and farming on a pedestal.

His criticism made me think: How does our food movement use language and imagery? How do the words and images best serve the issues? Do they break down or fortify existing barriers? Do they integrate values, vision, and best practices of what can be, without degrading, excluding, or simply being too precious?

Jean-François Millet's 1857 oil painting *The Gleaners* sympathetically depicts peasant women harvesting crops. It romanticizes them as well, in soft light, compassionate tones. Yet the French elite of the time forbade the painting from view.

More recently, there's the Cesar Chavez–inspired public art that adorns the walls of migrant farmworker centers and the street corners where workers wait today for their bus rides out to the fields. Have you seen the local food movement's quintessential image? It's a photograph of outstretched hands (calloused, dirt under the fingernails) cupping a clutch of farm-fresh blue and green chicken eggs as if they came from the House of Fabergé's cloaca, thoroughly bejeweled and speckled with henhouse litter. (Mea culpa. I published a version of that image, too. If memory doesn't fail me, there was even flannel involved.)

In their own way, such images uplift and reveal. Backlit by a photographer's golden hour, they give dignity to the mostly unnoticed and the quiet, by paying homage to nature's sublime and wonderful miracles. We do need to shed light, and the lighting is nice. But how much romance and soft focus is too much? What messages are we sending to whom? Is there a place for all of it? What do you think?

>×<

> "Going to where the silence is. That is the responsibility of a journalist: giving a voice to those who have been forgotten, forsaken, and beaten down by the powerful."
>
> — Amy Goodman, founder and host of *Democracy Now!*

RADIO

I think radio is a beautiful medium. It floats through the air and lands without a trace except in the listener's imagination. No mass mailings of pounds of paper that will likely end up in landfills. To me, good radio is visual. I can smell, taste, and feel it on my skin when it's right. With no images, I get to fill them in myself, led by the storyteller's words, sounds, and narrative. I've heard other radio lovers say they won't eat crunchy foods during their favorite programs so that they won't miss a word. I know exactly what it means to put down that chip while *On the Media* and *Latino USA* are on the air.

With its mix of voices and ambient sounds, radio — despite all the new innovations in technology and the Internet — is one of the most basic and accessible points of entry to tell the stories about your local food systems. And as Jay Allison (see page 199) says, "The equipment required to get broadcast quality is inexpensive and readily available, and basic recording and interviewing skills are easily mastered."

> "I want to make radio/audio for listeners . . . [to] make them look at their home in a new way or help them understand their own role in re-imagining where they live." — Zak Rosen, Transom.org

ON ENTERING THE WORLD OF RADIO

Elspeth Hay admits that when she started The Local Food Report *on the public radio stations WCAI (Cape Cod and the Islands) and WNAN (Nantucket), she had no idea what she was doing. That was years ago. Since then she's interviewed fisher- men, farmers, teachers, cooks, and more, all from her local food community. She also writes the blog* Diary of a Locavore. *Here, Elspeth writes about entering the world of radio, the local food movement, and what it means to her.*

When I approached Jay Allison and Viki Merrick about doing a radio show on local food, I had never held radio gear. I had no idea what ProTools was, or mixing, or levels, or fades. I knew that I was passionate about local food and encouraging people to connect to place and community through the meals on their tables, and I knew that I loved to write. Somehow, it did not occur to me that radio would be any different.

My beginning lessons were in recording. The first time I brought in audio from the farmers' market Jay told me that it sounded like I was standing sev- eral states too far away. I understood what he meant — instead of just one farmer's voice, I got the noises of every passing car, the slightest rustle of a shopping bag. Uncomfortable at first, I inched my mic closer and closer. I began to get over being shy about noises and feeling like I was invading peo- ple's space, and I found that the more comfortable I got with my gear, the less anyone else seemed to notice it.

In fact, the hard part turned out not to be recording everyone else, but recording myself. When I listen to the first few shows, I cringe. Do I really talk that high, and so monotone? I've had to work a lot with Viki in the recording studio. She tries to get me to lower my voice, but keep my energy up — a bal- ance that, for me, requires constant thought. One day, I came in wearing cor- duroys and square-toed boots, and we discovered that with my hands through the belt loops, I could almost channel John Wayne. Now I try to wear my cor- duroys every time I record my narration. I've also had to learn how to vary the way I read my sentences. I tend to read every phrase the same way, with my voice starting low and rising up and falling again at the end. Viki has me read each sentence a different way, changing my inflection several times before moving on, and it always surprises me later which ones I like best — often not what felt natural to me.

I've also had to work on my writing. I had assumed, having majored in writing, that this would be the easy part. But I've discovered that writing for radio is different from writing for print; I've had a hard time toning down the style and formality of my usual essays for the ear. I've ended up resorting to writing radio scripts from the more relaxed screen of my blog and copying them later to Word documents. Somehow, switching screens changes my frame of mind.

When we first started the show, everyone's biggest worry was that there wouldn't be enough material to carry us through the winter months. Happily, that is becoming more and more impossible every year. The local food movement has exploded on the Cape since we began. When we started the show, there were summer farmers' markets only; this year, winter markets opened in Plymouth and Marstons Mills. There is a growing coalition of young farmers and more and more people focusing on the fringe foods — things such as meat and grains and beans and dairy that have been so hard to get locally. The notebook I keep taped up with newspaper clippings and e-mails and notes scribbled down from farmers' markets and meetings gets fatter every day.

With each show, it's exciting to see new local food connections spring up. After a show on a young college student learning to raise grass-fed chickens in hopes of reviving his family's Truro farm, I got three e-mails from people well connected in the local food world wanting to help get him off the ground. After a show on a woman who inherited an orchard — and with it the dream of someone she'd never met — we got an e-mail from a local book group wanting to invite her to join them. They were reading *The Orchard* by Adele Robertson, a story about another woman's struggle to save her family apple trees, and they wanted to hear the perspective of someone who'd done it herself. Both sides left thrilled.

Connections like these are a good reminder that it's the local nature of the show that makes it work. I love that we can do a show on a certain kind of lettuce or tomato sold by only one vendor, and that listeners can seek it out at the farmers' market next week. The show may be part of a national movement, but it's the local stories that bring it home. — By Elspeth Hay

YOU CAN DO THIS

LEARN TO TELL STORIES

Treat yourself. Get going by attending a storytelling workshop. Here are a few options.

The Transom Story Workshop

Attend an eight-week residency at the Transom Story Workshop (transom.org) in Woods Hole, Massachusetts, to learn the art of storytelling. Students produce five original and different types of radio segments over the course.

The Salt Institute for Documentary Studies

The Salt Institute for Documentary Studies (salt.edu) in Portland, Maine, offers workshops in writing, radio, photography, and new media.

The International Storytelling Center

Located in Jonesborough, Tennessee, the International Storytelling Center (storytellingcenter.net) envisions and manifests the art, preservation, and performance of storytelling, to enrich the history and culture of place. Its National Storytelling Festival is a yearly event held in the fall.

EULOGIES

Eulogies are a particular kind of story we all will be called upon to tell. One of the best I've heard yet was for the musician Maynard Silva given by his friend, the storyteller Susan Klein. Her words settled his memory in my heart. Though I recall no specific quotes, Maynard, the man, his memory, and his music lives on for all of us who knew him and heard Susan's story. And now I get to tell you about him, too (see page 279).

TIP   Listen to the podcast *HowSound* for insights into radio storytelling, hosted by Rob Rosenthal.

JAY ALLISON

The award-winning radio producer and founder of the NPR stations WCAI/ WNAN, Jay Allison, first wrote up "The Basics" of radio broadcasting in the 1980s, and another version was published in the Whole Earth Review *in 1991. The 2013 update, from which this is excerpted, is available on the wonderful website Transom (transom.org). Give credit and make radio!*

If you are unsatisfied with the way your public radio system portrays life as you know it, consider doing the portraying yourself. What is going on where you live? What are the important stories? Whose voices should be heard? Consider taking on the role of Citizen Storyteller, and working on a grassroots level to make public radio more truly "public." . . .

One advantage to working in radio is that you are low-impact. When setting up interviews by phone, remind your interviewees you are not a film/TV crew. It's just you and a tape recorder — non-intimidating. (They'll still ask you what channel it'll be on.)

BECOME COMFORTABLE with your equipment. If you are, everyone else will be. Check, clean, and test all your equipment before you go out. Put in fresh batteries. Make test recordings. Be over-prepared. Be a Boy Scout. Have everything set up before you walk in.

FOR VOX POP, go where people are waiting. If it seems appropriate, walk right up with your sentence about what you're doing and attach the first question to it. I've heard it suggested that the best tape comes from people in funny hats.

REMEMBER EYE CONTACT. Don't let the mic be the focus — occupying the space between you and the person you're talking to so you have to stare through it. I usually begin by holding the mic casually, as though it's unimportant. Sometimes I'll rest it against my cheek to show it has no evil powers. I might start off with an innocuous question ("Geez, is this as bad as the smog ever gets out here?"), then slowly move the mic, from below, into position at the side of the person's mouth, but not blocking eye contact. You'll find your own way of being natural with the mic, but it is important.

— Excerpted with permission from Jay Allison, "The Basics"

"The key to getting good quotes from people is not making them forget you're there, but making them interested in the fact that you're there, making them an intimate acquaintance, if only for half an hour."

— Bill McKibben, "The Pen Is Easier than the Mic," Transom (transom.org)

LOW-POWER FM RADIO (LPFM)

As Julia Wierski of the Prometheus Radio Project (prometheusradio.org) has said, the "expansion of LPFM stations means that hundreds of non-profit organizations, schools, unions, and other community groups have a unique and low-cost opportunity to develop programming to meet their local and issue-based needs." In addition to Prometheus Radio, here are some other grassroots groups supporting community radio, with its "truly local" news:

» Common Frequency (commonfrequency.org)

» Coalition of Immokalee Workers' Radio Conciencia, in Spanish (concienciaradio.com)

» Media Action Grassroots Network (mag-net.org)

» Center for Media Justice (centerformediajustice.org)

CAPITALIST POEM #5

"We used to tell long stories in poetry, and over the years the novel and film co-opted all the territory of poetry," says poet Campbell McGrath. "But I don't think poets have to stand for that."

I was at the 7-11

I ate a burrito.

I drank a Slurpee.

I was tired. It was late, after work washing dishes.

The burrito was good. I had another.

I did it every day for a week.

I did it every day for a month.

To cook a burrito you tear off the plastic wrapper.

You push button #3 on the microwave.

Burritos are large, small, or medium.

Red or green chili peppers.

Beef or bean or both.

There are 7-11's all across the nation.

On the way out I bought a quart of beer for $1.39.

I was aware of social injustice

In only the vaguest possible way.

— Reprinted with permission by Campbell McGrath, from his collection *Capitalism*

YOU CAN DO THIS

HOLD A POETRY WORKSHOP
....

At *Edible Vineyard*, we sponsored local farmers to attend a poetry workshop and write about their livestock, especially chickens. This event was initiated by local poet Samantha Barrow and was another kind of offshoot from the humane mobile poultry-processing trailer (page 104) that rolls through our farming community. Barrow was inspired by and curious about another poet (though some would say not-poet) named Nancy Luce, who lived in West Tisbury, Massachusetts, from 1814 to 1880, with her birds. Apparently quite literally. She wrote poems and eulogies about them, and today, her gravestone is decorated tenderly with all sorts of bright plastic chickens.

> Everybody had something to say about poultry and our evening's local patron saint. It wasn't long before chicken tales started flying: stories of roosters jumping rope, inheriting chickens in strange ways, children's experiences with the slaughter and of course, new reasons why She crossed the road.
>
> — Samantha Barrow, poet, director of humanities in medicine at Sophie Davis School of Biomedical Education, City College of New York

The farmers had a blast at the workshop. It was a perfect midwinter gathering, and local chicken stew was served, of course. In the end, we published some of the farmer-poets' work in an article by Barrow in *Edible Vineyard*.

You could also organize a poetry slam or a storytelling fest focused around topics such as access (Clint Smith, page 206), cooking (Campbell McGrath, page 201), and farm animals (Howard Nemerov, page 103). Barrow offers these tips:

USE POETRY and the act of creating it to focus and start a conversation.

CREATE A SAFE SPACE and have a sense of humor. All participants should be valued and feel comfortable. This requires some thought, care, and community input.

POEMS CAN HELP disrupt embedded patterns of thought in creative ways. They are frequently short and perfect for careful and/or slow readers.

OFFER STRUCTURAL FORMS, such as an acrostic. Or a recipe. Even an obituary for a farmer's chicken.

ANIMATE an inanimate object, such as an apple, a clod of dirt, a fork.

HAVING GOOD EXAMPLES is key — this gets people into the space to write.

NOBODY LIKES TO FEEL not listened to. Leave all cell phones off or not even in the room. What makes you feel listened to? Hold the group and that space in those ways.

READ a poem a day.

>×<

NATIONAL POETRY MONTH

April has been National Poetry Month since the Academy of American Poets launched the concept in 1996. Schools and libraries, publishers and poets celebrate all month with special readings, festivals, and other events. Connect your food group, school, farmers' organization, or food-related concern to celebrate poetry every day in April, bringing light to what T. S. Eliot called "the cruelest month." For more, go to the American Academy of Poets (poets.org) and/or the Poetry Foundation (poetryfoundation.org).

PUBLISH

. . . .

Submit your original poems and writings about food-related subjects to one (or more!) of these publications.

Alimentum

The journal *Alimentum*, which began in 2005 as a print publication and continues now online, is dedicated to the arts and ideas of food. Submission guidelines are found at alimentumjournal.com.

Gastronomica

Gastronomica: The Journal of Critical Food Studies, a quarterly academic journal published by the University of California Press, covers wide topics from art and culture to food history and politics, long form to poetry. The issues are collectible. Follow submission guidelines online (gastronomica.org).

Edible _____ Magazine

Edible Communities magazines are locally owned and independently published magazines specific to a locale. With any luck, you'll find them in stacks outside your grocery store, in your public libraries, at restaurants, and supported by various other local and national businesses. (Full disclosure — as of this writing I am the co-owner of one of these, *Edible Vineyard*.) *Edible* publications focus on the growing and cooking of seasonal foods and local and regional culinary traditions and can be a resource for finding farmers' markets, restaurants, and co-ops. For more information and inquiries, go to ediblecommunities.com.

INSIDEOUT LITERARY ARTS PROJECT
Detroit, Michigan

The InsideOut Literary Arts Project (insideoutdetroit.org) places professional writers into Detroit public schools to help students write poetry
and learn that they, too, are poets. In an interview on the *PBS News Hour*,
U.S. poet laureate Natasha Trethewey recounted her experience with the
project at the Marcus Garvey Academy: "It was a sense of power that they
[the students] have from being able to imagine, and to create, to name
themselves, to speak for themselves."

The school's principal, James Hearn, had expected neither the huge
popularity of the program nor the positive impacts it would have on the
middle schoolers of Marcus Garvey. "Poetry really gets them truly motivated and excited. And I'm talking about my football players, my athletes,
my basketball players want poetry," Hearn said with a huge smile.

Imagine the power of such a program themed around food, cooking,
memory, mealtimes, and the potential to unleash youngsters' confidence,
voice, and imagination. InsideOut has been doing this for almost 20 years
in Detroit. They've got wisdom to share, no doubt.

— From "Young Detroiters Unlock Their Inner Poets, Claim Authorship of Their Experiences,"
PBS News Hour

PLACE MATTERS

Clint Smith, a teacher and poet from Maryland, said in an interview with Yvonne Brown (yvonne-brown.com) that poetry provides a unique opportunity to tell the stories of those who are not given a voice. It can also give insight into our common humanity by contextualizing each of our lives relative to those around us. It's a dynamic art form that challenges our perceptions and continually allows us to think outside of ourselves. That's what I love most about it — it is a medium that enhances our empathy. Smith's performance of his spoken poem, "Place Matters," excerpted on the following page, is the best definition of what a food desert really is. You can see his live performance on the web at clintsmithiii.com.

MAP OF LIFE EXPECTANCY

RWJF Commission to Build a Healthier America

Robert Wood Johnson Foundation

LAKEWOOD
NAVERRE
FAIRGROUNDS
80 YEARS*

NEW ORLEANS, LOUISIANA

SEVENTH WARD
MID CITY
66 YEARS*
MARIGNY

GERT TOWN
TULANE GRAVIER
IBERVILLE
55 YEARS*
FRENCH QUARTER
★ NEW ORLEANS

71 YEARS*
B.W. COOPER

BROADMOOR
75 YEARS*
CENTRAL CITY

1MI *Life expectancy at birth by zip code

Factors that impact the average life expectancy of any of us include the public health environment in which we live, economic circumstances and forces, and gender. The delineation is stark and it cannot be denied how disparate these factors are amongst us.

— Copyright 2013. Robert Wood Johnson Foundation. Used with permission from the Robert Wood Johnson Foundation.

These are my students. My warriors.

Fighting a battle against an enemy

They cannot clearly see.

These kings and queens

Meant to feast, not to fester,

But their zip code has already told them

That their life expectancies are 30 years

Shorter than the county seven miles away.

I can see the faults of my own ancestry

Shaking in their eyes.

Diabetes and high blood pressure run through the

Roots of my family tree.

Heart disease is as much a part of my history as

Shackles and segregation.

So from my father's kidney transplant to Olivia's asthma,

These things are more than mere coincidence.

Both grew up in places more accustomed to

Gunshots than gardens.

So tell me place doesn't matter.

That the neighborhoods that are predominantly healthy

Aren't the same ones that are predominantly wealthy.

Because when you're not choosing between buying

Your medicine and your groceries,

Health doesn't have to be a luxury.

Doesn't have to be an abstract concept

Presented in academic journals and policy briefs.

My students overcome more every day

Than I will in my lifetime.

They are the roses that grew from the concrete.

The budding oasis in the heart of the desert

And their lives are worth far much more

Than the things that this world

Has fed them.

— Excerpted with permission from Clint Smith,
the 2013 Christine D. Sarbanes Maryland Teacher of the Year

USE MEDIA

These days, there are a lot of ways to send your letter to the world.

Websites

Build a website for your blog with tools such as Squarespace, WordPress, Tumblr, and Blogspot. Commit to updates. Include a link to your blog (or publication or radio show) on your e-mail signature. Cross-post new entries on your other social media sites, such as Facebook or Twitter.

Multiple Platforms

Storify (storify.com) is a free multi-platform tool in which you can embed story elements from social media sites such as Twitter, Instagram, YouTube, Pinterest, and Facebook, as well as audio. The word on the street is that Storify is all the rage to use for anything from making radio to writing autobiographies.

Radio

The Public Radio Exchange (prx.org) is a dynamic and democratic wellspring and archive of radio stories. Designed for listeners, producers, and radio stations, this online marketplace allows you to publish your radio program, search for stories, connect to other publishers and stations, and download audio for your programming. Anyone can upload and license a story; any station can download one. Producers are paid through the exchange.

Video

The two big choices these days are YouTube and Vimeo. There are lots of cute baby animal YouTubes, and not so much on Vimeo, where there's less fluff and the videos are more narrowly niche oriented and organized, with fewer advertisers popping in and out. Vimeo also has password protections available. But if it's purely hits you're going for, and you've got a goat that can sing backup to Taylor Swift's song "I Knew You Were Trouble," then your YouTube video just might go viral and get over a million views.

Pictures

Instagram, like Twitter, is another stream of information, only a visual one. There's room for captions, and the filters make even the worst photographer's picture look cool. I know this from personal experience. Hashtags (#) apply, searchable by topic and by user. Examples include #YouHaveEverythingYouNeed and #VoteFood.

>><<

FILMS

Films are a great way to pique peoples' interest, tug at their hearts, and motivate them to action. Films that might leave people feeling depressed or helpless are best followed up with a discussion about how to pitch in, how to organize, how to make effective change.

It's relatively easy to find the producers of an independent film. Read the credits, Google them, go to their websites. They want their films seen, so they may very well come to your viewing. It helps them and you. As for the fees? You won't know until you ask.

>><<

MICROCINEMA

Microcinema is the short of the shorts. A microcinema film might be a mere 3 minutes long, so those 180 seconds have to be compelling. A microcinema theater may seat only 50 people. Like microbatch ice cream or beer, microcinema (whether it's the film or the theater) tends to be do-it-yourself, low budget, and indie. With advances in video and film technologies and camcorders more accessible to actors, commentators, directors, editors, writers, and producers (which in this case may likely be all the same person), microcinema is a relatively new niche. These films are often distributed over the Internet, viewed in microcinema festivals, or screened in small (sometimes movable) venues. Get small. Be focused. Cut right to the bone. Search: microcinema + food and farming.

>><<

THOMAS BENA

Looking to start a food film festival? Here's advice from the founder and executive director of the Martha's Vineyard Film Festival (tmvff.org):

START SMALL, be genuine. Accept help.

START by organizing a one-off; that is, one film, one night with a discussion following it. The hardest thing to do is find the right venue and "get butts in the seats."

MARKETING and promoting the film(s) take energy and time. Following up and showing up. So play something you believe in.

SO MANY TIMES interns are grateful to just be a part of something that is grounded in truth, asks hard questions, creates community. It's the magic of other people wanting to do the right thing.

SCREEN a film with another organization. (MVFF showed *Food Inc.* with the Martha's Vineyard Slow Food group.)

SELL GOOD FOOD at your screening.

SEND OUT a request for proposals (RFP) for food for your festival, if you grow that big. The MVFF takes 25 percent of the gross, which is apparently a standard.

IF THE FILM you are screening is child-friendly, offer age-appropriate activities related to the film, if you have a talk or Q&A after the film.

OFFER a sliding-scale ticket price to make it appealing and accessible to a broad audience.

ONLINE CLASSICS

Here are a few short, award-winning online movies to kick off your film festival.

» *The Meatrix*, by Sustainable Table

» *Food MythBusters* series by Anna Lappé (some are available in Spanish and Chinese)

» *The Story of Change*, by Annie Leonard

DOCUMENTARY FILM SITES

» Culture Unplugged (cultureunplugged.com)

» Fandor (fandor.com)

» International Movie Database (imdb.com)

» Top Documentary Films (topdocumentaryfilms.com)

CHAPTER 7

Harvest

NOW ALL THE hard work comes to fruition. The big payoff. The bounties of the land and the seas are before us, in overflowing baskets and bins and sacks: greens and squashes and tomatoes, meats, fish, lactage (a styling old word for dairy) of all sorts, fruits, and grains. But like many full moments, the harvest is rife with difficulty: How exactly is all the work to get done? How can it be done quickly enough that the food gets to those who need it, without waste? I'm starting this chapter with the easy-to-overlook part of harvesting known as gleaning. Gleaners go through the fields when everyone else is done. They look in the corners and harvest the food that wasn't quite ready along with the rest or was passed by for any number of reasons. Gleaners ensure that nothing is left to waste. Gleaning is a way of honoring all the effort that's come before. It's a commitment to endurance. It's an abundance of sharing.

You can learn from the gleaners of today to start your own network (page 215) and distribute the gleaned food to those in your community who need it. You can harvest the fruit from public lands (page 221), preserve it (page 224), and distribute it to those in your community who would benefit from it. You can hunt responsibly and distribute the venison to those in your community who cannot afford quality meat (page 229). In the harvest, be smart and thoughtful. Minimize food waste, so others may not be as hungry every day of the year.

FOOD WASTE & FOOD RECOVERY

19% CONSUMER LEVEL

AT LEAST 10% PRIMARY PRODUCTION LEVEL

10% RETAIL LEVEL

WHERE WASTE OCCURS (% OF TOTAL FOOD SUPPLY)

96 billion pounds of food is wasted in the United States annually: a loss worth approximately $165 million

50.1 MILLION

Americans are food insecure

1 OUT OF 6

people in this country do not have regular access to sufficient food for an active, healthy life

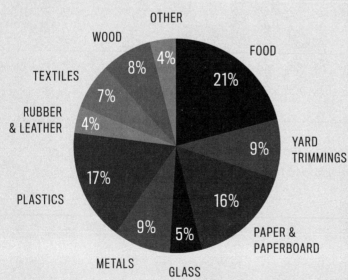

OTHER

WOOD

TEXTILES

RUBBER & LEATHER

PLASTICS

METALS

GLASS

FOOD

YARD TRIMMINGS

PAPER & PAPERBOARD

4%
8%
7%
4%
17%
9%
5%
16%
9%
21%

WHAT WE THROW AWAY

Food makes up the largest percentage of waste put into municipal landfills

— statistics from University of Arkansas School of Law's "Food Recovery: A Legal Guide"

CREATE A GLEANING NETWORK

This great advice about saving what might otherwise be wasted in your community is from Island Grown Gleaning's coordinator, Jamie O'Gorman.

Start small. Find a handful of volunteers (ideally at least one of whom is experienced with growing and harvesting vegetables). Talk to one or two farmers you have a personal connection with. Keep in mind that testing the waters and establishing systems while you are working with small quantities and small groups is easier.

VOLUNTEER MANAGEMENT

CREATE A SYSTEM for mobilizing volunteers on short notice — an e-mail list, Facebook page, or a phone tree. Most farmers offer 24 to 48 hours' notice.

INFORM VOLUNTEERS ahead of time what the crop will be, what they need to bring (gloves, pitchfork, knife, and so on), and be sure to give them directions and a meeting point at the farm.

MAKE IT EASY on farmers. Establish a key person whom the farmer will contact and who will lead the volunteers once in the field. Trust is built over time. In some cases the crop has been abandoned, so plant damage is not an issue; in other cases you are being offered a pick on plants that will continue to produce for the farmer.

BE SURE you know what you are allowed to harvest. Mark rows clearly, discuss which vegetables or fruit may be taken and which may not be. Then tread lightly and stay where you are supposed to be. Do not wander through the farm in other rows or areas without permission, and do not harvest anything else.

DECIDE AHEAD OF TIME if you will allow children or not. This can be a very important educational experience (for all involved), but you may want to wait until you have an established trust with the farmers. Children need to be closely supervised by their accompanying adult, especially when the crop is still producing.

>>

DISTRIBUTION

REUSE free empty boxes from your local grocer or liquor store. Beer boxes are ideal for holding 20 pounds of just about anything, although they may not be appropriate if you are using them in places where folks may be in recovery from addictions. Plastic kitchen trash bags will hold 7 to 10 pounds of produce, and work well for greens like lettuce, kale, bok choy. Empty feed bags are good for bulky crops like corn. Ask your local grocer to save the mesh bags that onions and potatoes ship in — they're really good for potatoes, as the dirt falls out and they can dry a little.

STANDARDIZE units of weight to make distribution to various places easier. If every box of squash weighs 20 pounds, you can count the boxes up rather than doing inordinate amounts of math!

FOLLOW UP with those whom you distribute to. Check on quantities. Can they use more? Or less? Do they have storage issues? Are there some crops that move better than others?

LET EVERYONE bring home some of the harvest for themselves. Bring paper or plastic grocery bags just for this purpose. Allowing folks to bring home food is a nice way to thank them for their services and may be a motivating factor in some cases. Promote this option in your food pantry or soup kitchen, and you may get a lot of helpers! "Do you want to bring some home

for dinner?" is a good question and suggests portion control. If someone seems to want extra, it's probably because they need it. In my experience, some people won't take anything, most take a little to try (a great way to introduce people to the goodness of fresh local food), and a few take a bagful. You will get to know which members of your harvest team/s are in need, if you don't already.

DELIVERING the produce the same day is usually easiest. Develop a system to let people know when the food will arrive. If they are on the volunteer recruitment e-mail list they will know anytime there is an upcoming glean. Some crops, such as greens, are highly perishable and will need to be refrigerated as soon as possible, while others can stay on the back of a truck in the shade overnight. There may be a walk-in cooler in the community that you can use to store things short term as needed. Ask around.

CREATE a tracking system. Weigh the produce and keep a list of how much of what crop goes to what organization. If you use an online spreadsheet, you can add farmers to it so they can track their own donations. If you are a nonprofit, be sure to send them a donation letter at the end of the season for tax purposes. We usually send quantities and let the farmer place the value.

GENERAL

RELATIONSHIPS are key. Endeavor to develop good working relationships with farmers, volunteers, and those who run the recipient programs or kitchens. We all need to work together for best results.

ONLY BASIC TOOLS are needed to start. You'll want some harvesting tools (pocket knives, a fork or two for root crops, and a scale; we used bathroom scales at first, but package scales work better — Uline has some good shipping ones). Gloves are nice for some crops, but some folks can bring their own. You need bags and boxes (ideally recycled and disposable that you can leave when you drop off the produce), and you'll want to have a first-aid kit, including some poison ivy wash and a snack or two for diabetic emergencies. A gallon of water and some Dixie cups are good for very hot weather when people forget to bring their own to the field. Now you're ready for anything!

KEEP program costs low. They should be proportionate to the amount you are harvesting. If your expenses are much over $1/pound for delivered food, you might as well buy farm seconds and save your volunteers a lot of work!

WHEN YOU ARE READY to grow, promote the program. Take photos to share, talk to the press, advertise in "things to do" listings online, on radio, and in print (see page 208). Create a flyer to share information about the program.

>⟩⟨⟨

Have fun! Gleaning is a joyful act of service.

— Printed with permission from Jamie O'Gorman

TIP : Have volunteers sign a permission and waiver form.

THE BILL EMERSON GOOD SAMARITAN FOOD DONATION ACT OF 1996

The Bill Emerson Good Samaritan Food Donation Act of 1996 exempts those who make good-faith donations of food and grocery products to nonprofit organizations that feed the hungry from liability for injuries arising from the consumption of the donated food. The U.S. Department of Agriculture has identified four basic types of food recovery: field gleaning, perishable produce rescue or salvage, perishable and prepared food rescue, and nonperishable processed food collection. The Bill Emerson Act provides liability protection for all four types of activities.

Purposes of the Bill Emerson Act

TO ESTABLISH a uniform national law to protect organizations and individuals when they donate food and grocery items in good faith.

TO ENCOURAGE the donation of food and grocery products to nonprofit organizations for distribution to needy individuals.

"PERSONS," "gleaners," and "nonprofit organizations" all receive protection from the Bill Emerson Act.

— Excerpted with permission from *Food Recovery: A Legal Guide,* by the LL.M. Program in Agricultural and Food Law at the University of Arkansas School of Law

RESOURCES FOR GLEANING

If you are going to start any kind of food recovery program, please do your legal homework. Understand the provisions of the Bill Emerson Act (see opposite page). *Food Recovery: A Legal Guide,* produced by the LL.M. Program in Agricultural and Food Law at the University of Arkansas School of Law with generous support from the University of Arkansas Women's Giving Circle, is a good place to start. Note, though, that it does not replace licensed legal advice in your state and should not be used as such.

THE U.S. DEPARTMENT OF AGRICULTURE has some good resources on this topic. Look for its *Citizen's Guide to Food Recovery* (1999) and online Food Safety Information.

DANA GUNDERS, of the Natural Resources Defense Council, has an excellent paper that shows how a great deal of our food problem begins with waste. See *Wasted: How America Is Losing Up to 40 Percent of Its Food from Farm to Fork to Landfill* (August 2011).

THE SOCIETY OF ST. ANDREW'S website (endhunger.org) lists local gleaning programs and other resources, and you can list your program there.

AMPLE HARVEST (ampleharvest.org) connects backyard gardeners with food pantries so that excess produce can be shared with those in need.

A GLEANING REPORT

This account of a week of October gleaning on Martha's Vineyard in 2013 is from Jamie O'Gorman to her Googlegroup (a handy way to organize a group, by the way). When does gleaning peak where you live?

Island Grown Gleaning organized seven gleans last week at three different farms . . . for a total of 3,853 pounds of produce — all distributed at no cost to our recipient organizations! **3,853 pounds — can you believe it?!** Just imagine what might have happened to all of that nutritious, delicious food if it were not for the generosity of our local farmers and our volunteer harvesting crew.

We started the week off right — by bagging and distributing 1,000 pounds of sweet potatoes from North Tabor Farm on Monday morning. They were beautiful and perfect, with the largest weighing several pounds each!

Later that same day, we made an inspiring visit to the prolific pepper patch at Whippoorwill Farm and drove away with 640 pounds of the sweet, lovely fruit.

Our regular Tuesday glean at Morning Glory was graced by four new volunteers, and we needed their help for sure! It was a veritable gleaning buffet of lettuce, bok choy, corn, arugula, and radishes (totaling 736 pounds).

On Wednesday, Nicole Cabot of Island Grown Schools helped facilitate a gleaning field trip for the 5th graders from West Tisbury School. The energy of the students was amazing — they picked almost 500 pounds of tomatoes and peppers in less than an hour! The next day's pre-frost glean at Whippoorwill yielded 300 pounds of peppers and some healthy kale as well.

But our volunteers did not stop there — Marjorie, Carol, Jeanne, and Janet headed directly from Whippoorwill to Morning Glory, where they knew more tomatoes were at risk of being lost to the impending frost. They harvested 315 pounds, delivered to the Edgartown School, the high school, and Woodside Village and then used the rest to make sauce for free community meals this winter.

By the time Friday rolled around, Simon Athearn called us to say that they had some extra corn (already picked). Priya and Uma came through and made sure that 360 pounds of sweet corn would be put to good use by seniors and disabled folks living at Woodside and Hillside Village, and those in sober living/recovery at Island House.

The Saturday morning rainbow summed our week up perfectly. I am so proud and so grateful to be a witness to this wonderful work. Here's to the future success of our farmers, and to the good health of our volunteers!

— Excerpted with permission from Jamie O'Gorman

HARVEST PUBLIC FRUIT TREES

Public fruit trees and edible plants can be harvested. In fact, anyone's trees can be harvested if they hang over a public street or sidewalk — though I'm not encouraging you to just grab fruit from your neighbors' trees unless you have permission! Under Roman law's concept of *usufruct,* plants can be harvested if no damage is caused to the owner. Public trees are part of our common good. If people stop and want to know what you're doing, explain. Offer them a taste!

City Fruit (see page 222) has a free, downloadable PDF of its booklet *Gather It! How to Organize an Urban Fruit Harvest.* The step-by-step guidance is based on Solid Ground's Community Fruit Tree Harvest Project, which started in 2005 in Seattle. Here is their condensed version of the steps that will help you plan for a volunteer-based harvest. See their booklet for full elaboration.

Planning

1. Decide on the scope

2. Set up a steering committee

3. Decide how to gather information

Laying the Ground Work

4. Recruit fruit tree donors

5. Find equipment and storage locations

6. Recruit and train volunteers

7. Decide how to use the fruit

Harvesting

8. Develop a scheduling plan

9. Harvest and deliver the fruit

Wrapping Up

10. Manage harvest data

11. Say thank you

— Excerpted with permission of Solid Ground

USUFRUCT

See the Latin roots of "use" and "fruit" in this word?

u·su·fruct |'yü–zə–frəkt,–sə–| noun: the right to enjoy the use and advantages of another's property, short of the destruction or waste of its substance.

CITY FRUIT
Seattle, Washington

The nonprofit City Fruit works to use and steward urban fruit trees as a community resource. According to its website (cityfruit.org), its goals are:

CONSERVATION: Preserve fruit trees on public and private properties; document historical orchards.

PRESERVATION OF THE URBAN TREE CANOPY: Increase fruit trees planted on public and private properties; map fruit trees.

STEWARDSHIP: Improve the care of fruit trees and reduce the impact of fruit pests and diseases using non-toxic methods.

HARVEST: Increase the amount of fruit harvested by supporting harvesting groups, developing the capacity of neighborhoods to harvest, and promoting harvesting by tree owners.

USING AND SHARING FRUIT: Develop the capacity of people and groups to preserve fruit; explore the income-generating potential of urban fruit; effectively link those who have fruit with those who need it.

COMMUNITY BUILDING: Build and strengthen connections within community groups through the planting, stewardship, harvest, and/or preservation of fruit.

FALLEN FRUIT
Los Angeles, California

The art collective Fallen Fruit is, according to its website (fallenfruit.org), "an art collaboration originally conceived in 2004 by David Burns, Matias Viegener, and Austin Young." Fallen Fruit got its start making maps of public fruit trees in Los Angeles, and the project continues today. The simple, hand-drawn maps depict a city block or two, or the public fruit trees around a public building, such as the L.A. County Museum of Art. They're micromaps of fruit to be had, made with local knowledge. Fallen Fruit has also hosted public Fruit Jams, where the public is invited "to transform homegrown or public fruit and join in communal jam-making as experimentation in personal narrative and sublime collaboration." Its Nocturnal Fruit Forages, an evening stroll through a neighborhood's fruit trees, explores the "boundaries of public and private space at the edge of darkness." Sounds fun!

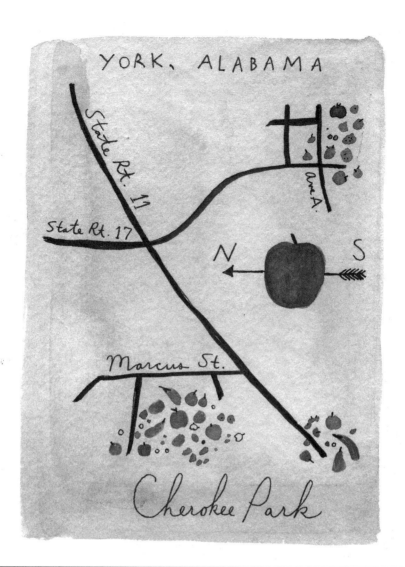

EATING ON THE ROAD

Traveling across the country or even in your own state? All you need is a zip code or a town name to help find farmers' markets, co-ops, products, or farms. And maybe you can help bring a farmers' market to a highway rest stop in your own area (page 95).

» Eat Well Guide (eatwellguide.org)

» Local Harvest (localharvest.org)

» Real Time Farms (realtimefarms.com)

EXTEND THE HARVEST

I've come across them on Facebook and read about them in e-mailed newsletters from organizations around the country: canneries, community kitchens, canning shares. Some are big and geared toward incubating small businesses and entrepreneurs, such as La Cocina in San Francisco (lacocinasf.org), and others are small pop-ups just for the harvest season when a neighborhood or a group of friends will get together with their own jars and lids, tomatoes and peaches, and canners and harvests, and put up the harvests to extend the season. Sometimes they're in church kitchens. Or a grange. And everyone pitches in for the rental fee of the kitchen and sharing such equipment as apple pulpers, food mills, and funnels for the day (or days) of work. The Mennonite Central Committee operates a mobile meat canner that travels across North America canning beef, pork, turkey, and chicken for hunger relief efforts (mcc.org).

There's no one-size-fits-all or one-vision-fits-all in local canneries or community kitchens (page 275). What's great about them is that they provide a place and a chance to learn how to can safely and extend the harvest.

Maybe you're ready to start a canning club or a canning swap (a great time to trade some dilly beans for some kimchi), organize a Discover You Can: Learn Make Share Program at your local farmers' market (page 243), or launch a food recovery program (page 250). If you're finding a rogue zucchini or summer squash left anonymously on the windshield of your car, your front door, or mailbox, maybe that's a sign that it's time to set up a local cannery.

DEFINE what it is you want to do in putting up your harvest: Is it for yourself or do you want to start a business? Who is the organizer, and what's the best way to communicate? Have a potluck with a purpose (page 23)!

FIND A PRACTICAL SPACE that reflects your vision. Consider the plumbing and the sink(s), the stove, cleanliness, space for canning, table space for cooling, refrigeration, access (stairs, handicap), hours, location, associated fees, and parking.

ASK your state Extension agent for guidelines to safe handling and safe canning practices. If you intend to give your put-up foods to a pantry or another outlet as a donation, find out their requirements before you start canning to make sure your process fits their criteria.

WILL YOU ASK for a monetary contribution from the canners? From a quick Internet search, I learned that some local canneries charge a processing fee of 15 cents per pint or quart jar, and $1 for a gallon, plus an annual fee to help offset space and shared equipment costs.

BEFORE the growing season starts, connect with local farmers during their quieter time to plan to get in on their second harvests or overages. Do this before they get super busy during the harvest season.

FORAGE WILD FOODS

Foraging for food is something I wish I had the confidence and know-how to do. Every time I walk my dog down a dirt road and I see a mushroom that looks like the edible chicken of the woods variety, I think, do it! Or the berries that ripen into almost-look-like wild blueberries, or seaweed that washes up on shore, I am tempted. But instead, I refrain, in a smart albeit fearful way, because I know that I am no wild food forager. Maybe someday I'll become one, but for now, I'm not stalking the wild asparagus. No matter if it's growing in a city, in a town, or in the forest. That, and much more, I'll leave to the local experts. Nevertheless, here's some advice about getting started. (Maybe I'll even take myself up on it!)

KNOW what's edible and what's not. Get a good guide and forage responsibly. Harvest only what you can eat, and don't take it all or it won't propagate. The general forager's rule of thumb is two out of three. Leave one-third behind.

THERE ARE some areas you want to avoid because of safety reasons and/or high pesticide use, such as under power lines, along big-box-store parking lots, railways, and the side of roadways.

ASK PERMISSION before you go foraging. Trespassing is trespassing. Learn what's endangered, what's toxic or poisonous. Go with someone more knowledgeable than you. Find a mentor. This is especially important when foraging for wild mushrooms!

WATCH OUT for loose rocks, branches that can't hold you, and poison ivy and ticks — the nonedibles!

ATTEND a local workshop or foraging hike. Check out arboretums and land conservation organizations in your area for educational opportunities.

INVITE a reputable forager to speak to your group about foraging.

CHECK OUT these sites for more info:

» Eat Here Now (eatherenow.org)
» Wild Edible (wildedible.com)
» Eat the Weeds (eattheweeds.com)

>|<

THE LOCAL WILD FOOD CHALLENGE

Founded in 2008, the Local Wild Food Challenge hosts its events in six locations around the world. The founders, Bill and Sarah Manson, work collaboratively with local contacts to help plan, promote, and run a challenge. They inspire chefs and home cooks of all ages (especially kids!) to create dishes with local, responsibly foraged ingredients. Dishes are judged (by wild locals, too) for ingredients, effort, taste, and presentation. The Local Wild Food Challenges are held in great spirit and for the fun of harvesting and cooking wild foods. They also connect people to their local environments and their community in new and unexpected ways. One example is the entry consisting of wild cranberry, Russian olive, and local honey-glazed mallard duck breast with confit duck leg, fried wild onion, whipped Jerusalem artichokes, sautéed chicken of the woods, and watercress salad with crab apple grape dressing that won Everett Whiting the grand prize in the 2013 challenge held on Martha's Vineyard.

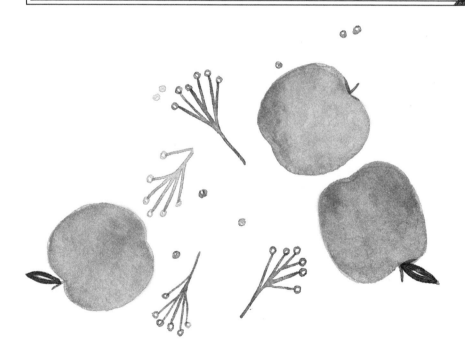

IT'S NOT FOR EVERYONE, BUT . . .

I remember telling a friend from Kentucky about the roadkill list we have here on Martha's Vineyard. I've never signed up for the list myself. I hear it's a long wait, and frankly it's not my cup of tea. But here it is: in the unfortunate occasion of a collision between a deer and a car that ends in the injury or fatality of the animal, if you're next on the list, you get a call to come collect the carcass to take home to butcher and stock your freezer. (Note: Meat from these instances is strictly for home use only. It is never for the marketplace.)

I thought it seemed a reasonable program to have. It's resourceful, and the deer's life is not a total waste. At least some of the venison can be salvaged, and some folks have an inexpensive way of getting meat. It's not quite turning a sow's ear into a silk purse or squeezing lemonade when life gives you lemons, but it's kind of close.

My friend listened, thought about it a minute or so, and summed it up as only he could, in his thick gravy of a Kentucky accent. "Oh, that is a sad shame. You poor people up there — you don't even know how to hunt for yourself. You gotta wait till a car does it for you."

WHAT'S GOING ON

THE INTERNATIONAL HUNTER EDUCATION ASSOCIATION-USA
Denver, Colorado

The time to learn how to hunt is not during hunting season, but well before. The International Hunter Education Association-USA (ihea.com) offers online courses and a database of the United States, Canada, and Mexico that provides important state-by-state information, such as the licensing agency, hunter education, and orange requirements. The association's *Hunter's Handbook* is available for free, and you can read the digital edition online.

HUNTERS FOR THE HUNGRY
Big Island, Virginia

Since its inception in 1991, Hunters for the Hungry (h4hungry.org) has donated over five million pounds of commercially processed venison to those in need throughout the state of Virginia. That's 20.9 million servings of this lean, high-protein meat. The average distribution is 400,000 pounds of venison a year. As a nonprofit that works throughout the entire state of Virginia, Hunters for the Hungry manages an up-to-date list of commercial processors to cut, wrap, and freeze the meat from the legally harvested, fully dressed deer that hunters donate. The venison is in turn donated to organizations as close to the source as possible.

FISHING

The first and last fish I ever caught was a bullhead, pulled out of the root-beer-colored water of Lake Wingra in Madison, Wisconsin. It gulped my spitball of Wonder Bread bait that hung from my tree-branch rod. Scared of its whiskers and convinced I'd get stung, I rode home as fast as I could on my pink-orange Schwinn Varsity, the fish dangling from the hook. With every other feverish downpedal, the dead fish bounced off the front wheel's spokes. Finally, with the fish bruised and battered, and myself adrenaline rushed, I pulled into the front yard, jumped off my bike, found Paul (my father), and proudly showed him my first catch ever.

My father was a sometime fisherman, and I knew he'd know what to do with my trophy, such as it was, including taking it off the hook. He did know what to do — and he made me do it, step by step. I had to follow his instructions, beginning with sharpening the knife and pulling out the hook, and proceeding to gutting and cleaning the fish. By the end of my tutorial, a measly three-inch fillet was all that was left, and that's probably this fisherman's exaggeration at that. He made me eat it, dredged in more Wonder Bread crumbs and fried in fat, for our 6:00 p.m.–sharp family dinner.

That bullhead and my father made a persuasive pair. They taught me early on that all the fish in the sea, and in the rivers, lakes, and streams, won't have to worry about me putting another line in their waters. Taking a creature's life, especially a wild one, even if it does have scary whiskers and it can be dinner, is not something I want to do.

START A FILLET PROGRAM

The Martha's Vineyard Striped Bass & Bluefish Derby (mvderby.com) has been an annual event on the island since the end of World War II. In addition to the general camaraderie and fun stirred up by the month-long event, "Derby," as it is affectionately called, is committed to community outreach, and one of their programs donates fresh fish to local senior citizens. Utilizing mostly volunteers, the Derby assembles a team that is responsible for filleting, then transporting the fish to local centers. The result? Each year, 5,000 to 7,000 ready-to-cook fresh fish are donated to happy elders.

><<

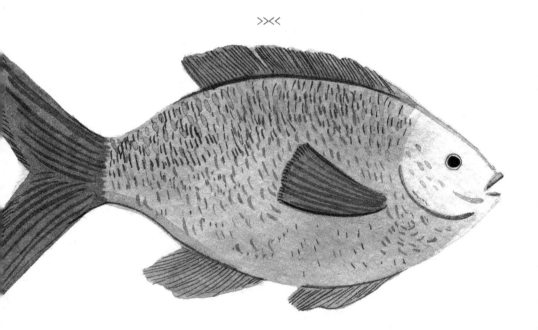

TIP As with hunting, take some steps to learn how to fish *before* you throw a hook in the water. This includes rules, regulations, and licenses. Contact your state's fish and wildlife agency to get started. This applies to harvesting shellfish as well.

YOU CAN DO THIS

CHOOSE FISH WISELY

The next big push in the good food movement needs to get out to sea, for the sake of oceans, wildlife, fishermen, and consumers — and our planet. This is an appeal from an admitted landlubber for more focus, diversity, and adaptability across boundaries and boats, technologies, and policies regarding seafood and fisheries. And all your magical action takes place down below, in water that we can't breathe, for fish we can't see.

As an eater, one thing I try to do and you can, too, is to eat seasonal, local fish, and all kinds of it. Not just cod, tuna, or salmon. Shop like you mean it, as you already may be doing with the other fresh foods in your basket. Seafoodwatch.org is host to updated sustainable seafood information, and the Northwest Atlantic Marine Alliance (NAMA) offers these guides to negotiating the fishmonger's best, wherever you live:

SEVEN PRINCIPLES FOR CHOOSING SEAFOOD

1. BUY from local fishermen whenever possible.

2. CHOOSE seafood that has traveled the least distance.

3. CHOOSE WILD seafood whenever possible.

4. AVOID farmed finfish and shrimp.

5. AVOID FAKE or imitation seafood products.

6. GET INVOLVED in a Community Supported Fishery (CSF).

7. ASK HOW, where, and when your seafood was caught.

— Northwest Atlantic Marine Alliance (namanet.org)

CHAPTER 8

Feed

NOT A DAY goes by that we are not fed by someone or something such as a business, food bank, or a corporation. Whether we give, produce, or provide food for ourselves or for others, it's inevitable and intractable: we feed one another. In a book like this, one that looks at how you can do one or many things to improve your food communities, ask this very simple question: If all were equal, would people choose to have no access to healthy food?

In my view, that's a quick and easy answer. No.

No one would choose to have limited access to fresh fruits and vegetables, quality protein and dairy, for themselves and their families. That's an absurd notion. But pitifully, things are not equal. Generations are being raised on the sugar, salt, and fat of highly processed foods. Frankly, there's a lot of bleak out there. Still, light shines through. And it does in the form of innovative food entrepreneurs. We need more of such people and businesses, such as local grocery stores (page 236), food desert grocers (page 242), and food recovery projects (page 250). Much about choice and access has to do with real-life living wages. By raising the minimum wage (page 248) while supporting education at the same time (chapter 2, page 30), the gaps will come together, closer and closer. We can do this.

NAVIGATING THE AISLES

Grocery stores are fascinating. All kinds of them. From big-box to bodegas, and not just for the food but for how people walk through them and what they choose, for the music that's playing or not playing, what condition the produce is in, what kind of meat is sold, what's stacked up at the aisle ends, the lighting, the refrigeration, how they display the most sugary cereals and snacks in glow-in-the-dark packaging, right at kids' eye level. Once you break supermarkets' code — from their prime product placement on low shelves and end caps, to the coupons pushing processed foods — it becomes obvious who's in charge of our food choices: it's agribusinesses. This includes direct marketing to children, by using cartoon characters to hawk candylike cereals, sugar-filled yogurts, and Lunchables. For all of us hipsters, millennials, mamas, papas, baby boomers, and kids, there are marketing strategies and products designed to attract our dollars, too. Businesses have something they're trying to sell you and your target market demographic.

The typical grocery store appears as though it has tremendous variety. Walking through aisles of well-packaged choices with items on sale, and maybe coupons in hand, is dizzying. It's overwhelming even, with the fluorescent light-ing and bright packaging. It seems as though you, the consumer, have choices, and if you're clever, you can save money — double-couponing, rebates, and all. You can also save time by purchasing processed or ready-to-eat meals, snacks, and other convenience items so you have more time to do whatever else is more important.

But the reality is, grocery stores provide a lot less choice than it seems. About ten corporations own what we think are different and independent brands. For example, Coca-Cola owns Dasani and Vitaminwater. General Mills owns Lucky Charms and Green Giant. The other big eight are Johnson & Johnson, Kellogg's, Mondelēz International, Mars, Nestlé, PepsiCo, Procter & Gamble, and Unilever. And meat and poultry? According to Grace Communications Foundation, as of 2007, just four companies controlled more than 80 percent of the country's beef processing, and three of these same companies (with an additional fourth) processed more than 60 percent of our pork. For chicken, the situation is not quite as extreme, but still the four main chicken companies process more than half of the country's chickens.

SHOPPING TIPS

Anyone who's ever gone into the grocery store with a child knows who is in charge of what goes in your cart. Feed your kids before you go in. You're less likely to have a battle in the cereal aisle.

For that matter, feed yourself before you go grocery shopping. You'll buy better food and less sugar, salt, and fat.

Shop the borders of the grocery store. That's where you'll find whole foods. The processed and frozen foods tend to be placed in the middle.

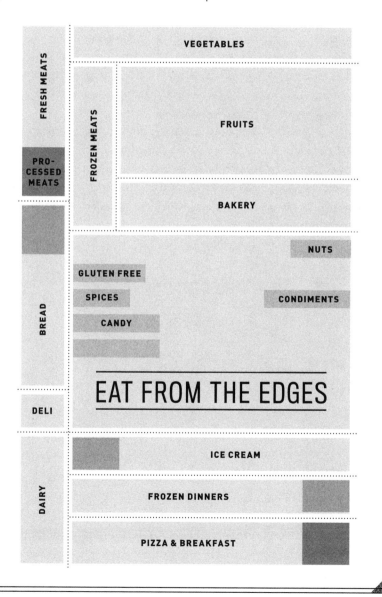

FRESH MEATS

PROCESSED MEATS

FROZEN MEATS

VEGETABLES

FRUITS

BAKERY

NUTS

GLUTEN FREE

SPICES

CONDIMENTS

CANDY

BREAD

EAT FROM THE EDGES

DELI

ICE CREAM

DAIRY

FROZEN DINNERS

PIZZA & BREAKFAST

YOU CAN DO THIS

SUPPORT A LOCAL GROCERY STORE

Shift the shop. Instead of purchasing couponed convenience, find community and sustenance at a locally owned and independently operated grocer.

Grocery stores are community bedrock. They reflect us. Is your neighborhood store (if you have one) convenient and someplace where you want to shop? Does it pay and treat its employees fairly? Does it feel safe? What's the quality of the fresh food like? Does it even offer fresh food? Is it a pleasurable shopping experience, or do you feel scammed every time you go there?

Introduce yourself or your organization to the owners or managers of your local grocery store. Let them know you want healthy whole foods. As in any other institution, from a school cafeteria to a hospital, change in the grocery industry can be difficult if not downright threatening. Demystify and clarify your intentions and purpose, diplomatically. "The customer is always right," it's said. You are the customer.

>×<

START A FOOD MILES LABELING PROGRAM

Metcalfe's Market (shopmetcalfes.com), which operates four stores in Wisconsin, has an innovative way of announcing local produce and products. It puts a food miles label on many of its goods. Produce, beverages, dairy, meats, fish, chicken, and small-batch items such as chocolate, condiments, crackers, and desserts get special signage that includes the town of origin and how far the product traveled to get to the store. It's so simple and effective. And instead of promoting specific farmers and producers with portrait posters — which are beautiful and do put a face on the local farmer, grower, or producer but are expensive to print and maintain — these food miles signs give buyers easy and immediate information about where their food comes from and allow buyers, not someone else, to decide what is local.

Food miles labels illustrate the inextricable link between food and energy and provide a launching point for talking about why some foods travel more miles than others. Coffee, for one, is going to keep coming from far away. Distances are relative based on seasonality, consumer demand, distribution routes, and infrastructure or lack of it, as in access to slaughterhouses (page 104) for small family farmers or commercial kitchens. Wouldn't it be great to have food miles labeling in grocers around the country, celebrating and raising awareness of how far food is traveling from anywhere to anywhere else? It would shed light on personal decision making, spark discussion, and prompt action.

Nature abhors a vacuum. So do local food systems. Showing how far food has to travel may very well stimulate and encourage new farmers; new growers; new value-added producers such as cheese, ice cream, and beverage makers; and new business incubator kitchens to support them.

A NONPROFIT GROCERY STORE: FARE & SQUARE
Chester, Pennsylvania

Fare & Square (fareandsquare.org), in Chester, Pennsylvania, is the first nonprofit supermarket in the United States. It provides consistent quality and access to health foods in a town that hadn't had a grocer since 2001. In the first ten weeks of Fare & Square's opening in 2012, its membership reached 47,000. With free membership enrollment, individuals and families receive special discounts, and a percentage of purchases is applied as a discount toward future buys. This is one way to incentivize healthy food purchases and engage regular customers.

The New Markets Tax Credit helped give this nonprofit grocery, which is a project of the traditional food bank Philabundance (philabundance .org), the credibility it needed to secure funders. What's more, 45 jobs were created, and Fare & Square fills those positions with locals as much as it can. This is a small grocer model for other food deserts and the non-profits that work in those communities.

FINANCING HEALTHY FOOD PROJECTS

SEARCH the Healthy Food Access Portal (healthyfoodaccess.org). This online resource for food retailers, brought to you by The Food Trust, The Reinvestment Fund, and PolicyLink, was launched in 2013. A veritable wealth of good food and public health information resides here, including retail strategies, information about mobile markets (like the one in Worcester, Massachusetts, page 107), incentives, loans, policy efforts, grants, webinars on food hubs (page 86), and model programs across the country.

THE NEW MARKETS TAX CREDIT, available through the Community Development Financial Institutions (CDFI) Fund (cdfifund.gov) of the U.S. Department of the Treasury, is well suited to large projects such as "food desert" grocers in the 60,000- to 70,000-square-foot range (page 242). Smaller projects may find the application process cumbersome.

LOOK for other CDFI funds, like The Reinvestment Fund (trfund.com), which played a role in the development of the public/private project Fare & Square Market (page 237). The CDFI's "Financing Healthy Food Options Resource Bank" is a wealth of web-based information, including training curriculums and webinars such as "Understanding the Grocery Industry," "Underwriting Supermarkets and Grocery Stores," and "Identifying Optimal Areas for Supermarket Development."

THE HEALTHY FOOD FINANCING INITIATIVE (HFFI) is a federal financing initiative to spur community economic development projects in areas recognized as food deserts. The HFFI is supported by the U.S. Department of Agriculture, the U.S. Treasury, and the U.S. Department of Health and Human Services, and its goal is to increase access to underserved communities through funding local private/public partnerships and businesses focused on grocers, small retailers such as corner stores and bodegas, and farmers' markets. Businesses, local tribes, nonprofits, universities, and community development corporations are a few of the kinds of organizations that may be eligible. For more information about grant opportunities, go to the Let's Move website (letsmove.gov).

UPLIFT SOLUTIONS
Westfield, New Jersey

Founded in 2008 by CEO Jeff Brown of Brown's Super Stores (page 242), UpLift Solutions (upliftsolutions.org) works on projects all over the country and all types of formats, including small and large stores, community cooperative-owned, nonprofit/food bank–owned, and Internet delivery services. According to Brown, he and his colleagues quickly learned that every situation really requires a different solution.

Regardless of geography, store format, or ownership structure, UpLift offers technical assistance that includes obtaining public and private support and financing and any other support needed, such as recruiting and training a management team.

RED TOMATO
Plainville, Massachusetts

Red Tomato (redtomato.org) was founded in 1996, when Michael Rozyne, one of the founders of the fair trade cooperative Equal Exchange, decided to apply the lessons learned working for fair trade of coffee to produce. This nonprofit works to connect regional farmers with the marketplace to bring fresh, sustainably grown produce into local grocery stores at wholesale prices. For me, I think of Red Tomato as a hybrid between a nonprofit (like La Semilla, page 88) that works to improve the PAD value chain (page 87) and a smart, savvy business enterprise that knows there's demand from the consumer for fresh, traceable, safe, and whole food and who figures out how to get it to them and pays the farmer a fair price for her food. Red Tomato has posted a great two-minute video on YouTube called "Local Food in Every Shopping Cart" that explains what they're up to in language even a kid can understand.

DISTRIBUTION

Distributing food on a local level is like building a sand castle every day, all day. Like what most of our food system is based on, distribution becomes more cost-effective at a large scale, which is why it may be cheaper to ship sweet potatoes from California to South Carolina than to grow culturally appropriate, indigenous sweet potatoes and get them out to local and regional markets. Distributors are efficient at shipping hard green tomatoes, a product more road-durable than a Hostess Strawberry Sno Ball, from Florida across the country. But getting the food value chain (page 90) to become efficient at shipping, say, vine-ripe tomatoes is another thing altogether. With rising fuel costs, economies of local and regional scale, technologies in mapping, and healthy food initiatives, a change in distribution is a necessity — and that's a good thing. So as they say about Vegas, perhaps what grows in California should stay (mostly!) in California, and what grows in South Carolina should feed people locally.

WHAT'S GOING ON

FOODHUB
Portland, Oregon

FoodHub (food-hub.org) is a project of the nonprofit EcoTrust in Portland, Oregon. It's both a marketplace and an interactive directory. As of this writing, it's free to join. If you're a buyer, seller, organization, nonprofit, government agency, food or agriculture trade association, or distributor, this is the place to find each other, do business, and make connections.

FoodHub is currently operating in Oregon, Washington, Idaho, Montana, Alaska, and California, but its Local Food/Tech Landscape resource transcends state borders.

YOU CAN DO THIS

MAKE FOOD DISTRIBUTION EFFICIENT

In preparing its report *Creating a Regional Food Hub: Assessments and Recommendations for Dona Ana County,* La Semilla Food Center in New Mexico found that distribution is usually "the most expensive component" of the processing, aggregation, and distribution triad (or PAD, page 87) for organizations and enterprises, especially for those working with highly perishable items; tomatoes, for example. Here are some of La Semilla's suggestions.

COSTS can be covered and net revenue is possible with careful planning of delivery times and routes.

THE MOST IMPORTANT determinant of net costs is whether or not delivery trucks are full. Plan accordingly.

MOST FOOD SHIPPERS charge a per-case delivery fee; the more cases that are on the truck, the more revenue is generated. Local and regional distribution systems have an advantage over national distribution, by being able to charge less and remain competitive.

COSTS OF DELIVERY include rental or lease costs of vehicles, or loan payments and maintenance costs, fuel/oil, road and vehicle taxes and fees, and insurance.

OTHER CONSIDERATIONS for distributions are proper refrigeration temperatures, secure wrapping of pallets, proper loading, dock timing for deliveries, driver training, and following Federal Highway Safety Administration rules.

— Excerpted from *Creating a Regional Food Hub: Assessments and Recommendations for Dona Ana County,* La Semilla Food Center (lasemillafoodcenter.org)

BECOME A FOOD DESERT GROCER

Jeff Brown is the president and CEO of Brown's Super Stores, a chain of 11 stores operating as ShopRite supermarkets, 7 of which are in former food deserts in the Philadelphia area. Jeff also started the nonprofit UpLift Solutions (see page 239) to support grocery stores of all shapes and sizes in becoming financially sustainable in underserved communities around the country, be they rural or urban. He is a practical, innovative entrepreneur who offers the following sage business advice and encouragement for the innovative grocer.

Ideally, the best outcomes include a great, proven grocery entrepreneur with lots of experience in the retail supermarket business, maybe even multiple generations. Location is everything in retail stores. Food desert locations are best with dense population, at the intersection of two major roads, with traffic lights so you can get to the store from every direction, and, most importantly, fantastic access to public transportation. It's pretty normal for 50 percent of the food desert population not to have cars, so they depend on public transportation. Supply chain is important: a low-cost wholesaler or cooperative will allow the store to have competitive pricing and marketing programs. Many people of the least means aspire to have a store that measures up to the standards of price, variety, quality, and appearance that you see in more affluent neighborhoods. Offering less is seen as disrespect to the community.

Because the level of diversity, widely varying family income, and the suspicion that society generally acts as if only more affluent people know what's best, rich and personal community engagement is critical. In my work, from the beginning of evaluating a location/community, through design and construction, and on an ongoing basis after the store is open, an entrepreneur needs to deeply understand the community's way of looking at things, what their challenges are, and not just food access. If a trusting relationship develops, there will be a lot to learn, including issues of formerly incarcerated people, violence, drugs, religious conflicts, and so forth.

I have found that all of these community challenges need to be considered in an entrepreneur's plans. If a challenge is ignored, it will end up being a bigger problem. In our work, we have strategies to deal with graffiti, gun violence, predatory financial service, inadequate availability of health care, employment of the formerly incarcerated, job opportunities, religious conflict, and so forth. Besides the social and moral benefits of this work, it turns out to significantly accelerate the success of the store. If you have a personal relationship with community leaders, you will also learn about differences that require special products and/or services. For example, I have learned about and have authentic products for our Muslim/Jewish customers, western African, Jamaican, southern African American, and so on. Similar to the additional services, it significantly accelerates sales.

Financial Sustainability

In my experience, almost no food desert stores can achieve financial success without some form of public investment. Every project should start with an expert sales study to project sales based on plans and competition. The next step is to produce financial projections based on the sales study, wholesaler, competitive pricing analysis, store format, and projected sales, gross profit and labor costs of each offered department and service. After you have a solid projection, you will have an idea of the financial gap, or shortfall, for the store to be financially sustainable. Then it's time to work with local nonprofits, Community Development Financial Institutions (CDFIs), and the public sector to obtain upfront assistance until the projection shows an industry average level of financial performance. It's bad for everybody to open a store that will ultimately fail.

— Jeff Brown, CEO of Brown's Super Stores (shoprite.com)

DISCOVER YOU CAN
Springfield, Missouri

A few years back, the Greater Springfield Farmers' Market teamed up with the national Discover You Can — Learn Make Share Program, sponsored by the makers of Ball products and the Farmers Market Coalition (FMC). The market holds regular canning workshops and education programs throughout the season, and the country, spreading the word about the ease of preserving your own food. This market even teamed up with a local art club to paint a mural as a backdrop for the canning workshops. Channeling an early-20th-century home kitchen, the mural depicts the time period when the Ball jar was first introduced. The workshops include everything from home pickling to salsa making. To find participating FMC markets nationwide, go to farmersmarketcoalition.org or freshpreserving.com.

SHOP AT YOUR LOCAL FARMERS' MARKET

It sounds so obvious, doesn't it? Just go shopping. (Actually, it sounds like George Bush's advice after 9/11 . . .) But farmers' markets are like town centers and community happenings. They're more than anonymous consumer purchasing power at mega-box stores. They are chances to meet face to face the people who grow the food you're about to eat. They're personal. So here's some advice to shoppers, eaters, and all of us who go to farmers' markets from my sister, Ann Bliss, who is a member of the Forsyth Community Food Consortium Advisory Council in Winston-Salem, North Carolina.

DO . . .

THINK about what you bring to the market just by being there. This is not the isolated, acquire-and-abscond experience that big-box superstores are set up for. What you add to the marketplace by your presence and your participation is just as important as what you will take home. If you went out of your way to come to the market, you've already chosen care over mere convenience, and commitment over mindless consumption. Care and commitment look good on you. Accessorize them with patience, respect, good humor, and good manners while you shop. Everyone will notice.

BUY only what you will consume between now and the next market day. It makes you a better customer. If you buy more than you reasonably expect to consume or preserve, others won't get any. It means you can look forward to coming back next week — to find new items and new varieties that have ripened and come to harvest as the season progresses. That's the key to integrating local, seasonal eating into your shopping routine, and what ultimately sustains the market and the growers who depend on it for sales. Markets love their loyal "weeklies."

TIP At farmers' markets and farm stands, look for the less-than-perfect produce, which is usually for sale at a lower price. They're the same tomatoes and peas; they're just not going to win the beauty pageant.

LOOK OUT FOR . . .

NEW VENDORS and give them a chance! Markets need growers, and growers need sales. Everyone has favorites, but do try to spread your shopping dollars around. This is another good reason to come back every week.

SOCIAL MEDIA. Markets get reviews just like every other business does — from fans, fanatics, and fools. If you have a serious complaint about a vendor or think something needs to change, seek out the market manager or lead organizer to speak with directly rather than posting a public comment. It's unfair to turn others away based on a one-off incident or encounter that could be addressed internally in a constructive, remedial approach.

NEVER . . .

COMPLAIN about a product without first going to the vendor who sold it to you. Use the vendor's website to e-mail them or set up a phone call rather than waiting until the next market day and turning what could be a reasonable conversation into a public confrontation. Be accurate, polite, and fair. If you don't get a fair, polite response, then go to the market manager or organizers to let them know of the situation.

ASK A VENDOR to bend or break market rules for your convenience or advantage. Doing so is profoundly unkind to the vendor because it puts him or her in an uncomfortable spot. It marks you as a selfish consumer, and it can ultimately contribute to the market's demise. If you think that getting a vendor to sell to you before the market officially opens gets you the better pick, or is just a harmless favor, don't be surprised when your market shuts down because no one else comes there to shop.

BRING PETS to the market unless you have determined in advance that they are welcome. You cannot expect volunteers at the information tent to babysit Rover while you shop, and you certainly know better than to lock him in a hot car. Certified companion animals are always the exception, and this should be provided for in the market's rules.

>×<

"We've had some success in passing policies that support farmers' markets, but really the numbers are pretty small compared to the huge support that flows to big commodity crops. Policy makers are slowly catching up with the public on the benefits of supporting local agriculture, but we have a long way to go before the playing field is really leveled."

— Maine congresswoman Chellie Pingree

ACCEPT SNAP

. . . .

The Supplemental Nutrition Assistance Program (SNAP) is the official name for the food stamp program administered by the federal government. Farmers' markets and local co-ops can accept food stamps, too. Go to the U.S. Department of Agriculture's Food and Nutrition Service, the authorizing agency. The information is also in Spanish.

» Google hint: USDA, Food and Nutrition Service, SNAP

» Or go directly to the SNAP website (www.fns.usda.gov/snap)

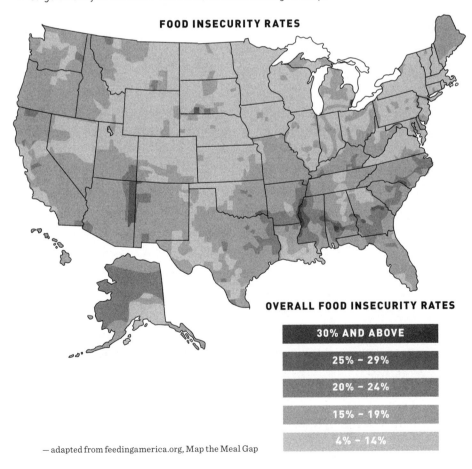

FOOD INSECURITY RATES

OVERALL FOOD INSECURITY RATES

| 30% AND ABOVE |
| 25% – 29% |
| 20% – 24% |
| 15% – 19% |
| 4% – 14% |

— adapted from feedingamerica.org, Map the Meal Gap

SNAP STATS

OF ALL FOOD STAMP households in the United States, 76 percent include children, elderly persons, or disabled persons.

THE FOOD STAMP PROGRAM has the lowest fraud rate of any federal government program.

EVERY DOLLAR of food stamps spent returns roughly $2 to the economy.

— "SNAP (Food Stamps): Facts, Myths, and Realities," Feeding America (feedingamerica.org)

APPLYING FOR SNAP BENEFITS

Start with the USDA's prescreening tool (www.snap-step1.usda.gov/fns) to find out if you qualify. The tool is also available in Spanish.

You may qualify for other benefits besides SNAP. To learn about those, go to Benefits.gov (benefits.gov/benefits).

IN THE FIRST PERSON

BURNIN' IT DOWN

"Burning It Down" by Steve Earle, from the recording *The Low Highway*

I'm thinkin' bout burnin' it down, boys

Thinkin' bout burnin' it down

Nothin's ever gonna be the same in this town

I'm thinkin' bout burnin' the Walmart down.

On the surface, it's a song about a guy who's turned his car into a bomb, and he's about to drive it into the wall of a Walmart, blow the thing sky high. But, really, there's a choice you have to make . . . and that's beneath the story line. Listen to it. It's really about jobs versus bigger and cheaper flat-screen TVs; paying people a living wage so they can exist with dignity, or else slip into what is rapidly becoming a third-world country. It comes down to that. So many people we don't see because they're in these small towns, and they're suffering because our economy is now flipping burgers and parking cars and making change, because the factory jobs and the small local businesses are falling away and that's all that's left.

— Steve Earle to Holly Gleason, *Lone Star Music Magazine*

YOU CAN DO THIS

CAMPAIGN TO RAISE THE MINIMUM WAGE

Stores like Walmart have contributed to the demise of local, small family-run food businesses and the rise of food deserts in their absence. But there are a number of things we can do to help food deserts get water and shrink. One is working for a fair living wage. Raising the minimum wage will help people, particularly those living in food deserts, have money to spend on healthier food choices. Efforts to raise the minimum wage should go hand in hand with educational efforts (see Educate, page 30).

Get the Facts

The following information is from Raise the Minimum Wage (raisethe minimumwage.com), a project of the National Employment Law Project.

AS OF THIS WRITING, the federal minimum wage, established in 2009, is $7.25 per hour, which translates to $15,080 for a full-time, year-round worker.

THE VALUE of the minimum wage has fallen sharply over the past 40 years. In 1968, for example, the federal minimum wage was $1.60 per hour, but with accounting for inflation, that figure translated to approximately $10.70 in 2013 dollars.

IT IS GENERALLY UNDERSTOOD that the minimum wage — even in states with higher-than-federal rates — is inadequate to support a family of any size. As a result, the concept of a "living wage" has gained popularity, as advocates, academics, and policymakers have explored other ways of defining a wage level adequate to support a decent standard of living in America.

What's Happening in Your State?

Campaigns abound across the country; examples include Raise Michigan, Give Arkansas a Raise, and Alaskans for a Fair Minimum Wage.

Raise Awareness

TELL your story (page 198).

BE a witness (page 191).

>×<

START A CAMPAIGN
TO TAX UNHEALTHY FOOD

As we do with tobacco, we should tax highly processed, sugar–salt–fat–laden foods and drinks that make people sick and use the money to subsidize positive initiatives in sustainable agriculture (page 106), good-food education (page 30), local/regional food hubs (page 88), and innovative businesses like food desert grocery stores (page 242).

WHAT IS A HUNGER-FREE COMMUNITY?

The nonprofit Hunger Free Communities Network (hungerfreecommunities .org) offers the following description of what a hunger-free community looks like: a place where no one, no matter of what age or social standing, is worried about having enough money to buy healthy food.

IT IS A PLACE where those who are suffering know they can get help, without feeling shamed or judged.

IT IS A PLACE where the agencies charged with helping those in need provide assistance with transparency and accountability, and always seek the meaningful participation and partnership of those who are struggling.

IT IS A PLACE where there is no discrimination, where people are positively connected beyond the usual social boundaries of race and ethnicity, class, social status, disability, age, and neighborhood.

A HUNGER-FREE COMMUNITY can be a workplace, a neighborhood, a network of people, a university, a hospital, a city. It can be any group of people that works together to ensure all families are economically secure and have a voice in policies that affect their lives.

— Excerpted with permission from hungerfreecommunities.org

FOOD BANKS

In a YouTube video featuring Rachel Bristol of the Oregon Food Bank, it is striking how in 10 minutes one can learn the history of how food banking has dramatically changed in the last few decades. What started out as a way to keep good food out of the landfills and to provide emergency food for people who needed it in exigent circumstances has turned into something quite different. Today, food banks are expected to fulfill a family's nutritional needs over an extended period of undetermined time.

That's a dramatic shift. Food banks have become part of a high-stakes parallel distribution system that is expected to meet the day-to-day nutritional needs of families. Cuts in SNAP benefits threaten more people's food security and bring more people to food banks. Federal policies (see #VoteFood, page 303) and a low minimum wage (see page 248) contribute to the recent changes and higher demands put onto food banks such as the Oregon Food Bank. Let's take heed of history lessons of this venerable institution and take action so that more people can lead independent, healthy, active, citizen lives.

START A FOOD RECOVERY PROGRAM

The Greenhouse in Harrisburg, Pennsylvania, collects food from local farmers, then does one better. To extend the life of this good food, its members preserve, can, pickle, and freeze it, capturing precious nutrients at their peak before redistributing their efforts to their community's underserved citizens. This excerpt is from "How to Start a Food Recovery Program 101," written by Ashlee Shelton, founder of the Greenhouse, for the skill-sharing website Homegrown .org (homegrown.org). Steal this recipe, and start your own food recovery program!

1. SET THE STAGE (a.k.a. get folks excited and gather resources): Since we don't have a physical location, we have to rent commercial kitchen space. In order to make that financially possible, we threw a fund-raiser and equipment-gathering endeavor early on called Stuff the Bus. This event served as a way to educate the community about the need we had identified and afforded us the chance to engage potential volunteers in person. This event gave us a platform to explain our ideas in a way that enticed folks to participate in the hard work to come. We held Stuff the Bus at a local park and decked out the basketball court like a house. Folks enjoyed sweet potatoes and homemade vegetarian chili in the dining room, and we had overflow seating on the back porch, under the clothes line, and next to the fire ring. Attendees brought cases of canning jars and other canning equipment, and we stuffed our trusty Greenhouse school bus to the gills.

2. IDENTIFY RECIPIENTS: We agreed from the beginning that we wanted to donate the food we collected to direct-service providers in our community. The organizations we choose to support serve people within the food desert but do not limit their service recipients to subscribers of any particular religion. One of our group members works in the mental health field and knows all too well about the linkages between that issue and food insecurity. She recommended Shalom House because she saw firsthand the important services they offer. In addition to serving as a shelter from domestic violence, Shalom House also provides a transitional housing program for female veterans and their children who are experiencing homelessness. We also share food with the Boys and Girls Clubs of Harrisburg and the St. Francis of Assisi Soup Kitchen. The Greenhouse remains open to suggestions and has a number of events slated to serve new, as well as repeat, organizations.

3. FIND A KITCHEN: We worked at the Village Acres Farm Food Shed in Mifflintown, Pennsylvania, for our first two preservation events. Village Acres is a certified organic CSA that has a unique and desirable community space. Because we were using the space for an awesome cause, they allowed us to rent the kitchen at a discounted rate. The Greenhouse was very fortunate to have access to their environmentally friendly facility, and their staff even gave our volunteers tours of the farm via hayride!

4. NETWORK WITH AND LEARN FROM FARMERS: Early on in the process, we realized that, while we had a great idea and good intentions, we certainly were not experts on farming or what goes into supporting a farm's gleaning efforts. So, we asked a lot of questions and learned as we went. For the first two events, we relied on donations of vegetables and fruits from farmers. In the near future, we plan to start mobilizing gleaning teams to go to farms and collect the fallen crops. The farmers we've been working with seem to be grateful to have an outlet where they can contribute their unsold produce. They've also been an abundant source of suggestions and education, especially on effective timing for our projects.

>>

5. RALLY SUPPORT: We were able to drum up substantial financial and volunteer support through an online publicity campaign. Since we don't have a Greenhouse website yet, we rely heavily on our Facebook page. We also had enormous success with Smore.com's online flyers, which you can seamlessly sync with other social media outlets. We've submitted our events to online community calendars and online news services; the ideal timing for such calendars is six to eight weeks prior to the event date. We also sent links to our online flyers to a variety of like-minded community groups and asked those groups to distribute our event info to their e-mail lists. We sent out traditional media advisories one week prior to each event, as well as press releases on the morning of each event.

We've secured volunteers through all of the above channels, too. Typically volunteers can choose between shifts we lay out ahead of time. This system assures our volunteers that their time is valuable and lets them know in advance what tasks we need help with. We also lucked out in finding two top-notch graphic designers who work with us pro bono. People are amazingly generous, I tell you. Sometimes you just have to ask for help! Some examples of our volunteer tasks include:

» sorting/cleaning

» cutting

» cooking

» canning

» storage/delivery

6. PRESERVE THE FOOD: There are a few different options as far as what types of food preservation methods to use. We chose to cook and can applesauce in early November and called the event Yes We Can. In mid-January, we made a delicious squash soup and prepared it for freezing at an event called Squash Hunger. Dehydrating would also be an option, though we haven't tried it yet. Because no one in our core group considered themselves a "master canner," we reached out to a number of folks who had expertise and insight to share. We also did a lot of research and practiced some recipes and canning techniques at home and during Farm Nights.

Don't Get Intimidated, Do Read Widely, and Ask for Help

You might notice a theme in these experiences: We didn't start out as experts in any of the above-mentioned tasks. Not everyone in your group needs to be a food expert, a canning guru, or a marketing professional — but a willingness to reach out to folks who have those skills is key. We found that being honest about our gifts as well as our limitations allowed us to expand our volunteer base in a way that made the most sense.

— Excerpted with permission from "How to Start a Food Recovery Program 101," by Ashlee Shelton

>×<

STARTING AN ONLINE CO-OP

My sister helped found the wonderful Triad Buying Co-op (tbcoop.org), in Winston-Salem, North Carolina. Its members can get healthy food in a system that shifts the paradigm away from grocery stores. Ann has always been thrifty—something we inherited from our parents, I suppose. Saving and reusing plastic bags, twist ties, the wax paper wrapped around sticks of butter, just like our grandmother and home ec teacher, Elva Coulter, used to teach her students in Iowa City. Ann has applied both her love of food and cooking and her law degree to creating and organizing this food co-op. What I know is how happy it makes her to be a member of a food co-op she loves. Here, she shares her knowledge for people interested in starting an online co-op of their own.

Using a web-based ordering system developed by one of its founding members, the Triad Buying Co-op provides shareholders with monthly delivery of high-quality, locally sourced natural foods and all the same brands and varieties of organic products typically available at specialized retail stores.

Do you worry about giving something up to shop with an online co-op? Retail therapy is woven into contemporary American life in ways most of us are unaware of. Grocery store advertising is meant to make you want to go there, to feel good about yourself as a smart shopper and a conscientious provider for those you love and care for. If shopping makes you feel good, you don't have to give it up. It's unlikely to go away as a legitimate use of our time and energy, as media, marketing, and the culture of consumption combine to deepen their hold on our American society. It takes time and applied decision making to shift away from the see it/want it/buy it pattern, to which we are all accustomed, and toward the online co-op buying alternative.

If, on the other hand, you come away from shopping trips feeling manipulated, even assaulted or in despair, then buying through a food cooperative might bring you hope.

A three-hour work shift realistically takes half a day to fulfill, if you count the other activities or commitments it displaces. Bulk buying assumes you have appropriate food storage capacities and equipment, as well as the cooking skills to use the products you buy in a timely way. Planning meals in advance, and sticking to that plan, can be tough at times. For many, the initial cash outlay to pay for a bulk order may be challenging — even if in the long run it saves money on specialty products needed to satisfy restricted diets.

>>

Take a Quiz

This short quiz is designed to help potential members of the Triad Buying Co-op self-assess their reasons for joining and the likelihood of staying in long enough to find benefit. The survey helps you decide: Should I really spend $35 of my hard-earned money to join?

CHECK ALL THAT APPLY, FOR EACH MEMBER OF YOUR FAMILY:

☐ Vegan (5)
☐ Vegetarian (5)
☐ Dairy free (5)

☐ Gluten free (5)
☐ Raw (5)
☐ Kosher (5)

☐ Halal (5)
☐ Other (7, explain)

SUBTOTAL:

I KEEP A PANTRY/HOME FREEZER

☐ To be prepared for emergencies (5)
☐ Because I plan meals in advance (5)
☐ To take advantage of bargains (3)
☐ To preserve seasonal harvest, such as strawberries (3)
☐ An extra jar of peanut butter is all I need (1)
☐ I just run to the grocery whenever I need something (1)

SUBTOTAL:

I THINK ABOUT FOOD

☐ When they ask me if I want fries with that (1)
☐ Enough to read the ingredient list on my kid's cereal box (3)
☐ When I want to try a new recipe (5)
☐ Because I think my buying dollars impact the whole world (5)

SUBTOTAL:

I'M INTERESTED IN BEING PART OF THE CO-OP BECAUSE

☐ I want to pay less for food (3)
☐ I'm curious (3)
☐ My friend is a member (3)
☐ I want to change the way I buy and consume food (5)
☐ I'm willing to show up and work my shift (7)
☐ I'm interested in a non-working membership for now (7)

SUBTOTAL:

GRAND TOTAL:

Scoring (just between you and the doorpost):

10 POINTS OR LESS: Maybe that $35 is better spent on a nice dinner out.

10 TO 20: We might be a fit for you. Why not talk to one of our member mentors first?

20+: You look a lot like some of our happiest members.

How It Works

All members of the co-op are shareholders of the "Triad Buying Co-operative, Inc." (TBC). All members work a co-op job that the board either creates or recognizes, unless they have agreed to pay an increased mark-up (known as the "bump") on their purchases. All the work needed to set up, execute, and complete the monthly delivery cycle is done by members. All management, accounting, and other organizational work is done entirely within the co-op, by its members. One member serves as the co-op's executive director. She is paid on a contract basis for the hours that those responsibilities require over and above the minimum 3-hour-per-month commitment that is the standard for all other co-op jobs.

Why It Works

Great prices on foods and products that represent commitments to conscience, personal preference, or health needs may be the first reason a member joins. But the opportunity to become an active and engaged member of a food community is what long-term members identify as their most important benefit. "Shareholder" is the legal term that describes the relationship between the incorporated business entity and its owners. "Membership" is the sense of participation, contribution, and engagement that keeps the co-op alive and thriving.

Each member makes their individual food choices online from the TBC ordering website. The site is built from two catalogs: locally sourced goods (primarily produce, meat, and eggs from local and regional growers, but also prepared foods from restaurants, bakers, and other providers who have met our approval) and the United Foods web catalog (nationally recognized brands of organic and "natural" food products you'd see in a store). Members may also buy from the Frontier Natural Products Co-op through the monthly TBC aggregate order. The co-op buys at wholesale prices, and passes that price on to members. At check out, members pay an additional "bump" on their total purchase. Bump percentages are determined by the board each year based on budget projections.

A member who selects and orders a United Foods product on the TBC website — for example, two jars of a particular brand of pasta sauce out of a case flat of six — shares that flat by making the remaining four jars available to other members to add to their own order on the website. Or, a member can buy an entire case if they want to.

>>

The computer program that ties the member selections together from both catalog sources into a single member order and tracks subscriptions took the place of the monthly gathering around someone's kitchen table, using a paper catalog to aggregate purchases and place the combined order. But the feeling of "sharing" knowledge and good food choices is almost the same, since all members still see what other members have chosen when a flat of spaghetti sauce is up for grabs. TBC's computer program is available to others, but the local buying component in the software would have to be adapted and customized.

On pickup day, it's pretty common that members visit while they help each other juggle kids and cartons and ice chests back into their cars. You hear them ask each other: What is that like? How do you fix it? Do your kids eat it? Along with all the other simple, civil exchanges that make us a cooperative community: How's your mom? Did the job come through? When did you join? We are each other's greeters, baggers, nutrition advisors, and recipe exchange, all in one.

Buying food as part of a co-op turned out to be a wonderful way to feel individually enabled to make positive economic and environmental change and to create access to whole, healthy foods in an economically sustainable way.

Why It Continues

When TBC grew from a few families who met once a month to pool their orders, it needed a larger food preparation area and more floor space for distribution. A local church agreed to let the co-op use its kitchen and meeting area in exchange for cleaning services and the shared use of TBC's upright freezer. On delivery day, TBC workers came in early to arrange the church's folding chairs into three rows, alphabetized according to the member's name, stuck on the back of each chair with a magnetized tag. That chair was the landing place for all the items ordered by the member whose name it wore. As items were weighed or counted in the church kitchen, like blocks of feta or bags of almonds, other workers distributed products to each member's chair. Pickup days were a glorious, bustling 48-hour phenomenon, with everybody working to get everything ready for pickup, which opened and closed once a month on Thursday afternoon. When delivery was over the tags came off; the chairs were cleaned, folded, and put back in storage. Cleanup workers vacuumed, scoured the kitchen, and generally put the church back into the Church by making sure it was presentable for Sunday services. The last one out took care of taking flattened boxes and other materials to the recycle station, turned out the lights, and locked the door.

Co-op delivery operations today retain the same vibe. Instead of chairs, we used our new space to build long open counters with taped-out "slots" — a space for each member's order that month. Just as before, many food goods are taken home in plain paper bags, cloth drawstring sacks, or clear plastic bags. Each is weighed or counted out and labeled by members during their work shift. Produce is often delivered in the boxes it came in. For cold food items (meats, cheeses, and frozen goods), members now take the printout of their order to a separate room where porters gather these products from our collection of used and donated freezers and refrigerators. And while they wait, there's lots of conversing, catching up, and introductions between new and seasoned members.

Food from the co-op has my name on it. What could be better than that?

The desire for, and commitment to, our food community extends to our vendors and suppliers. When growers come in to deliver their monthly order of eggs, meat, or seasonal produce, they are greeted personally. When a grower needs extra hands at harvest, the co-op sends an e-mail invitation to members to come out and help. And they do.

Legal and Financial Realities

The co-op is a corporation. That "Inc." at the end of its name represents a choice of business entity that ensures the co-op complies with all external regulatory requirements. It also provided an architecture for internal participation in co-op governance, ensured accountability to the membership from those who hold office, and gave legal protection for those individuals willing to take leadership responsibility. More important, by incorporating, the co-op bound itself publicly to its mission and the co-operative business model.

After incorporation, the board's first act was to produce a written set of bylaws delineating the board's power to make policy, commit the co-op's resources, and control the co-op's operations. The bylaws also detailed share-owner's rights, including the right to vote. The bylaws reiterate the co-op's mission and built out an internal organizational structure to be consistent with that mission. Members can read the bylaws anytime, as they are posted on the member's section of the TBC website.

>>

Insurance

The co-op is insured. It files the forms needed to comply with tax reporting requirements. It collects and pays state sales taxes on the goods members purchase. It pays income tax at corporate rates. Because the co-op's business operations did not fall within any of the definitions of a "charitable organization" recognized by the Internal Revenue Code, it could not qualify for tax-exempt status.

Key Principles

TBC made two commitments when it decided to limit eligibility for co-op membership. The first remains unchanged from the moment the co-op started: "The Co-op shall not discriminate on the basis of sex, race, religion, color, national origin or ancestry, age, physical appearance, sexual orientation, handicap/disability, marital status, familial status, occupation, source of income or political belief."

The second requirement was to build an approval process for membership. At the time the bylaws were written, membership required every member to work. TBC's business model is designed to reduce each individual member's purchase price for food by relying exclusively on the membership at large as its labor force. Therefore, every potential member completed an application that included information about their skill set, their availability for shift hours, and any physical limitations, such as lifting or carrying. Sometimes the membership committee of the board invented a new job in order to capitalize on the applicant's skills. Sometimes that new applicant was willing to take on a job someone else wanted out of, or couldn't do anymore. The co-op reinvented its labor pool and staffing schedule as often as needed, the better to meet our mission and accept new members.

Learning Lessons in Growth

New jobs and new capacities were added as the base of time, talent, and labor that comprised our membership grew deeper and more diverse. As public interest in food sourcing and safety grew, so did interest in TBC. As dietary and health awareness expanded, so did the need for exactly the kind of high-quality food products that TBC offered, and at affordable prices. Those advantages were available to you, if you could work a co-op job.

The co-op had grown and thrived since it incorporated. It sponsored a new, producers-only farmers' market for the downtown area, making the co-op more "public" than ever. It moved from the church kitchen into its own suite of rooms in a converted factory building, located in a central area of the city. It expanded its delivery schedule, its inventory, and its member services. Its core group of active leaders also increased, with each new contributor bringing ideas for programs and initiatives that would further the TBC mission.

At the same time, the co-op's need for revenue to meet fixed expenses, such as rent and insurance premiums, also hardened. Growth became desirable, possible, and necessary. Deep discussions began at board meetings and among members: What about people who couldn't join because they couldn't work, but needed access to these kinds of foods? Was it fair to allow a member to "buy" out of the work requirement by paying a higher bump? What about the value of work in simple monetary terms, and the value of work hours in building relationship between members?

The work requirement excluded many people from membership. Individuals with disabilities as well as people with incompatible employment hours or other conflicting demands on their time could not join.

TBC shareholders voted almost unanimously to change the bylaws to create alternative membership categories. Membership has surged, from that kitchen-table-sized group of first founders, to the 93 current shareholder families that now channel over $125,000 worth of food through the co-op distributive model each year.

— Excerpted with permission from Ann Bliss

COOKING FOR THE HOSPITAL PATIENT

The young man was mugged, dragged down an alley, and left for dead. He spent 24 hours in Bellevue Hospital in New York City as John Doe before his family tracked him down. He'd already had emergency brain surgery for multiple skull fractures. Michael (not his real name) was a chef, coming home late after a night shift, getting out of the subway in Brooklyn, when he was hit on his head and robbed. All the assailant took were a cell phone and the meager contents of Michael's wallet, about $40. Someone found him, called an ambulance, and saved his life. He was a healthy 23-year-old who was fine one minute, and his life as he knew it was gone the next.

His friends, a mother-and-daughter team, cooked every day to feed him as he lay recovering in the neurointensive care unit. They made smoothies out of fresh organic vegetables from the greengrocer. Eventually he could eat again. They roasted clean, farm-raised, and humanely slaughtered chicken. Organic meat. Flavors, spices, and herbs tasted good to him. Nearly every day for the first couple of months his friends cooked in their small city apartment and took the meals to the hospital; then they'd all eat together in his hospital room. "The worst thing," one of the friends remembers, "was using the microwave on the hospital floor. To reheat what we'd made. You know how microwaves make food smell really good? Well, we'd have to walk down the hall, past all the other patients, with this amazing-smelling food. It made me feel awful."

She went on: "It strikes me as beautiful and ironic that together we united in this marathon endeavor to put everything that had slipped, bruised, and been assaulted back in its station through kindness, humanity, and love — via food. This is what I have some kind of control over, and it feeds me."

This story has a happy ending: Michael has healed and is back working in the restaurant business in the New York area.

"Let food be thy medicine and medicine be thy food."

— Hippocrates

A POTENT TRIUMVIRATE

What if the Internal Revenue Service, farmers, and hospitals all got together to make institutional food better?

For hospitals to maintain their nonprofit status, they must provide information to the IRS that they support public health and do provide a community service. Institutional food service is being scrutinized. The IRS is requiring hospitals to complete a survey, the "Community Health Needs Assessment," in order to keep their nonprofit status. And here is the crack "where the light comes through," as Leonard Cohen sings. It is the potency of the intersection between public health, fresh healthy food, and local farmers, joining together to impact diets, health, economies, and food systems.

The New England Farmers Union (newenglandfarmersunion.org) recommends these steps to connect local farmers to hospital cafeterias and kitchens:

1. Approach your hospital's CEO, board members, and the personnel who handle community benefit programs (usually within the department of community relations).

2. Start by building relationships. Invite these people to farm and food events in your community, where they can learn about agriculture and why it matters to human health.

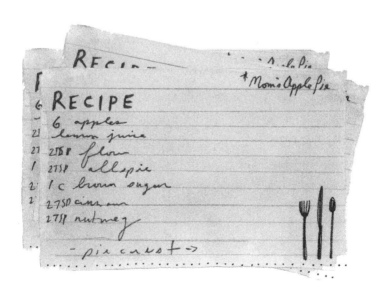

GOOD HOSPITAL FOOD

Tulane Medical School

Med students are run ragged: long days, high stress, lack of sleep, and probably not great food. You can see all of this in one episode of *House*. But why wouldn't good food cooking be a part of a med student's education? Seems obvious, doesn't it? Dr. Benjamin Sachs, the dean of Tulane Medical School, says, "Nutrition isn't often taught in medical schools, and if it is, it's glossed over. Unless you can explain to your patients about nutrition in the sense of culinary science, you're not going to get anywhere. But if you truly understand what goes into cooking and how ingredients change with temperature — what's good, what's bad — it's a wonderful goal." And with such an addition to their education those run-ragged medical students would have something delicious to eat, and something more to pass on to their future patients: recipe cards.

— John Pope, "Tulane University Medical Students to Don Chef Jackets," nola.com

Novant Health Brunswick Medical Center

The idea that you'd voluntarily go to the hospital to enjoy a good meal of, say, a wood-fired pizza or a crisp salad bar is just catching on. Creating an atmosphere in which people can eat good food together is a whole other way hospitals can help caregivers and support communities. In Bolivia, North Carolina, the Novant Health Brunswick Medical Center is doing just that. "You wouldn't know it's hospital food," says Pauline Benton, a regular diner at the hospital cafeteria.

Novant Health recognized that by switching up its food service to provide improved fresher, healthier meals, it could attract more paying customers, especially in the area around the hospital, which reportedly has not much more to offer than fast-food joints.

— Jason Gonzales, "Cafeteria Breaking Hospital Food Stereotype," *StarNews Online*

"We believe that food is nurturing."

— Zach Erickson, Warrenton, Virginia, Fauquier Health's director of nutrition services, quoted in Julie Rovner, "Hospital Food So Fresh, Even the Healthy Come to Dine," *The Salt,* National Public Radio, May 2012.

BRING GOOD FOOD TO HOSPITALS

In the case of the injured chef (page 260), his friends were in the fortunate position to be able to buy, cook, and deliver whole, fresh foods to aid in his recovery. But not all patients are so lucky. Not all hospitals are located near good food. And not all friends and family members can manage this type of day-to-day care.

So why not do what we do in schools? What Kate Adamick of Cook for America® (see page 48) does? If we can have Lunch Teachers® in schools educating kids on how to eat well, why can't we do the same in hospitals? Let's support "Lunch Doctors" — cafeteria directors and staff who purchase from local and regional farmers, cook it, and serve it to provide sustenance and healing for patients. "Lunch Doctor" has a nice ring to it, doesn't it?

Here's how to start changing your local hospital's food, courtesy of Health Care Without Harm.

1. Start a conversation about healthy food. Pull together a team.

2. Contract with a group purchasing organization (GPO), distributor, or food service provider that supports healthy food. For example, facilities can use the contracting process to distinguish which food service contractors develop seasonal menus to support local and fresh produce. Health systems can contract with those GPOs that not only source but support sustainable food options for their member facilities.

Similarly, health systems and GPOs can require distributors to fit the unique needs of a facility's healthy food program. For example, electronic distributor catalogs might be tailored to screen out products such as highly processed foods and meats raised with nontherapeutic antibiotics. Alternatively, they might be designed to allow a facility to search for desired criteria such as local, seasonal, organic, fair trade, or other certifications. Purchasing tools are available on the Health Care Without Harm website (noharm-uscanada.org).

3. Institute purchasing policies for meat and poultry raised without nontherapeutic antibiotics. Work with your GPO, particularly with chicken at no cost premium and some pork products as well.

>>

4. Model local, nutritious, sustainable food at conferences, meetings, and workshops. See "Guidelines to Increase the Use of Local Foods at Meetings," under Resources and Relationships, at the website of the Society for Nutrition Education and Behavior (sneb.org).

5. Buy milk produced without recombinant bovine growth hormone (rBGH), also known as recombinant bovine somatotropin (rBST).

6. Buy organic and other certified food. The Food Alliance, Protected Harvest, Humane Farm Animal Care, and Fair Trade USA are examples of organizations with certification systems. Good certification systems are verifiable, are transparent, avoid conflict of interest, and disclose organizational structure and funding sources.

7. Consider establishing an overarching food policy. Health facilities may want to begin their food work by laying out a broad, integrated food policy. An aspirational policy or goal may then guide your facility's future efforts. Conversely, you may elect to build excitement and momentum one step at a time and tackle a broader food policy for your facility by building on your success. Through an understanding that healthy food includes more than nutritional quality, health-care facilities and systems can play an important role in supporting the health of their staff, patients, and local and global communities.

8. Buy from local producers. Some health-care systems purchase their food through a supplier or contract with a private food service company distributor. In either case, it is worth learning what locally produced foods your vendor currently provides. Express a preference for purchasing fresh, locally grown, and sustainable food from your vendors, and ask them to provide these options. Some health-care systems are able to buy vegetables, dairy, coffee, and other products through local suppliers without violating their prime contracts. Finally, when your contract is up for renewal, use this as a time to negotiate the off-contract percentage purchases.

9. Become a fast-food-free zone. Hospitals can review the food service operations within their facilities (patient food, cafeteria food, catering, vending machines, and coffee carts) and evaluate whether the food choices offered are consistent with the promotion of healthy dietary patterns for patients, staff, and the larger community. Food service operations and distributors that do not meet the criteria set forth by the hospital can be removed and replaced with those companies that can commit to offering high-quality, nutritious food that does not compromise the health of visitors and staff.

10. Limit use of vending machines, and replace unhealthy snacks with healthy choices. Hospitals can draft a policy that outlines the types of food that would be acceptable in vending machines (e.g., no trans fats, low in processed sugars and fats, no artificial ingredients, and no preservatives) as well as outlining food packaging standards and energy efficiency of machines. This type of policy can be used in negotiations when vending machine contracts come up for review.

11. Host a farmers' market or a CSA on hospital grounds. [Author note: Tips, profiles of existing model programs, and stated benefits to the hospital community and the local community are available at Health Care Without Harm (noharm-uscanada.org), in their PDF entitled "Farmers' Markets and CSAs on Hospital Grounds." Also see tips on organizing a farmers' market on page 94.]

12. Create hospital gardens to grow fresh produce and flowers. Hospital gardens can also serve as demonstration gardens to educate the community about organic growing methods, integrated pest management, and the incredible variety of foods that can be cultivated in a small urban space.

13. Compost, divert, and reduce food waste. Food waste comprises approximately 10 percent of a hospital's waste stream. Food and other organic waste can be diverted, composted, or otherwise beneficially reused instead of being landfilled. Fresh but unwanted food can be donated to local soup kitchens or food pantries. À la carte programs are reducing food purchase and disposal costs. Through reductions in food waste volumes, composting has been demonstrated to be cost-effective.

14. Buy certified coffee. Coffee is the United States' largest food import and second most valuable commodity after oil. Most coffee is grown in developing countries under conditions that require clear-cutting and heavy use of pesticides and where agricultural workers toil for little pay. There are many different types of certified coffee that can address these issues, like fair trade, shade-grown, and organic. Buying certified coffee supports community development, health, and environmental stewardship.

— Excerpted with permission from "Healthy Food in Health Care: A Menu of Options."

>×<

TIP

Look for the PDF "Hospital Farm Direct Purchasing: A Guide to Ensuring Safe & Sustainable Food" at FoodHub (food-hub.org). This guide was developed by the Oregon Healthy Food in Health Care Project of Oregon Physicians for Social Responsibility (oregonpsr.org). It is a two-part document and questionnaire: Part One for the hospital, and Part Two for farmers about on-farm food safety. Yeah!

REDUCE FOOD WASTE
AT RESTAURANTS

According to a 2002 study at the University of Arizona, in the United States each day there are 49,296,540 pounds of food wasted at full-service restaurants and 85,063,390 pounds of food wasted at fast-food restaurants. Those numbers are so mind-boggling they just make your eyes cross and your teeth itch, they're so disturbing.

The Food Waste Reduction Alliance (foodwastealliance.org) has published a 25-page educational guide to increase awareness about the relationship of food waste at restaurants and food insecurity, "Best Practices and Emerging Solutions Toolkit." This guide has three goals in mind: reduce the amount of wasted food, increase the amount of nutritious food getting to those who need it, and recycle unavoidable food waste to divert it from landfills. The tool kit includes examples and links to get started, such as "Perform a Waste Stream Audit" and "Inventory Food and Track Waste."

"60 percent say reducing food waste at restaurants and grocery stores is the best way to increase food availability in the U.S."

— Sustainable America Food/Fuel Public Poll, March 2013
(sustainableamerica.org/downloadspresentations/SustainableAmericaFinalDeck.pdf)

37 DEGREES FROM HUNGER
Los Angeles, California

A few students from the Thomas Starr King Middle School in LA got themselves a refrigerator. That was the key piece of equipment they needed to ensure that unused food, such as fruit and dairy, from their school cafeteria could be collected and distributed safely to food banks via collaborators such as the Los Angeles Regional Food Bank and the First Southern Baptist Church in Hollywood. It's also how they named their organization: 37°F is the ideal temperature of a refrigerator. Their fridge was acquired through a grant from the home improvement retailer Lowe's.

This all started with three kids (McKenna Greenleaf Faulk, Fabian Samayoa, and Erick Sanchez) and a challenge from their environmental studies teacher. The assignment was to identify a community need that impacted the environment, and the students chose food insecurity. McKenna was quoted in the local press as saying, "Even though we are starting off small in our community, we are hoping it will spread out all over the country."

THE FOOD RECOVERY HIERARCHY

MOST PREFERRED

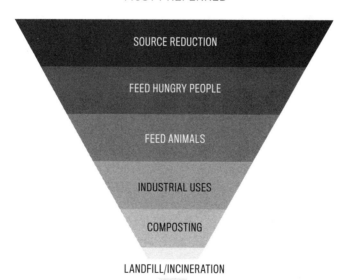

SOURCE REDUCTION

FEED HUNGRY PEOPLE

FEED ANIMALS

INDUSTRIAL USES

COMPOSTING

LANDFILL/INCINERATION

— epa.gov/foodrecovery

LEAST PREFERRED

CHAPTER 9

Cook

I BELIEVE IN THE blue flame. I believe that cooking is a transformative act and that eating together is the metamorphosis. I believe that after 19-year-old Jahmari was handed the cool, gray-tinged flesh of a just-caught bluefish fillet to prep it for dinner, the transformative act beyond the heat of the blue flame actually happened around the dinner table, when we all stopped talking to eat and taste his dish.

The metamorphoses happened as Taija set the table, as Imani hulled ripe summer strawberries for dessert, as Deshawn grilled potatoes like a master, as salad was tossed with homemade dressing over Elijah's farm-grown greens, and as we all sat down, gathered together for the evening meal. Metamorphosis happened as Ben, Zoli, and Alec did the dishes, cleaned the counters, swept the floor, and put the kitchen to bed. The blue flame, the instigator of it all, transformed raw resources into delicious sustenance. And how lucky any of us can be, for all hands to share in the process. That's what I believe in: the transformative powers, wonders, and connections that are cooking. The blue flame.

Sometimes social movements — the local food movement included — can make us feel shackled and tied. As if whatever it is we're doing, we're not doing it well enough or enough of it. There's plenty of judgment out there. The books about cooking and eating within some number of miles, like 50 or 100, from your home, make for interesting challenges and great reads, but they are unrealistic for the average anyone. Same with growing a significant amount of our own food: it is impractical for many. Aspirational can trump inspirational and scare people away. Choosing seasonal and regional foods is a wonderful thing, but you don't have to feel shame about not doing it enough. What I've been saying throughout this book goes for cooking, too: start small.

Plan meals (page 271), gather food (page 272), and cook and eat together on a Sunday. Love your kitchen; start a community kitchen (page 275) or a cooking club (page 276), or cook for someone with cancer (page 279). Host events (pages 280 and 281). Then clean up (page 285) and do it again. Amen.

MAKE SMALL CHANGES

Weaning anyone off processed food — a teenager, a boyfriend or girlfriend, a mom, a dad — to whole, fresh, healthy food and home cooking takes time. "A year," my colleague Claire says, from experience. One of the evil geniuses of super-processed food is its damn consistency. No matter where or when you go, what country you're in or what time of day it is, a fast-food burger is going to be the same everywhere, all the time. So if you're trying to shift toward more whole, fresh foods — foods that deviate from the norm, that don't come from the fast-food joint — that food is going to challenge a palate that's come to expect the consistency of highly processed food.

Most important, what we eat when we're young determines taste and sensory memories and compelling emotional pulls. We've lost generations of people to comfort foods from the dollar menu and not the home kitchen. Hey, I still crave a Tombstone frozen pizza or a can of Campbell's chicken soup once in a while. But it's not my regular fare. So when introducing new whole, fresh foods, start with small changes, and take the time to cook — for a full year, day by day. In the meantime, don't knock the occasional Oreo.

START COOKING with a couple of things you and your family members prefer. If it's eggs, use farm-fresh eggs. If it's spaghetti, make a simple sauce from scratch that's not an overly dramatic departure from sauce from a jar.

EAT MEALS TOGETHER at the table sans television or smartphones.

INCLUDE EVERYONE in setting the table, cleaning up, composting, and taking out the recycling and the garbage.

COOK together.

PICK YOUR BATTLES. Let the convenience store sweet rolls and boxed donuts come into the house sometimes. Then, at other times, go to the bakery to get the real deal.

IF YOUR LOVED ONES SAY, "I don't like onions," you might try, "But you eat pizza and the sauce has onions in it. You like them on burgers. Why not eat them in other things?" Reasoning won't always get you a win the first time around, but it plants a seed. That's a lot.

INSTEAD OF BUYING artificially flavored and colored sodas and sports drinks, make a refreshing beverage at home: Add the juice of one or two citrus fruits to a quart of water. Add half a teaspoon of salt. Finish with a natural sweetener of choice (honey, maple syrup, sorghum), to taste. Stir, shake, keep in the fridge.

MAKE a homemade fast-food burger. See Make Over McDonald's on page 54.

> "We need to realize that our taste buds are conditioned and can be re-conditioned. When we only eat for taste we become slaves to taste alone. And as we learn from seeing far too many of our relatives sick and miserable and overweight and diseased, eating for taste without regard to health leads to self-destruction. We can eat healthy on a hood budget. We deserve the best and we can start living like we understand our value by choosing to adopt healthier habits. When the hood is strong, we are truly unstoppable. Salute!

— 7 Ways to Eat Good While on a Hood Budget, by Stic of Dead Prez, founder of RBG Fit Club (rbgfitclub.com)

PLAN MEALS

. . . .

You will save money and time by planning the day's or week's meals. And you'll probably waste less food as well. Whole Foods Market has an excellent "Healthy Eating Handbook," downloadable for free off its website (wholefoodsmarket.com/healthy-eating/getting-started), and available to you whether you shop there or not. It includes a sample shopping list, how to start a cooking journal, a weekly meal plan, cooking guides for a wide range of beans and grains, and great tips for riffing on homemade dressings and marinades, all suitable for culturally diverse palates. Also check out your local Whole Foods Markets for their cooking classes. Schedules and topics vary from store to store.

>><<

GROCERY SHOP

. . . .

Before you have that dinner, you're going grocery shopping somewhere. Here are some tips to start eating better by shopping better.

BUY IN BULK. Search out grocery stores that give you the option of buying things like rice, flour, sugar, beans, pasta, spices and herbs, nut butters, maple syrup, and honey out of bins or other large containers, taking what you need without paying for special packaging and marketing. Bulk doesn't mean you have to buy pounds at a time — buy only what you can eat without it going bad. Store bulk items in sturdy containers to keep away pests like moths or mice.

LOOK FOR seasonally fresh produce, and plan your meals around those vegetables instead of the meat. Refocus the meal around vegetables and legumes.

FREEZE OR CAN excess items. (Want to learn how to eat out of your pantry and can more? Check out Sherri Brooks Vinton's book *Put 'Em Up*.)

MAKING A SUNDAY DINNER can mean leftovers for the week.

COOK UP YOUR BULK STAPLES and use them throughout the week. For example, a pot of beans can mean quesadillas, soups, and salad fixings, as well as a full meal, maybe combining the beans with corn and squash.

>✕<

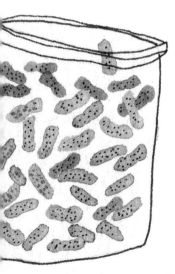

CHOPCHOP
Watertown, Massachusetts

Named the James Beard Foundation Publication of the Year in 2013, *ChopChop* magazine is one of the finest examples of inclusion, tested recipes, and accessibility of information. *ChopChop*'s recipes tend to start off with this basic step: Wash your hands well with soap and water. Its focus is teaching kids how to cook healthy foods, and it takes caregivers along for the ride. Available in English and Spanish, thanks to its support- ers, such as the New Balance Foundation and the American Academy of Pediatrics, *ChopChop* can found for free in pediatricians' offices, after- school programs, health centers, Indian reservations, and community centers around the country. It is also available by subscription, and its website (chopchopmag.org) is host to all its content for free. At *ChopChop*, they believe that "cooking and eating together as a family is a vital step in resolving the obesity and hunger epidemics." Wouldn't it be great to offer this valuable resource in more languages?

> "Getting kids to cook is essential in every way. It bonds kids with their adults, and encourages responsibility. It increases understanding of other cultures, and fosters reading, math and science. We believe *this* is what will help resolve the obesity crisis. But we need your help. Families need role models they can relate to across all media. They need stories . . . images . . . and conversations that celebrate simple, healthy, accessible approaches to cooking. They need to see that it is possible to feed themselves well and with joy."
>
> — Sally Sampson, founder of *ChopChop* magazine

"I begin with the proposition that eating is an agricultural act."

— Wendell Berry, "The Pleasures of Eating"

U-PICK APPLES

I have memories of my *oma* making *apfelkuchen*, and my mom still bakes the cake when I come home. The names of apples — Pink Pearl, Hidden Rose, Spitzenburg — read like little verses. I love walking in my favorite orchard, especially when the bees and blossoms are out. And I go cross-country skiing through those craggy hilltop rows of resilient trees in the winter. It's the same orchard where my youngest son and his friend Zoli played one October, eating along the way, not knowing as little boys that you couldn't just pick apples without paying but feeling free enough to do just that. It's where the Honeycrisps grow. My oldest was happy to be able to bite into a fresh one after his braces finally came off.

These autumn days I like apple slices with smudges of almond butter for a snack and make applesauce flavored with nutmeg and sweetened with maple syrup to serve with potato pancakes.

"Do you like apples?" I asked the tall quiet young man who'd come to our dinner table and stayed.

"No. I hate apples. Nasty," he said, shaking his head.

"Really. Why?"

"I don't know why. I just do," he said, closed.

And all went quiet. Still.

"Did you say we can go and pick them?" he asked.

"Yes. We can go."

"Okay."

"But soon. Now's the season," I said.

"Okay," he said.

>×<

START A COMMUNITY KITCHEN

Community kitchens mean different things to different people and different communities. Are you interested in creating a space where people can come to can their extra zucchinis or make jams, jellies, or sauerkraut together (page 224)? Is it a teaching kitchen and, if so, for whom? Children, adults, people with disabilities? Is it a commercial space — meaning, is the food coming out of it legally salable? Is it an incubator kitchen for burgeoning food entrepreneurs? These are all very different things.

How to Have a Successful Community Kitchen

1. Identify goals and needs for the community kitchen at an early stage. Offer the right equipment for the set of clients identified.

2. Organize a group of committed leaders who will rally support for the kitchen.

3. Market the kitchen to a variety of clients.

4. Set rental rates close to market rates at the beginning of operation, rather than starting lower and then raising them. The latter strategy can prove devastating for the clients.

5. Involve local, state, and federal regulatory agencies in planning the facility, and identify start-up and long-term sources of financial support.

6. Provide technical and marketing assistance in addition to kitchen facilities. Incubators with successful clients also tend to be successful.

7. Plan for adequate storage, both dry and refrigerator/freezer.

8. Manage conflicts between clients over time, cleanliness, or products.

9. Try to find a stable funding source to subsidize the operation or lease the facilities or operate as debt-free as possible.

10. Consider using existing community facilities such as churches or community buildings and tap into technical resources for marketing, labeling, and insurance.

— Contributed by the University of Wisconsin–Madison Center for Integrated Agricultural Systems

>×<

START A COOKING CLUB

These days, you can find out how to do pretty much anything online. For example, if you Google "How to start a cooking club," you will immediately find a terrific wikiHow entry that'll get you going. Check it out. It breaks down the process (summarized here) and offers a lot of great advice.

CONSIDER what you want to get out of a club.

FIND fellow foodists.

TRY to have a monthly meeting — but build flexibility into that.

DECIDE how to run the sessions. Do you want to choose a theme? Are you into ethnic cooking, whole grains, confections?

COOK enough so that you have extra meals to freeze.

MAKE preserves of any kind together.

COMBINE book club and cooking club.

TAKE turns. Focus on friendship.

— wikiHow

"The production of meat, especially beef (and dairy as well), has a large environmental impact. According to the U.N., animal agriculture is a major source of greenhouse gases and climate change. It also wastes resources. It takes 7,000 kg of grain to make 1,000 kg of beef. In addition, beef production requires a lot of water, fertilizer, fossil fuels, and pesticides."

— USDA "Greening Headquarters Update," July 23, 2012 (Author note: This is the reference to industrially raised beef, not sustainable meat production)

TIP

When a recipe fails in your opinion, try to figure out why and make adjustments. Write in the margins what happened and where. Failures are part of the learning curve and what makes cooking fun and creative anyway.

GO MEATLESS ON MONDAYS

The idea of Meatless Mondays has roots back in World Wars I and II, when people needed to cut back on all various and sundry consumptions. The Meatless Monday project (meatlessmonday .com) was reintroduced in 2003 to address the fact that Americans eat copious amounts of industrially raised meat, which has a huge environmental impact, as well as a detrimental effect on our overall health. Giving up that burger, chicken, or pork cutlet just one day a week has been embraced now by everyone from Oprah to the organizers of Mardi Gras celebrations (with the exception of the meat industry and its politicians, not surprisingly).

When the U.S. Department of Agriculture suggested in July 2012, in its internal e-newsletter "Greening Headquarters Update," that going meatless for one meal, one day a week, at their cafeterias may have positive benefits, vocal proponents of the meat industry cried foul.

"One simple way to reduce your environmental impact while dining at our cafeterias is to participate in the 'Meatless Monday' initiative," it read, pointing out that Meatless Mondays is an international effort, in association with the Johns Hopkins School of Public Health. Tucked in on page three, it was sandwiched in between stories of the barber shop's new cost-saving energy-efficient lightbulbs and how local honey would now be available for tea, toast, and coffee at the cafeterias. It read like an innocent, healthy meal suggestion with a side of environmental consciousness. But it riled up the Cattlemen's Beef Association (a lobby group) and Representative Steve King, Republican of Iowa, who tweeted: "USDA HQ meatless Mondays!! At the Dept. of Agriculture? Heresy! I'm not grazing there. I will have the double rib-eye Mondays instead."

The immediate pressure and outcry was so loud that the USDA folded and even removed the supposedly damning suggestion from its newsletter. But because whatever goes on the Internet stays on the Internet, it's out there still, though now as a sad vestige piece of incriminating evidence as to who really controls our USDA.

Try Meatless Monday as a way both to diversify your diet and to save money.

KING OF THE GRILL

Small and portable, the George Foreman Grill comes in all kinds of colors. It doesn't take much up space. It has the same wattage as a lamp. Its clamshell design, with hot plates that cook simultaneously on top and bottom, are connected by a hinge that, like the jaw of snake, adjusts to varying thicknesses of food, from thick grilled cheeses, to burgers, to broccoli, to slices of pineapple. It's easy to clean, with its patented tilts-away-grease design. Sold for about $40, the George Forman Grill is one of the preferred items of the homeless and people living in shelters — people who have no kitchens. The grill launched in 1994 and sold over 100 million units in its first 15 years.

> "In 1977 when I left boxing, I realized I didn't have any friends. People weren't pouring into my home anymore. And I noticed that if I barbequed something, they would come over. Even the guys would go fishing, I wanted them to stay and come back so much, I would always clean the fish, do all the cooking, I found that more satisfying than even winning boxing matches when people would lick their fingers, and say my food was good. That grill, I'm just happy that it's helped so many people. And it helped me of course."
>
> — George Foreman, Houston, Texas

"You make a kitchen for yourself so that you can survive."

— Shelter resident in "An Unexpected Kitchen: The George Foreman Grill"
by the Kitchen Sisters, Hidden Kitchen series

TIP   Eat mostly seasonal ripe and tasty fruits and vegetables from your region. Don't make yourself go crazy with judgments. But try to eat less meat, and better meat when you do, like organic or from local/regional farmers and ranchers.

COOK FOR SOMEONE WITH CANCER

I remember seeing Maynard Silva in the grocery store, wearing his signature red high-top Chuck Taylors and prowling, as was his wont, sick with cancer or not, the frozen food aisle. "Italian lemon ice," he growled. Maynard was a blues guitarist who lost his gritty voice and then his life to throat cancer after beating it once, twice, but not three times. The cruel irony was not lost on him. Lemon ice was all that he could eat, all that tasted good to him, he told me. I miss that man. He was gravity. Though he had shied away from any musical benefit to be held in his honor, later he said in a local paper, "When people help you it's actually a joyous thing for both of you. I always thought asking for help was shameful, a weakness. I learned that to be connected to people that way was a joy, and that they liked it as much as I liked it. That made the way I relate to everybody different, including other musicians I play with and the people I play for." Had I known what or how to cook for him, it would've been a gift to do so. So here's to you, Maynard!

Cancer can kill taste buds, the sense of smell, and appetite along its cruel path. It can manifest itself in food aversions, temperature sensitivities, cravings, digestion and swallowing problems, dry and/or sore mouth, and weight fluctuations before, during, and after treatments. If and when patients don't eat well, or get enough good fats and calories, battling the disease is even harder. Food is love. Cook with the intention of healing both of you, the patient and the caregiver. And never stop the music.

>>

COOK TO HEAL, TOGETHER

COMFORT THEM. Find out if the person has any special requests. Instead of just showing up with chocolate cake, ask, "What can I make you? What sounds good?" A comforting taste memory can be just as important for the emotional well-being as to the physical. Set a beautiful place setting.

ASK to help with groceries or offer to do the dishes. Or the laundry, or take their pets to the vet. Help out.

COOKED VEGETABLES such as kale, broccoli, collards, string beans, or carrots may be easier to eat and digest than raw.

PULL TOGETHER a "survival kit" in a cooler, filled with healthy, digestible snacks and drinks, for times when no one wants to get out of bed or when travel is needed. Include nuts, fresh or dried fruits or berries, dark chocolate, seaweed snacks, and crackers.

INSTEAD OF MAKING one big thing such as a casserole or a meal, prepare individual servings to freeze and reheat. Soups!

WASH YOUR HANDS carefully, make sure all meats and eggs are fully cooked, and take care to avoid any kind of contamination, which can be dangerous for people with weakened immune systems. Use the freshest, cleanest, healthiest meat, fish, poultry, and eggs you can find.

— Tips adapted from the American Cancer Society

>╳<

YOU CAN DO THIS

HOST A DINNER-AND-A-MOVIE POTLUCK

. . . .

Ask some friends to cook dishes from a movie of your choosing. Gather, then watch and eat together. Here are some movies to cook by.

» *Babette's Feast*

» *Big Night*

» *King Corn*

» *Seeds of Freedom*

» *Tampopo*

» *Chocolat*

» *Fed Up*

» *Jiro Dreams of Sushi*

» *Food Chains*

» *Mostly Martha*

>╳<

THE CHEFS COLLABORATIVE
Boston, Massachusetts

The Chefs Collaborative (chefscollaborative.org) is a national nonprofit network of chefs that works to change the sustainable food landscape. It's a great concept, connecting chefs, the frontliners of the culinary scene, to best practices, educational resources, and a national network of growers, distributors, and chefs across the country. One of the collaborative's most innovative programs is in line with seafood. The Trash Fish Dinners, held from Sarasota, Florida, to Denver, Colorado, challenges chefs to cook with lesser-known fish in order to help diversify our collective fish palates.

YOU CAN DO THIS

HOST A GROW-OUT

Tomatoes all seem to come ripe at the same time and flood the markets. But what if chefs and farmers got together to grow a wide variety of just as delicious heirloom varieties that taste and look and feel different? A "grow-out," as outlined below by the generosity of the Chefs Collaborative (see above), is one way to diversify crops; delve into local culinary histories and places; strengthen relationships between farmers, chefs, and community; and appeal to new markets, new customers. Check out these tips.

How Does a Grow-Out Work?

At its core, it's simple: Farmers grow selected varieties of rare, regionally significant, unusual, and heirloom vegetables, and chefs buy the locally grown produce and celebrate the unusual varieties by featuring them on their menus. In doing so, the grow-out revives endangered varieties of vegetables and boosts local food systems as chefs and farmers form partnerships.

>>

While a grow-out can be simple or involved, depending on your resources and your community, it will likely involve the following steps:

1. Recruiting participants, including chefs, farmers, and other partners

2. Deciding on vegetable varieties to grow and finding sources of seed

3. Holding events, activities, and celebrations

4. Evaluating the project

Chefs

Start by contacting a few chefs who are well known for working directly with local farmers and using lots of fresh, local vegetables in their kitchens. Ask them for recommendations of other chefs and restaurants who might be interested in joining the grow-out. The grow-out has room for restaurants of any size, type, and price point to participate, but it is important that participating chefs have an interest in the mission. When talking with chefs, make sure they are clear on what the benefits and responsibilities are.

Benefits include:

» Increased/enhanced relationships with local farmers

» The chance to work with delicious and special vegetables with interesting histories (see page 284)

» Participation in events that can bring in new customers

» Media attention for the project and participants

» The opportunity to help renew local agriculture, biodiversity, and regional agricultural heritage

Responsibilities include:

» A sincere commitment to buy vegetables from the participant farmers

» Participation in grow-out events

» Getting the word out to customers and networks about the events and varieties

"I think it is a wonderful community-building project. It involves a lot of partners — landowners, farmers, chefs — and a lot of young people who could be motivated by this kind of thing. It was really a wonderful community-building activity." — Grow-Out Farmer

Farmers

Similarly, start with a few farmers who are already growing diversified vegetables, preferably at least a few farmers who are already selling to restaurants. Ask them to recommend others who might be interested. If there is a buy-local organization, farmers' market, or other food and farm network in your area, send out an invitation through their mailing list as well. Again, it is great to involve farms of various sizes. Let them know about the benefits and responsibilities of participating.

Benefits include:

» Increased relationships with local chefs

» Introduction to new varieties of vegetables with interesting regional histories

» Participation in delicious and fun events that provide a chance to meet new customers

» Media attention for the project and participants

» The opportunity to help renew bio-diversity and regional agricultural heritage

Responsibilities include:

» Growing at least one of the selected varieties

» A sincere commitment to selling vegetables to participating chefs

» Getting the word out to customers and networks about the events and varieties

Partners

Just as important as having a strong group of committed participants is having partners who can help plan events, spread the word about grow-out activities, get media attention for participants, recruit volunteers when needed, and generally contribute to the success of the project.

VARIETY IS THE SPICE

Here are the 11 varieties that Chefs Collaborative included in the 2010 New England Grow-Out.

» **Boothby's Blond Cucumber:** From the Boothby family in Maine, a crispy yellow-cream slicing cuke.

» **Boston Marrow Squash:** Red-orange winter squash with sweet moist flesh, popular in Boston in the 1800s.

» **Forellenschuss Lettuce:** Also known as "Speckled Trout," a romaine lettuce with juicy speckled leaves.

» **Gilfeather Turnip:** Actually a rutabaga bred by a Vermont farmer, egg-shaped with a sweet, creamy mild taste.

» **Jimmy Nardello's Sweet Italian Frying Pepper:** Brought from Italy by the Nardello family in 1887, a long crimson pepper, creamy and soft when fried.

» **Long Pie Pumpkin:** First brought to Nantucket on a whaling ship in 1832 and still considered the best pumpkin for pie today.

» **Marfax Bean:** The favorite of Maine logging camp cooks, a small golden bean great for baking or soups.

» **Oka Muskmelon:** An orange-fleshed muskmelon bred by monks in Quebec with sweet, aromatic fruit.

» **Trophy Tomato:** An excellent slicing tomato, the seeds sold for $5 per packet in 1870, the equivalent of $70 today.

» **True Red Cranberry Bean:** One of the oldest American bean varieties, a pole bean with green pods and purple beans inside.

» **Wethersfield Onion:** Once the main cash crop of Wethersfield, Connecticut, a flattened red onion perfect for slicing on top of burgers.

— Excerpted with permission from Chefs Collaborative (chefscollaborative.org)

YOU CAN DO THIS

CLEAN UP

· · · · · · · · · · · · · · ·

When you cook, you're going to be cleaning. Or someone is. As my husband will attest, I am not the most orderly person in our home. He is. I can leave a house with dishes in the sink, but I hate coming home to them. The solution in our household, for everyone's peace of mind, is to clean up after every cup of coffee, every bowl of cereal, after every meal. It's aspirational. Not that we get it right all the time. We don't. But it's hard to be motivated to cook when you come home to a messy kitchen. So keeping it clean means you're more likely to cook it up. Here are some tips:

A MIXTURE of white vinegar and water is good for just about everything, including small appliances like a coffeemaker or tea kettle.

WASH KNIVES and other sharps separately so that no one gets hurt. Always place them point down in the dishwasher.

A THIN LINE of boric acid where cockroaches scurry about should do the trick.

DE-CLUTTER kitchen counters. They're easier to clean that way.

A SLICED LEMON will make the stinkiest garbage disposal smell better.

STORE FOOD in glass jars to keep out pests like moths, ants, and mice.

FOR MORE TIPS on keeping a kitchen free and clean, track down Jolie Kerr's books and writings; she's very entertaining.

>×<

TIP Make your kitchen comfortable to be in and work in. Put your pots and pans, spices, workspace, and trash/compost within reach. Follow your intuition.

CHAPTER 10

Engage

NONE OF THIS was my idea. I'm a crow. Attracted to things just out of reach, I reach. I am an adapter of ideas, a collector of connections. A gleaner, relating and associating people to ideas and ideas to programs. Funders to projects that make a difference. My stories to you. But never have I been so out of my element as when I was in the midst of the great thinkers and advocates of federal sustainable agriculture policy in Washington, D.C. These people speak another language. They speak in acronyms. They read, write, and understand testimonies, public comments, and regulations. And they know how to work the politics and the money.

They are unsung heroes and the hope in the concrete political jungle of our nation's capital. After just a dip into the world they inhabit, I was exhausted from treading in their deep waters. They're like great whales. They live most of their lives out of sight. But then they'll come up to breach just when we think they don't exist, displaying all the good in political advocacy for us to see and take action. It's time to shed more light on them and on how you, too, can become an advocate.

Become a food policy giant of the sea. First, start from where the world is (page 288). Be an active citizen (page 290); run for a board (page 293). Connect food policy councils with planners (page 298), engage with your community leaders (page 300), get to know your members of Congress (page 301), and learn from adversity.

You don't have to live in D.C. to be a policy leviathan. You do, however, need to keep your phone charged. Maria Moreira (see page 120) taught me that much and more.

START FROM WHERE THE WORLD IS

Activists will find a lot to think about in this quote from Saul Alinsky, who is considered the father of community organizing. In his *Rules for Radicals,* he wrote:

> As an organizer I start from where the world is, as it is, not as I would like it to be. That we accept the world as it is does not in any sense weaken our desire to change it into what we believe it should be — it is necessary to begin where the world is if we are going to change it to what we think it should be. That means working in the system.

>>< <

WOMEN ADVOCATES FOR GOOD FOOD

I admire both the men and the women who are food activists. But it is especially the women who inspire me. Old and young, these policy thinkers and advocates are doing great, deep-diving, holding-their-breath kind of work. Some I've met, others I follow. Here are a few of my contemporaries (in alphabetical order): Traci Bruckner (Center for Rural Affairs, Nebraska); Georgia Good (Rural Coalition, South Carolina); Alicia Harvie (Farm Aid, Massachusetts); Steph Larsen (Center for Rural Affairs, Montana); Kathleen Merrigan (former U.S. Department of Agriculture deputy secretary, now with the Sustainability Institute, Washington, D.C.); Maria Moreira (a farmer and a slaughterhouse owner/operator with World Farmers [worldfarmers.org, page 119], in Massachusetts, and the Rural Coalition in Washington, D.C.); Julia Olmstead (University of Wisconsin Extension, Cooperative Extension); Lorette Picciano (Rural Coalition, Washington, D.C.); Susan Prolman (Defenders of Wildlife, Washington, D.C.); Shirley Sherrod (former Georgia State Director of Rural Development for the U.S. Department of Agriculture); and Aimee Witteman (formerly with the National Sustainable Agriculture Coalition, Washington, D.C., now with the McKnight Foundation, Minnesota).

ORAN HESTERMAN
Fair Food Network

Oran Hesterman is the author of *Fair Food* and the executive director of Fair Food Network, a nonprofit headquartered in southeast Michigan whose mission is the mission of this book: to help create better access to healthy, fresh, and whole sustainably grown food for everyone. In an interview with Bill Moyers, Hesterman was asked that looming question: What's the one thing people can do to make a difference?

> The most important action is to make the shift from conscious consumer to engaged citizen. And what I mean by that is for us to stop thinking that by simply eating local and organic and focusing on our own diet that we're going to change the system, but instead to expand that and realize that no matter where we live, work, play or worship, we have opportunities to shift the system on a larger scale.

Q: How can people do that? What are some ways that you can make an impact outside of your own refrigerator?

> Start where you are. If you're a parent with children in schools, public or private schools, start learning more about what are they eating and where it comes from and get together with other parents who care about this to make school food good food for your kids.
>
> If you're a student at a college or university, or you're a parent or grandparent of a student, talk with them about getting involved in the Real Food Challenge, which is working to shift 20 percent of all university and college dining hall purchases to local and sustainable sources. Or if you're in the health-care world, take a look at Health Care Without Harm and the Healthy Food in Health Care movement that is shifting purchases of food to local and sustainable sources for hospital and health-care situations.

> — Excerpted from an interview with Theresa Riley on *Bill Moyers & Company,* April 27, 2012

YOU CAN DO THIS

BE AN ACTIVE CITIZEN

I have spent a good part of my adult life living in the refrain: "What is worth doing?" This mantra and its timing came about after I had a child. Because until that point in my life, I don't think I thought much about what was worth doing. I did what I wanted to do. But the "why" of my refrain doesn't matter, whether it was induced at conception, labor, or my son's first breath. All I do know is that it's not about me anymore. So as the answers to my question, "What is worth doing?" get tweaked day to day, month to month, year to year, this gets me to check in and circle back to how can I live a wholehearted life that's rooted in peace, fairness, justice, respect, kindness, and dignity for people, animals, and the environment for generations to come. Because I do think that that is worth doing, even if I don't always know yet how best to do it. And perhaps I may not see some of the fruits of my labors in this short sweet life, and a lot is never going to be perfect, and I know I'm not always going to get it right. But I do know that planting some good seeds is worth doing. That getting out of my comfort zone and disturbing the status quo, that is worth doing. That taking action, that is worth doing. And for me, part of what's worth doing includes being an engaged citizen.

>>

"And we would go into the fields where people were working in the fields and try to convince some of the field workers. We would go into beauty shops, the barber shops, knock on the doors of people's homes trying to get them to become a participant, to get involved, to come to a rally, come to a mass meeting. . . . We would say to people, you know, you've been living here for 40 years, for 50 years. Your street is not paved. You have a dirt road. You don't have clean water. If you want to change that, you must register and you must vote. You can get someone else elected."

— Congressman John Lewis of Georgia, on his participation in the Civil Rights Movement, *Fresh Air* interview with Terry Gross, National Public Radio

VOTE. If you haven't registered, do so in plenty of time before an election. My mom grew up under the fascist totalitarian government of Nazi Germany. She moved to the United States in 1953 and became a naturalized citizen on June 19, 1956. She raised my brother, sister, and me to vote. She also made sure we knew that it's not anyone's business how you vote, because it's a secret ballot, but that the most important thing, the imperative, is to exercise your right to vote.

TO FIND OUT where to vote, go to the Voter Participation Center (voter participation.org), a national nonpartisan nonprofit. The center's focus is to increase the registration of eligible voters, specifically unmarried women, people of color, and the age group of 18- to 29-year-olds. According to the center's website, these three groups represent 53 percent of the eligible but not registered people in America.

SIGN ONLINE PETITIONS. Add your own comments. Your comment will have greater impact if it's modified, personalized, story-fied with your own (polite) powerful words.

CALL your representatives and voice your opinion. Tell them why an issue is important to you and how it affects you, your family, and your community. Explain how they can help.

WRITE LETTERS to your representatives, the more personal about how an issue affects you, the better.

ATTEND MEETINGS and public forums where your representatives are speaking. Introduce yourself and discuss the areas of your concern. Face-to-face meetings are the best.

GO TO WASHINGTON. Whether you are a farmer or whether you're a citizen concerned about food safety, SNAP, or another issue, knock on your representative's door, tell him or her what you care about and what can be done to help, then go visit the Lincoln Memorial.

SUPPORT A COALITION GROUP that best represents your interests in D.C. It's not possible for each and every one of us to fly in to meet with members of Congress, so align yourself with those advocacy/coalition organizations in Washington that do have political access to the senators and representatives who are involved, or who need to be involved, in the issues you care about. Look at their members list for organizations that you can work with, which may be closer to your home. Here are some D.C.-based nonprofits:

» The Rural Coalition (ruralco.org)

» The Humane Society (humanesociety.org)

» Supermoms Against Superbugs, a project of the Pew Campaign on Human Health and Industrial Farming (pewhealth.org)

» National Latino Farmers and Ranchers Trade Association (NLFRTA.org)

» Association of Farmworker Opportunity Programs (afop.org)

>><<

MEET

A MODERN FARMER IN CONGRESS

By the time Chellie Pingree was elected to represent Maine's first district in the U.S. House of Representatives in 2008, she had already amassed more than 30 years of farming experience in the state. Her agrarian CV includes starting an organic farm on North Haven, an island off the coast of Maine; running a successful yarn company that used wool from the sheep on her farm; serving on the Agriculture Committee in the Maine State Senate; and renewing her penchant for organic farming with the acquisition and renovation of Turner Farm in 2008. Now Chellie is in her third congressional term, and in her five-year tenure she has served on both the Agriculture Committee and the Agriculture Subcommittee of the Appropriations Committee.

Q: There is a tendency to view the local food movement as elitist. Yet, Maine is 38th in GDP per capita in the United States and is nevertheless among a few other states that are leading the way for the local food movement. What does that say about the alleged elitism of farmers' markets, CSAs, and other community-driven agriculture?

> **A:** Frankly, that's one of my favorite statistics. In a state like ours that isn't, when compared with other states, wealthy but where people really want to eat well and cook healthy foods . . . if people in our state are flocking to farmers' markets or the local foods section of their grocery store or seek out the farmer who grows organic food, it shows that even on limited dollars people want to have good, healthy food. People have been really interested in the programs that make it possible to take your SNAP cards to the farmers' markets or to join a CSA with your SNAP benefits.
>
> And I find that anecdotally. If I'm talking to a group of Mainers at a town meeting or a high school graduation, and I start talking about local, healthy foods, about getting more locally grown foods in the school lunch program, making it easier for people at all income levels to buy locally grown foods, people perk right up. They want good-tasting food, and they want to keep farmers and farms in their area. I don't think that's something that's specific to rich people. I think that's relevant for people who love their community. Maine is very rural, very small-town-oriented, and nothing makes people happier than to see a farm move into the community or come back to life again, and being able to take their kids and grandkids there to visit.
>
> — Excerpted with permission from an interview by Tom Wolf in *Modern Farmer* (modernfarmer.com), June 14, 2013

CHANGELAB SOLUTIONS
Oakland, California

ChangeLab Solutions is the winning ticket, the bees' knees, the pot of gold at the end of the rainbow. The amount of information and guidance this nonprofit offers is staggering. If your town, school, or city wants to implement healthier public policies, from getting the junk food out of vending machines to eliminating food and beverage advertising in schools (see page 46), visit changelabsolutions.org for help with how to do it. Fact sheets and guides are available to download for free. And its report about what's changing for the better in Birmingham, Alabama, is quietly revolutionary. In its own words, ChangeLab is "pioneering a new approach to public health advocacy by fostering collaboration between public health officials dedicated to chronic disease prevention and local planning officials."

SERVE ON A BOARD OR COMMISSION

One of ChangeLab Solutions' propositions is that concerned citizens should get involved with boards and commissions to work to create healthy communities. Here is the organization's advice about how to join an advisory board or commission.

Citizens have many opportunities to get involved in local government to make their voices heard on issues that affect health — everything from how transportation dollars are allocated and where new jobs and housing should be located to whether or not there are local stores that sell healthy food.

Serving on an advisory board or commission is one way for public health advocates and other community leaders to influence local policies.

>>

"Every land use decision that is made affects public health. Because this way of thinking is new to many government agencies, you have to be persistent to get this message across." — Member, Neighborhood Plan Community Advisory Council

We use the term "boards and commissions" here to describe any advisory group that provides oversight on and recommendations to a legislative body or other group of decision makers (such as a public agency). Members are typically volunteers appointed to serve for a defined term. (A group of elected officials may also be called a "board" or "commission" — for instance, a school board or a board of supervisors — but these groups have different responsibilities and are not included here.)

Why Join a Board or Commission?

Most elected officials want what is best for their communities, but they may not fully understand how policies affect their constituents. Boards and commissions are meant to serve as a bridge between the community and government, ensuring oversight and raising awareness on important community issues.

Public health advocates have an especially critical role to play in this process, since many people working in local government may not be accustomed to thinking about how their work influences health. For instance, economic development departments are generally focused on supporting local businesses and creating jobs. Staff may not have thought about how they can help improve nutrition by bringing a grocery store into the community or by working with retailers to stock healthier foods. Advocates can share data on health priorities and help engage residents in developing sustainable solutions.

Serving on an advisory board or commission may require more in-depth involvement than other forms of public participation, such as attending public hearings, meeting with local officials, or writing comment letters. In return, members enjoy more direct access to their policymakers and may have the chance to shape proposals early in their development. Over time, this can yield stronger working relationships and help ensure that health concerns are considered in all-important local policies.

Step 1: Research and Connect

How can you identify opportunities to join boards or commissions that match your interests? Looking on local government websites or asking around can be a great start. In most communities, local governments are required to post announcements for openings on boards and commissions publicly, in their offices and online. You may also be able to call your local city or county clerk for a listing of all current openings.

People find out about opportunities in many ways. They may see a posted announcement in an agency newsletter. They may hear about the opportunity from a community-based organization that is interested in seeing more diverse members in the group. Or they may be actively recruited by an elected official or an agency staff member.

To get a feel for a board or commission, you may want to attend a public meeting, review past meeting notes, or talk to current and past members and others familiar with the group.

Step 2: Assess

Once you've identified a board or commission to join, think about the skills, experience, and connections you have that will strengthen your application. The Iowa Commission on the Status of Women has published an excellent guide on applying to boards and commissions, with worksheets to help you assess your skills and put together an application.

Qualifications for appointment may vary depending on your location, local regulations that govern public participation, and the nature of the board or commission itself.

Step 3: Apply

The application process can vary, even within a single community. You may need to submit materials (résumé, application, letters of support) and meet with staff for an interview. Or you may get appointed after a single meeting with an elected official.

>>

In some cases, appointments are made based on recommendations and connections rather than a formal application process. For this reason, it may be important to develop a relationship with an agency in order to be considered a strong candidate.

If your application is rejected, do not take it too personally — it is possible the overseeing agency had a specific type of person in mind, or there was another candidate with previous connections to the policymakers. If you feel comfortable doing so, consider following up to ask about other ways to get involved, or for recommendations of other groups that may be a good fit.

> "The process was very simple — I submitted a short application to the city clerk, was interviewed by a staff member, and was then nominated and confirmed at the next city council meeting." — *Community Development Commissioner*

Step 4: Serve

Once you've been appointed, it's time to start getting oriented and building stronger connections with other members, policymakers, and relevant organizations. It's also a good idea to develop your expertise in the group's key issues and policies.

We recommend becoming familiar with your group's bylaws to learn more about its scope and responsibilities.

> — Reprinted with permission from ChangeLab Solutions, changelabsolutions.org.
> This work originally funded by Kaiser Foundation Hospitals.

WHAT'S GOING ON

FARM-TO-CONSUMER LEGAL DEFENSE FUND
Falls Church, Virginia

The national nonprofit Farm-to-Consumer Legal Defense Fund (farmtoconsumer.org) will always hold a special place in my heart because when I was in the thick of building and operating a mobile poultry-processing trailer (page 104) and was between a rock and a hard place with no one to turn to, these guys picked up their phone and helped me suss it out. Their focus is mainly on raw milk issues — supporting family farms and defending a consumer's access to nutrient-dense foods. It is well worth becoming a member as an individual or as a farmer.

LEGAL SERVICES FOOD HUB

Boston, Massachusetts

The Legal Services Food Hub (legalservicesfoodhub.org) is a program of the Conservation Law Foundation (clf.org). What a brilliant idea, to provide a hub of legal services to farmers, food entrepeneurs, nonprofits, and community organizations! Legal transactions, leases, navigating insurance — these are all areas the program works in to help with referrals and networking. Currently this is a regional program based in New England. Expand it westward.

FUND EFFECTIVE PROGRAMS

The Sustainable Agriculture and Food Systems Funders (SAFSF) is a nonprofit that assists donors (and donors only) in connecting with an international network of grantmakers to responsible programs, projects, and people in the areas of sustainable agriculture and just and equitable community food systems. Its website (safsf.org) is host to a wealth of information available to the public because education is a large part of its mission.

Many of its events are for funders only — a good thing, don't you agree? To have an informed, safe, and confidential place to honestly discuss distribution of funds. And as it states on the organization's website: "Members may not use their participation in SAFSF for promotional purposes or for private gain."

CONNECT FOOD POLICY COUNCILS AND TOWN PLANNERS

Food policy councils vary in their organizational relationships and structures. But usually they're connected to some agency, perhaps a department of agriculture. There are many advantages to connecting with planning departments, as either the host or sponsor, or to having a planner be on the board of a food policy council (FPC). Planners tend not to be community food system people, and food system people tend not to be planners. But together, as those two mind-sets join, much good and benefit can come to communities. See the potential, outlined here by the American Planning Association, based on seven of the commonly held objectives of FPCs, followed by the possible roles for planners in enacting those aims.

1. ADVOCATE for policy change to improve a community's food system.

Recommend new policies or changes to policy language that impact the food system, such as beekeeping and backyard chicken ordinances.

Serve as a liaison between the FPC and local government by helping FPCs understand the political context that policies operate within.

2. DEVELOP PROGRAMS that address gaps in a community's food system.

Identify legal barriers to new or existing food system programs, such as outdated land-use regulations or restrictive zoning codes.

Find applicable funding sources for food system programs, such as Community Development Block Grant funds.

3. STRATEGIZE SOLUTIONS that have wide applicability to the food system.

Incorporate food system objectives into comprehensive and strategic plans by using FPC knowledge in conjunction with the planner's systems-thinking approach and long-term perspective.

Devise win-win solutions to food problems, such as using regional scale transfer of development rights for farming urban land or bridging urban-rural divides through direct-to-consumer outlets like farmers' markets.

4. RESEARCH AND ANALYZE the existing conditions of a community's food system.

Examine existing policies for their positive or negative impact on food related goals and objectives, such as improved food access.

Conduct food system assessments by gathering baseline data about the state of food system sectors or stakeholders in a given community.

Conduct land assessments, such as inventories of city-owned vacant parcels or inventories of brownfields.

5. COMMUNICATE INFORMATION about a community's food system.

Raise awareness of a community's food system to local government and residents by sharing information about FPC activities at public forums.

Explain policy language to FPC members and community residents; for example, by translating zoning codes or breaking down technical jargon.

Convey information to elected officials and the public through such visually engaging mediums as GIS maps.

6. CULTIVATE PARTNERSHIPS among a community's five food sectors (production, processing, distribution, consumption, and waste recovery).

Highlight common goals within the food framework by helping planners and other professionals see their own work through a food "lens."

Foster trust among stakeholders through an objective perspective and a professional manner.

7. CONVENE MEETINGS that draw diverse stakeholders of a community's food system.

Encourage community participation in food system decisions by helping FPCs coordinate outreach efforts such as conducting surveys or hosting guest speakers at FPC meetings.

Facilitate meetings, including community visioning sessions.

— See also the American Planning Association (planning.org), "Policy Guide on Community and Regional Food Planning" (a PDF), and *Zoning Issues* (an online publication)

>×<

ENGAGE WITH BOARDS AND COMMISSIONS

There are many ways to communicate your opinions to a board or commission, even if you are not a member.

LEARN ABOUT AND MONITOR THE PROCESS. Find out when and where meetings take place and what will be discussed. In most communities, this information should be posted publicly. Track progress over time on the issues you care about most.

GET TO KNOW MEMBERS. If there are members who are likely to share your opinions, reach out to them and offer your support. You may get more context about the policies and issues from them, while the board member or commissioner may be able to cite your support during the decision-making process.

SPEAK AT A MEETING. Giving public comments at a meeting or submitting letters to the board/commission and other relevant government officials can be a great way to raise visibility of health and equity during the policy process. These strategies are especially effective as part of a longer-term campaign that involves engaging and building coalitions with community-based organizations, residents, and board/commission members who share your values. If you are planning to speak at a meeting, be sure to rehearse your statement and stick to any applicable time limits. Think about who should deliver your message: for instance, if you come from a community-based organization, decide who will have the most credibility or impact.

VOLUNTEER. Some groups have workgroups or subcommittees that do not require that you sit on the board/commission in order to participate. This can provide an opportunity for you to learn more about the group's work, contribute your expertise, and build relationships with members and other community stakeholders.

FIND OTHER WAYS TO VOICE YOUR OPINIONS. For highly contentious issues, you may want to expand your outreach: in addition to contacting the board or commission, you may also want to voice your perspectives to the overseeing agency or legislative group, elected officials, and local media outlets. Find allies and other organizations that share your views and work with them to engage residents to voice their opinions.

RECRUIT COMMUNITY MEMBERS. Urban Habitat, a nonprofit in Oakland, California, runs an innovative Boards & Commissions Leadership Institute (urbanhabitat.org) that is perhaps the most extensive program of its kind in the nation: it recruits, trains, and helps place low-income people and people of color in high-impact boards and commissions around the region with the goal of promoting equitable planning processes. A program of this depth and intensity may not be possible everywhere, but without too much effort a community-based group or a coalition of organizations could follow and build relationships with relevant agencies over time to help recruit new members.

ORGANIZE TO START A NEW BOARD. If a new or pressing need arises that doesn't fall neatly within the jurisdiction of current agencies, boards, or commissions, you might consider working with local government to assess the feasibility of starting a new advisory group. Some communities have started food policy councils or food access workgroups to create a multidisciplinary, interagency forum for new policies and programs aimed at improving community food systems. Similarly, many cities, counties, and states have started a youth commission or council to advise government officials on policies affecting young people. Getting new advisory bodies off the ground will involve recruiting champions both within local government and among the larger community.

— Reprinted with permission from ChangeLab Solutions, changelabsolutions.org. This work was originally funded by Kaiser Foundation Hospitals.

KNOW YOUR MEMBERS OF CONGRESS

The Senate and the House of Representatives make up the U.S. Congress. To find your senators, your representatives, and their district maps, go to GovTrack.us (govtrack.us) and click on the "Members of Congress" button. You'll find contact information, Twitter handles, report cards, committee membership, bills sponsored, and voting records.

"We must say wake up America, wake up! For we cannot stop, and we will not and cannot be patient."

— John Lewis, representing the Student Nonviolent Coordinating Committee at the Civil Rights March on Washington, 1963

YOU CAN DO THIS

SPEAK OUT
. . . .

Use your voice. Here are some tips, so it doesn't tremble so much. In all cases, be clear, concise, polite, and accurate.

TIPS ON SPEAKING AT TOWN MEETINGS

START by saying thank you and stating your name, affiliation, and town, if you are representing one.

KNOW the agenda items, as well as the purpose and tone of the meeting.

PREPARE your succinct presentation. Do your homework; write notes for relevant info or stats you need to make your case. Use up-to-date information to make your case. Know who you are talking to (their history, position in community, etc.).

HAVE your supporting documentation, such as written copies of your presentation, ready to give to the board.

TIPS FOR SUBMITTING PUBLIC COMMENTS

DO YOUR RESEARCH. Include specific examples of the issue and/or the names or identification numbers of the law or regulation on which you are commenting.

READ other organizations' comments. Do this by joining newsletters and action alerts. Follow their model for clear, concise language. A public comment period is usually short and, like a screenplay or set of submission guidelines, follows a specific formula.

Your comment will make more of an impact if you learn and adopt the style, formatting, language, and organization of a comment. It's a unique beast.

CHECK OUT this free, online resource: "Step-by-Step Tips for Writing Effective Public Comments," found at the Environmental Law Institute Ocean Program's website (eli-ocean.org).

TIPS FOR WRITING LETTERS TO THE EDITOR

IDENTIFY the issue and make your case regarding it; include evidence.

STATE what you think should be done about the issue.

SIGN THE LETTER with your full name, address, and e-mail address.

>×<

#VOTEFOOD
· · · · · · · · · · · · · · · · · · ·

"As soon as one legislator loses their job over how they vote on food issues, we're going to send a clear message to Congress that we're organized and we're viable and strong," Tom Colicchio said. "We're going to make clear that, yes, we do have a food movement — and that it's coming for you."

You may know Tom Colicchio from the television show *Top Chef*, from his New York City restaurants, or from his cookbooks. He's also a powerhouse of an activist. After participating in the making of the movie *A Place at the Table*, Tom has been working to end hunger in the United States. He's also making the point that we should be actively supporting and voting for the politicians who actively support and vote for good food policies at the local, state, and federal levels. That's where his involvement with Food Policy Action (foodpolicyaction.org) comes in.

Food Policy Action was started in 2012 by a group of national food policy leaders to hold elected officials accountable for their votes. Their goal is to "change the national dialogue on food policy by educating the public on how elected officials are voting on these issues." Their National Food Policy Scorecard arms people with the "information they need to vote with their forks and elect more food policy leaders across the country." #VoteFood is the twitterverse for more information and to use when posting about your representatives' food platform scorecards.

>×<

This is not all there is. Not even close. A book can only hold so much. The rest is up to you. Be hope. Use what's here, find out more. Write in the margins, dog-ear the pages you like, don't like, and want more of. Be the next book. Don't stop. Do things that haven't been said here. Do things beyond your imagination. Do not be dissuaded. Stand tall, stand firm. If everyone did something, that's something. Still, do more. We can do this together. You have everything you need.

ACKNOWLEDGMENTS

SOJOURNING INTO THE Good Food Movement started for me unconsciously after I became a mother, way before any book deal was inked. Consequently, many more organizations and inspirations informed this book than made it onto the page. Any errors or omissions are mine. My deepest gratitude and admiration for your work, contributions, permissions, and support, whether you know my name or not:

350.org

Agroecology in Action

American Cancer Society

American Farmland Trust

American Planning Association

Animal Welfare Approved

Anson Mills

Association of Fundraising Professionals

Atlantic Public Media

Wendell Berry

Grace Lee Boggs

Brown's Super Stores

Ben Burkett

Betty Burton

Center for High Impact Philanthropy

The Center for Rural Affairs

Center for Science in the Public Interest

Centro De Los Trabajadores Agrícolas Fronterizos

ChangeLab Solutions

Chefs Collaborative

Mariana Chilton

ChopChop magazine

Coalition of Immokalee Workers

Community Cinema

Cook for America

CropCircle Kitchen

Larisa Demos

Drexel University Center for Hunger Free Communities

Edible Media

Farm Aid

Farm-to-Consumer Legal Defense Fund

Farmers Market Coalition

Farmer Veteran Coalition

Betsy and Jesse Fink

Ron Finley

First Nations Development Institute

Flats Mentor Farm

Food & Water Watch

Food Chain Workers Alliance

FoodCorps

FoodHub

Food Policy Action

Food Waste Reduction Alliance

Global Animal Partnerships

Grace Communications Foundation

GreenFaith

Hazon

Helping Hands

Oran Hesterman

Annette Higby

Howard Hinterthuer

Elizabeth Hoover

Hudson Valley Seed Library

Huffington Post Religion

InsideOut Literary Arts Project

Institute for Agriculture and Trade Policy

Iowa Public Radio

Island Food Pantry

Island Grown Initiative

Island Grown Schools

Kitchen Gardeners International

Land for Good

Anna Lappé

La Semilla Food Center

Destin Layne

LL.M. Program in Agricultural & Food Law at the University of Arkansas

Massachusetts Department of Agriculture Resources

Bill McKibben

Media Voices for Children

Metcalfe's Market

Migrant Legal Action Program

MigrantStudents.org

Modern Farmer

MV Ag Society

MV Shellfish Group

MV Vision Fellowship

National Center for Farmworker Health

National Council of Non-Profits

National Family Farm Coalition

National Farm to School Network

National Latino Farmers & Ranchers

National Policy & Legal Analysis Network to Prevent Childhood Obesity

National Sustainable Agriculture Coalition

Native Seed/SEARCH

Nelson and Pade Inc.

New York Coalition Against Hunger

Marion Nestle

Niche Meat Processor Assistance Network

Northeast Sustainable Agriculture Research and Education

Northwest Atlantic Marine Alliance

Jamie Oliver's Food Revolution Community

OnBeing.org

Rainforest Alliance

RAWtools.org

Red Tomato

Regional Environmental Council

Rural Advancement Fund

Rural Coalition

Tracey Ryder and Carole Topalain

Slow Food USA

Strolling of the Heifers

Sustainable Agriculture and Food Systems Funders

TEDxManhattan

University of Arkansas Women's Giving Circle

UpLift Solutions

USDA

Vermont FEED

Vermont's Agency of Agriculture, Food & Markets

Weston A. Price Foundation

Witnesses to Hunger

White House Rural Council

Whole Foods Market

World Farmers

Many gave their time, voice, candor, and advice and shared their knowledge, experiences, and encouragement along the way:

Carrie Abels

Darnell Adams

Krysten Aguilar

Kaila Allen-Posin

Jay Allison

Emily Armstrong

Rudy Arredondo

John Ash

Jim Athearn

Terrie Bad Hand

Samantha Barrow

Michael Becker

Julie Beliel

Thomas Bena

Ann Bliss

Robert Booz

Jeff Brown

Doug Brush

Marla Camp

Mariana Chilton

Krishana Collins

Tina and Ted Cramer

Joanna Creed

Laurie David

Melinda Rabbitt DeFeo

Bruce Dunlop

Anna Edey

Anthony Gardner

Georgia Good

Eugenia Gratto

Ken Greene

Lauren Gwin

Viki and Armen Hanjian

Jessica B. Harris

Elspeth Hay

Ebba Hierta

Ferd Hoefner

Louise Holland

Joy Hought

Ruth Katz

Jerusha Klemperer

Sarah Kornhauser

Marina Lent

Carlos Marentes

Michael Martin

Pati L. Martinson

Liz McMullan

Maria and Manny Moreira

Len and Georgia Morris

Gary Nabhan

Becky Nelson and John Pade

Michel Nischan

Jamie O'Gorman

Julia Olmstead

Lorette Picciano

Paul Raushenbush

Glenn Roberts

Robin Romano

Kathryn Z. Ruhf

Catherine Sands

Dan Sauer and Wenonah Madison

Jacob Seigel

Aaron Sharratt

Ashlee Shelton

Maynard Silva

Chelsey Simpson

Scott Soares

Noli Taylor

Sherri Brooks Vinton

Kate Warner

Greg Watson

Rowen White

Rebecca Wiggins-Reinhard

Aimee Witteman

For a book like this, I took to the road. Public libraries became and still remain my office, my sanctuary. Shout-outs go to the these towns' library stacks, for their heating, air-conditioning, and plumbing systems, as well as their stalwart Internet connections:

West Tisbury, MA

Putney, VT

Woods Hole, MA

Oak Bluffs, MA

Bellows Falls, VT

Madison, WI

Chilmark, MA

What team *Edible Vineyard* did in keeping our magazine timely, beautiful, and on deadline while I was away is all because of Sydney Bender, Dan Cabot, Elizabeth Cecil, Lauren Dreier, Carrie Gee, Emily Kennedy, Claire Lindsey, and Emily Portman (this book's research assistant). Thank you, and see you soon at the Ocean View.

Family, friends, and community, thank you for holding me up:

Kate Adamick

Richard Andre

Jennifer Bender

Marge Berlow

Rabbi Caryn Broitman

Geraldine Brooks

Nicole Cabot

Kimberley Cartwright

Patricia Cliggott

Janet Davis

Daniele Dominick

Mollie Doyle

Paul, Emy, and Dan Gartzke

Holly Gleason

Abby Jones

Peter and Kate Karafotas

Carol Kenney

Julia Kidd

Fae Kontje-Gibbs

Lena Lenček

Jim and Peg McLaughlin

Claudia Mens

Mermaid Farm

Viki Merrick

Tina Miller

Jefferson Munroe

North End Butchers

Kathie Olsen

Liz Packer

Zephir Plume

Corky Pollan

Michael Pollan

Walter Robb

The Scottish Bakehouse

Deb Shumlin

Pete and Patty Stickney

To the songwriters, poets, writers: Steve Earle, Campbell McGrath, Howard Nemerov, Clint Smith, Patti Smith, Tillie Olsen. And to the beauty in the practical that is Storey's brilliance. I thank my lucky star Arcturus to have worked with editors Deb Burns and Pam Thompson. You are guides on moonless nights, patient, and, most important, artful.

To Temple Grandin, always. Alice Randall for inviting me to come out and play, and Binky Urban, agent extraordinaire.

Dear family: The time of "fake it 'til you make it" has drawn to a close. Deshawn James, our most remarkable third son — you are brave, a gift, and a hero. Embrace this today and every day. Sam, Max, Elijah, and D — believe the hardcore troubadour Earle's words: Art is war. Wage yours. The laundry can wait. For a while, at least. You are the loves of my life. I am one lucky woman.

Index

Page numbers in *italic* indicate illustrations; page numbers in **bold** indicate charts.

C

cafeteria, school, 15, 17, 58
Calvo, Luz, 182
cancer, cooking for someone with, 277
canning, 224–25
Capitalist Poem #5, 201
Center for High Impact Philanthropy, 82
Center for Hunger-Free Communities, 190
Center for Rural Affairs, 108
Center for Science in the Public Interest (CSPI), 64
Center for Veterans Issues, 164
Centro de los Trabajadores Agrícolas Fronterizos, 76–77
certification, food handler, 42
certified food/coffee, 264, 265
Champions for Change Network for a Healthier California, 50
ChangeLab Solutions, 46, 64, 293
chefs, grow-outs and, 282
Chefs Collaborative, 281, 284
Cherichello, Genna, 54, 55
chicken(s)
        as gateway livestock, 104
        processing of, 10
childhood nutrition director (CND), 56
childhood obesity, 46, 98
child workers, 157, 158
Chilton, Mariana, 190
ChopChop, 273
citizens, political action and, 290–91
City Fruit, 222
city spaces, greening of, 116
Clark, Sean, 60

classism, 69
clean up, 285
"Clearing" (poem), 19
clergy, 186
climate-just food system, 71
club(s). See also youth groups
        book, 14
        cooking, 276
        garden, 131–32, 137
Coalición Rural, 106
coalition groups, 291
Coalition of Immokalee Workers (CIW), 75
coffee, certified, 265
Colicchio, Tom, 303
College Assistance Migrant Program (CAMP), 161
college farm, starting, 60–63
Collins, Krishana, 112
commercial aquaponics, 124–26
commissions. See boards/commissions
communication
        community food system and, 299
        community gardens and, 139
        letter writing, 15, 291, 303
Communities in Schools (CIS), 56
community, meaning of, 67
community awareness, 43
community building
        about, 19
        grow-outs and, 282
        public fruit trees and, 222
community composting, 141
community development, 70
Community Development Financial Institutions (CDFI) Fund, 238, 243

community food security, 70
community gardens, 131–140, 134
        additions to, 136
        budget for, 136
        celebration of, 138
        composting and, 139, 141
        elements of, basic, 135
        funding/materials for, 136–37
        garden infrastructure, 137
        growing plants/food in, 137–38
        irrigation for, 135, 137
        land for, 132
        landowner and, 133
        leases and liability, 134
        planning, 134
        soil testing and, 133
        troubleshooting and, 138–140
        turnover/dropout and, 140
        water and, 133
        weed management and, 140
community kitchens, 275
community members, recruitment of, 300–301
community radio, 200
community supported agriculture. See CSAs
Community Supported Fishery (CSF), 231
Compost Community, 141
composting
        community gardens and, 135, 137, 139, 141
        hospitals and, 265
        school gardens and, 39
conferences, 44
conflict-of-interest policy, 80–81

OTHER STOREY BOOKS
YOU WILL ENJOY

100 Skills You'll Need for the End of the World (as We Know It)
by Ana Maria Spagna

Prepare yourself for the end times, however they may come, with this wonderfully illustrated checklist of essential skills for self-reliance.

224 pages. Paper. ISBN 978-1-61212-456-8.

Greenhorns
Edited by Zoë Ida Bradbury, Severine von Tscharner Fleming, and Paula Manalo

Fifty original essays written by a new generation of farmers.

256 pages. Paper. ISBN 978-1-60342-772-2.

Reclaiming Our Food
by Tanya Denckla Cobb

Stories of more than 50 groups across America that are finding innovative ways to provide local food to their communities.

320 pages. Paper. ISBN 978-1-60342-799-9.

The Good Life Lab
by Wendy Jehanara Tremayne

Follow and learn from the adventures of a resourceful couple who ditched their careers and rebuilt their lives from the ground up, making their own fuel, structures, food, and medicine.

320 pages. Paper. 978-1-61212-101-7.

The Mobile Poultry Slaughterhouse
by Ali Berlow

A complete guide to building and using a humane processing unit for chickens and other poultry.

144 pages. Paper. ISBN 978-1-61212-129-1.

Soup Night
by Maggie Stuckey

Bring the neighborhood together with your own soup night, using real soup night stories and recipes from across the United States.

304 pages. Paper. 978-1-61212-099-7.

These and other books from Storey Publishing are available wherever quality books are sold or by calling 1-800-441-5700. Visit us at *www.storey.com* or sign up for our newsletter at *www.storey.com/signup*.